D1053280

FROM CRAYONS
TO CONDOMS

FROM CRAYONS
TO CONDOMS

THE UGLY TRUTH
ABOUT AMERICA'S PUBLIC SCHOOLS

STORIES EDITED AND COMPILED BY

Steve Baldwin &
Karen Holgate

WND BOOKS

FROM CRAYONS TO CONDOMS
A WND Books Book
Published by WorldNetDaily
Los Angeles, CA

Copyright © 2008 by Steve Baldwin and Karen Holgate

All rights reserved. No part of this book may be reproduced in any form or by any means, electronic, mechanical, photocopying, scanning, or otherwise, without permission in writing from the publisher, except by a reviewer who may quote brief passages in a review.

Jacket Design by Linda Daly

WND Books are distributed to the trade by:

Midpoint Trade Books
27 West 20th Street, Suite 1102
New York, NY 10011

WND Books are available at special discounts for bulk purchases. WorldNetDaily also publishes books in electronic formats. For more information call (310) 961-4170 or visit www.wndbooks.com.

First Edition

ISBN 10-Digit: 0979267110
ISBN 13-Digit: 9780979267116
LCCN: 2008920623

Printed in the United States of America

10 9 8 7 6 5 4 3 2 1

This book is dedicated to all the parents who have struggled against the public school monopoly to simply retain their rights as parents, to the students who have been subjected to inappropriate material and practices, and finally to teachers who have struggled to ensure that their pupils learn despite liberal legislators and their determination to use classrooms to indoctrinate instead of educate.

CONCORDIA UNIVERSITY LIBRARY
PORTLAND, OR 97211

CONTENTS

FOREWORD

By Phyllis Schlafly

The *American Citizens Handbook*, published fifty-eight years ago by the nation's largest teachers union, the National Education Association (NEA), offers a dramatic illustration of how public schools have changed. It's a sort of civics handbook written to promote citizenship among young people. It includes essays on citizenship, brief biographies of "heroes and heroines of American democracy," and reprints of historical documents that are the "great charters of American democracy."

One section entitled "A Golden Treasury for the Citizen" offers passages suitable for memorization by children. The *Handbook* advises the importance of students having "a like heritage of purpose, religious ideals, love of country, beauty, and wisdom to guide and inspire them." Numerous Old and New Testament selections are included, including the Ten Commandments, the Lord's Prayer, and the Golden Rule. The book unabashedly celebrates old-fashioned virtue and patriotism. The Boy Scout oath, national songs, and uplifting poems appear alongside geography facts and a household budget. This NEA *Handbook* embraces "the creation of national unity" and "Americanization" as explicit tasks for the schools.

The first *exposé* of big changes in the American public schools was *Why Johnny Can't Read* by Rudolf Flesch. In this 1955 book, he laid bare how public schools had abandoned the teaching of phonics (i.e., learning the sounds and syllables of the English language and how to put them together like building blocks), and substituted a method called "look-say" (i.e., recognizing and memorizing a few dozen whole words, usually from clues in pictures, and reading stories that repeat the same words *ad nauseam*).

Look-say took over the U.S. educational system with the elementary school readers entitled *Dick and Jane*.

The result was that students didn't learn how to read books without pictures and with polysyllabic words. The entire educational system was "dumbed down" to accommodate this new reality.

The public schools adamantly refused to reinstate the proven system of phonics. Twenty-five years after his landmark book, Rudolf Flesch wrote *Why Johnny Still Can't Read*. The schools had renamed look-say as "whole language" and to this day persist in stubborn hostility to phonics. We now have two or even three generations of Americans who are virtually blocked out from reading the great books written in the English language.

Sidney Simon's 1972 book *Values Clarification* had a profound effect on public school curriculum. Its message was that the school's mission was to get the children to create their own value system, preferably without reference to what their parents may have prescribed. The methodology was to present the students with a series of moral dilemmas and let them choose their own solutions, with the *caveat* that any choice is acceptable. Situation ethics became the norm.

The classroom became a place for children to confront all varieties of adult behaviors and depressing situations. Instead of acquiring basic knowledge of history, literature, math, and science, more and more classroom time was spent discussing feelings, attitudes, beliefs, and behaviors.

This change in the mission of public schools was best encapsulated by Samuel Hayakawa, president of San Francisco State College and later a U.S. senator from California, who stated: "An educational heresy has flourished, a heresy that rejects the idea of education as the acquisition of knowledge and skills…the heresy of which I speak regards the fundamental task in education as therapy."[1]

By the late 1970s, the most widely used schoolroom therapy was the nosy questionnaire, which required students to answer a long, specific list of leading questions about their personal behavior in regard to sex, drugs, and suicide. Parental outrage at this invasion of student privacy and parental rights resulted in passage of the federal Protection of Pupil Rights Amendment. The public school establishment's open hostility to this law, and the testimonies that detailed its need, are set forth in my 1984 book, *Child Abuse in the Classroom.*

This law has never been enforced and, by 2005, the schools had won the support of the federal courts for their right to inflict nosy questionnaires. The Ninth Circuit Court of Appeals ruled in *Fields v. Palmdale School District* that the fundamental right of parents over the care and upbringing of their children "does not extend beyond the threshold of the school door," and a public school has the right to give students "whatever information it wishes to provide, sexual or otherwise."

The *Palmdale* decision resurrected a Latin phrase, *parens patriae,* used centuries ago by British kings to mean the country is the parent. In the last several years, five federal circuits have handed down decisions that support the public schools in doing whatever they want regardless of parental and public objections. These decisions support not only mandatory nosy questionnaires but indoctrination about homosexuality, so-called "safe" sex, evolution, and Islam.

From Crayons to Condoms is a compilation of eloquent, often heartrending, testimonies of parents and teachers who tried to resist unwanted psychological manipulation of students. Dozens of examples are set forth of how behavior modification and ideological indoctrination are imposed on public school students in every kind of class, including history, civics, English, and even math. Students are promoted and given "A"s (to help their self-esteem) without being taught the essentials of American history, government, and arithmetic.

From Crayons to Condoms provides a firsthand look at defective curricula, assignment of books that are vulgar and depressive, psychological courses in death and suicide, explicit sex education courses, hate-America multiculturalism, and other inappropriate classroom assignments. The book also has a useful finale on what parents can do to protect their children. It is must reading for any parent who sends his child to a public school.

Phyllis Schlafly, B.A., M.A., J.D., is the author of twenty books, a radio commentator, and the president of Eagle Forum.

ACKNOWLEDGMENTS

We want to thank all those who contributed their personal stories to make this book a reality. We know that for many it was difficult to sit down and openly relive stressful and sometimes painful experiences. You all did a great job! Thank you.

Also, our deepest appreciation to Ami Naramor of WND Books. Her ongoing patience with all of our questions and changes should qualify her for sainthood. We couldn't have done this without her suggestions, advice, and comments.

And finally, we want to thank our own families: Patti and the boys and Steve and the girls for being so patient with us over the years and for their loving support during this whole process.

INTRODUCTION: IT'S A NATIONAL PROBLEM

EVERY DAY, parents confidently send their children to school trusting that they will spend the day learning their ABCs. For far too many, that trust is woefully misplaced. Unfortunately, unsuspecting parents don't know that many children are psychologically molested by classroom exercises, many of which focus on death and suicide, graphic sex, and invasive surveys. Some schools even force children to participate in religious practices which may be in direct opposition to the children's families' personal beliefs. Questionnaires ask questions about how children feel, their families, their religious beliefs, their political affiliations, and whether they or their family members take drugs or drink alcohol.

Schools too often shunt academics aside to make room for "support groups" that delve into children's psyches and waste valuable classroom time by having children in elementary school solve each other's personal problems.[1] Sometimes these exercises conclude with the admonishment not to discuss what happened with anyone outside of the classroom. One in-service facilitator told elementary school teachers that he would show them fun ways to teach children "confidentiality."[2] (He failed to say from whom the children were supposed to keep these confidences. Was it Mom and Dad?)

Today's education emphasizes the basic premise that the proper socialization of children is best accomplished by integrating "politically correct" attitudes and values into academics. Yet when schools water down academics to accommodate social agendas, the quality of academic subject matter can only suffer.

Senator Robert Byrd of West Virginia, in a speech before Congress on June 9, 1997, pointed out the controversial social issues integrated into today's textbooks. In what he referred to as "wacko" algebra, the senator gave one of the best examples of this new integration technique. Quoting from the algebra textbook *Secondary Math: An Integrated Approach: Focus on Algebra*, Senator Byrd said:

> Let me quote from the opening page. "In the twenty-first century, computers will do a lot of the work that people used to do. Even in today's workplace, there is little need for someone to add up daily invoices or compute sales tax. Engineers and scientists already use computer programs to do calculations and solve equations." What kind of message is sent by that brilliant opening salvo? It hardly impresses upon the student the importance of mastering the basics of mathematics or encourages them to dig in and prepare for the difficult work it takes to be a first-rate student in math...
>
> Page five of this same wondrous tome begins with a heading written in Spanish, English and Portuguese... This odd amalgam of math, geography and language masquerading as an algebra textbook goes on to intersperse each chapter with helpful comments and photos of children named Taktuk, Esteban and Minh. Although I don't know what happened to Dick and Jane, I do understand now why there are four multicultural reviewers for this book. However, I still don't quite grasp the necessity for political correctness in an algebra textbook. Nor do I understand the inclusion of the United Nations Universal Declaration of Human Rights in three languages...
>
> ...By the time we get around to defining an algebraic expression we are on page 107... From there we hurry on to lectures on endangered species, a discussion of air pollution, facts about the Dogon people of West Africa, chili recipes and a discussion of varieties of hot peppers... I was thoroughly dazed and unsure whether I was looking at a science book, a language book, a sociology book or a geography book.
>
> This textbook tries to be all things to all students in all subjects and the result is a mush of multiculturalism, environmental and political correctness...it is unfocused nonsense...
>
> Mathematics is about rules, memorized procedures and methodical thinking. We do memorize the multiplication tables, don't we?[3]

The practical result of these universal reforms is that they "dumb down" the curriculum. Under these reforms, students know they aren't being educated.

One angry ninth-grade girl, with tears streaming down her face, told how she had been asked to determine the circumference of a circle. She said each student received a piece of string, along with instructions to place the string around a circle and hold it up to a ruler. The teacher then required them to write about the process! "I did that in elementary school. How dare they treat us like first graders! I'm so mad! I know there's a way to use math to figure the circumference of a circle but they won't teach me!"[4]

Indeed—how dare they! And how dare we allow it to continue!

Whether in math—as with the tearful ninth grader—or in some other subject, no class is exempt from the dumbing down process that integrates core academics with the politically correct psychosocial agenda. The bottom line is that these new reforms breed academic failure. And for this reason, parents in every state across America are beginning to speak out.

A 1996 report published by the Office of Educational Research and Improvement said when talking about school principals, district superintendents, and regional administrators: "These executives typically operate with a keen sense of politics, both in understanding the process and knowing the players. *They are also willing to take risks and recognize that change demands time, mistakes and a tolerance of failure*" (emphasis added).[5]

That says it all. In their opinion, school reform is an experiment; if it fails—too bad! Our children are expendable. The educational bureaucracy is willing to tolerate failure for and from our children. The question is: Are we willing to tolerate their failure to educate our children, and will we continue sacrificing our children at the altar of experimental education?

Some teachers and administrators, however, will not admit that their social engineering experiments are even partly to blame for the academic failure we now see in our public schools. The prevailing view, espoused by the education establishment, is that our underachieving schools suffer from inadequate funding, an assertion that simple fact checking shows to be false. There is no correlation between performance and funding. Indeed, some of the lowest per-pupil funded states are the highest performing states whereas, conversely, the states spending the most money per pupil are at or near bottom nationwide in performance.[6] And, in fact, solid academics sometimes cost far less than experimental methodologies. For instance, *The Beginning Reading Instruction Study* reported that it cost $30 per pupil to teach phonics compared with $214 per pupil to teach whole language.[7]

Most parents, many educators (considered maverick because they adhere to the principle that schools should actually educate children), and a handful of school board members hold an alternative view: that our schools perform poorly because they no longer focus on academic achievement. Instead, they pursue faddish educational practices such as inventive spelling, whole language, constructivist[8] math, cooperative learning, self-esteem programs, and death education. Indeed, it is a common view among educators that public schools exist, not so much to teach academics, but to shape our children emotionally and psychologically in the proper politically correct image. Moreover, public schools are inundated with social studies curricula containing false and misleading concepts, and sex education programs whose main purpose apparently is to challenge societal norms. Academics take a back seat to social engineering.

Low performance is a nationwide problem that has escalated even further as a result of federal legislation. Today's school "reform" movement is an all-encompassing program that calls for total systemic change in every state, every district, and every school in America. In 1994, the Clinton administration passed two key pieces of federal legislation. These bills, the Goals 2000: Educate America Act and the School-to-Work Opportunities Act (STW)—now referred to as "career technical education" or some similar euphemism in many districts—mapped out the radical reform agenda that is still promulgated today.

While Goals 2000 and STW may have sounded good to their promoters, in reality the bills sacrificed academics and created the framework for "feeling-centered" or affective education. Called a paradigm shift, the new goals "shifted" education away from traditional core academics such as spelling, reading, math, science, history, athletics, and the arts, to the shaping of children's attitudes, values, beliefs, and behaviors.

STW should not be confused with traditional vocational education. While "voc-ed" incorporates job-training skills into traditionally sound academic coursework, STW refocused the purpose of education from a broad-based liberal arts education to narrow-focused entry-level job training. Sadly lacking in promoters of these radical reforms is the understanding that K-12 education should, in fact, provide the base upon which students can build their skills and knowledge for upwardly mobile career choices.

One of the least understood features of the original STW legislation was the requirement that students participate in "work-based" learning. Unlike the typical weekend or summer vacation work experience most parents think of when their children work part-time, work-based learning was encouraged *during classroom hours*. Under the plan, children would be allowed to leave campus during regular school hours to do their work-based learning at local businesses. If "career technical education" is ever fully implemented as originally designed, *all* children will be required to participate in "entry-level" job training—often at the expense of academics.

Unfortunately, federal involvement has only grown since that time, including the more recent passage of "No Child Left Behind." As with the other federal programs, this program has done little to improve academic performance. And today, politicians call for more federal education programs, never seeming to understand that a centralized approach to education *just doesn't work*.

The overall feeling of parents is that they, as taxpayers, are no longer in charge of our public schools—or of their own children. Instead, unelected elites, often backed by school boards, impose policies and practices irrespective of parental protests. In fact, it is clear the rights of parents have steadily eroded over the last few decades, and the abuses recorded here reflect this erosion. Unless steps are taken to wake citizens up as to what is happening in our public schools, these anti-academic trends will not only continue, but increase.

The movement to involve government in your child's life at an increasingly earlier age continues to grow. In an interview, actor Rob Reiner discussed an early intervention program called the I Am Your Child Campaign. His premise was that more government early childhood programs were needed because even parents with good instincts didn't know everything about child development.[9] Apparently, government bureaucrats now believe it is their place to tell you although it makes you wonder how parents have been able to raise children for thousands of years without government intervention.

Over the last few years, legislators have introduced numerous bills in states throughout the nation to strengthen and clarify parental rights. But often, with few exceptions, these bills have died along party lines. While school officials lament the lack of parental involvement, the reality is that unless parents heartily endorse every new education fad and unless they continue to ignore the failure of these experimental programs, parents are not wanted. In many cases, they are ridiculed, arrogantly dismissed as troublemakers, or ignored.

Many people wonder why parents are not more involved in our public schools. One possible reason is that when parents do get involved in any substantial way, they are gradually shut out of the process. The attitude of school administrators and some teachers seems to be that parents are useful only for organizing bake sales or rubber-stamping bureaucratic goals, but nothing else—and woe to parents who dare challenge those in "authority."

We challenge parents to find out what is going on in their schools and to ask themselves: *Have I read the curricula or the textbooks? How explicit is my child's sex education course? Does the school violate our family's value system? Has my child been told that parents whose belief system is different from what is taught in school are wrong? Have I read the books my child is reading? Is my child given surveys and questionnaires that ask intimate details about our family? Does my child's school teach phonics or whole language and math that focuses on computational skills, or does it use fuzzy, feel-good math integrated with social values? Does my state allow children to receive medical or mental health services without my knowledge or permission?*

A phone call or letter from a constituent carries a lot of weight. If every parent and teacher reading this book would call his or her state and federal legislators and demand that they end worthless federal and state programs and instead focus on basic skills, changes would occur. If parents questioned candidates about their stances on education, and then voted based on those candidates' stands—and held those candidates accountable for their votes—changes would occur. Until laws change or until parents demand that their legislators make those changes, educational malpractice will continue. It is our hope that *From Crayons to Condoms* will serve as a wakeup call for parents and encourage them to demand meaningful education reforms.

We present a book with two basic parts: First, we present personal stories from parents, teachers, students, and school board members from all over the country. Then we present some options parents can pursue if they want to challenge the *status quo*.

We encountered far more stories than those collected here, but due to space considerations, we selected only a small sampling. Most of the personal stories have never been reported, nor have they appeared anywhere else.

These stories are not only about bizarre textbooks or failed teaching practices but also about dangerous, even deadly, results. Some psychological procedures in the classroom are highly leading—and in death education may even contribute to suicide, as one of the stories included here so tragically demonstrates. Other stories deal with sex and AIDS education practices that promote high-risk behavior.

The stories are representative of a diverse population; they are from well-to-do parents and lower income inner-city parents, from parents living in rural and urban areas, and from parents of different ethnicities. The overwhelming sense of frustration so evident in these stories knows no financial, ethnic, or geographic boundaries. Parents who are not activists and who accidentally stumbled upon a bizarre teaching technique or ineffective methodology wrote most of the stories. In many cases, they quietly took their concerns to a teacher or administrator. Most of the time, they were ignored or told the incident was isolated and wouldn't happen again.

Many parents were labeled troublemakers and told, "You're the only parent with this problem." The overall message was that those who run the schools are the experts and parents shouldn't interfere. In many cases, the parents, frustrated, pulled their child from school and enrolled him or her in a private or home school. However, many parents can't afford to do this and thus some of the authors have asked for anonymity to protect their children from retribution.

Nearly all the parents we spoke with were not part of any anti-public school group. They truly wanted to improve their schools by exposing something they thought was improper. Most were shocked to find that what they considered improper was, in fact, standard practice. Nearly all of them remain frustrated, since their issue was never resolved and the treatment they received was usually less than cordial.

We ask that you read this book with an open mind. It is not meant to attack individuals or target specific schools; the purpose is to point out a growing trend in our nation's education system. We also want our readers to know that we struggled with whether or not to include some of the language this book contains. Some of it is sexually graphic and very crude. However, in the end, we decided that if the material is too vulgar for parents and other adults to read, then it is that much worse for our children to study in their classrooms. For that reason, we decided to let the filth speak for itself. We apologize in advance and warn you that some of the following information is pornographic in nature. Our hope is that as you read the following stories that rather than say, *that's not happening in my child's class,* you will instead ask: *Is that happening in my child's classroom?*

Steve Baldwin, former California State Assemblyman
Karen Holgate, former Director of Legislative Affairs, California Family Council

Sliding Academic Standards

CHAPTER ONE

THE CURRICULUM OF SOCIAL ENGINEERING

M ANY OF THE STORIES *detailed in the following section discuss programs dictated by the federal government which have affected school curricula nationwide. While some people may think that federal involvement in education is part of American history and culture, they are mistaken. The federal government's role in education is a modern idea and, indeed, many constitutional scholars believe it to be unconstitutional.*

President Jimmy Carter created the United States Department of Education (USDOE) in 1979 as a result of a deal made between his campaign and one of the Democrat Party's main power brokers: the teachers' union.[1] The union agreed to throw all its members' support and money behind Carter's candidacy in exchange for his agreeing to create the new federal agency.

One might argue that federal involvement with our schools has been a positive development; however, an argument can be made that just the opposite is true. We now have hundreds of federal programs and mandates burdening schools across the nation while the budget for the USDOE has grown massively. But despite the growth of the federal Department of Education, academic achievement during this same time period has been in decline by any measure.

The only reason the USDOE still exists is the love affair too many legislators have with a large, impersonal central government—the children be damned. The federal programs have placed unreasonable regulations upon our school districts, centralized policies and programs historically controlled by local schools, and diverted precious local resources in order to comply with federal dictates and programs which have repeatedly been proven worthless. The myriad of federal programs that now exist suffer from a one-

size-fits-all mentality and are driven by an elitist utopian philosophy that the federal bureaucrats know what's best for our children.

Integrated, nonacademic coursework begins at the earliest grades. An English curriculum for elementary students, Language Is Fun, Level One, Book One, includes a portfolio assignment that tells the young students: "Perhaps children don't always love their families...write a story about these times."² What parent would believe that schools should tell children that there are times when children don't love their families? Of what possible academic value is this type of curriculum?

As the following stories reveal, it isn't always easy for parents to monitor what schools teach in their children's classrooms. Titles of textbooks, curricula, or exercises may change, and often do, which is why it will be an ongoing challenge for parents to stay abreast of today's classrooms.

Human Interaction Program

Graduation requirements approved by our school board mandated students take a one-semester course entitled "Human Interaction (HI)." The course outline was sufficiently vague to keep parents in the dark about the curriculum's content, and labeled any parent who opposed the program a "right wing, religious extremist."

After much evasive action by district employees, the district finally allowed us to view HI's content and we were stunned by its pervasive invasion of students' privacy and that of their families. We were equally appalled by the district's presumption that all families were composed of dysfunctional, uncommunicative strangers who just happened to live in the same house. Based on our objections to these content areas, we immediately requested an exemption/waiver for both of our children from the graduation requirement.

The school district informed us that they only allowed students to "opt out" for objections based on religious beliefs or related to sex education. (Our objections were not based on religious beliefs, nor did we object to sex education—as long as it conveyed factual information about communicable diseases and AIDS.) The school district told us that they would not take up the question of waivers until the spring semester of a student's senior year. We questioned the policy and expressed our concern over students' inability to plan their courses under such unreasonable restrictions. While appealing the waiver process, our son did not attend an academic alternative class; instead the school assigned him as an "aide" to the school counselors.

We finally contacted the newspapers. Reporters approached us with preconceived ideas about who we were, our position, our politics, and our religious affiliations. When we showed them questions used in the classroom, including: "What presidential candidate did your mom vote for in 1980?" and "Who are your parents' closest friends?" they were quite surprised. These reporters soon learned that our objections centered on solid constitutional and confidentiality grounds. (We still question why 1980, when Ronald Reagan defeated Jimmy Carter, was chosen as the pivotal year. What did the school hope to learn about the students' families?)

A popular columnist in our area, Debra Saunders, highlighted the proposed "waiver" our district asked us to sign. This "waiver" required us to give our reasons for opting our children out of the class and made us "declare" that we would provide an "appropriate alternative education experience" comparable with HI's content. This waiver carried the legal consequences of forcing us to sign "under penalty of perjury." As Saunders said, "The sentence for committing perjury, by the by, is up to four years."[3]

As other parents encouraged us to continue our opposition, our district's position became increasingly inflexible. They took the position that the psychological probing found in HI would prevent abuse and the spread of AIDS, and would encourage all families to discuss sex, religion, and politics.

The district repeatedly refused to acknowledge our allegations that teachers collected and read the surveys in the classrooms—with complete answers. District officials and members of the board were embarrassed when the publicity surrounding the case revealed that this practice was indeed conducted in "HI." The district defended itself by saying that teachers didn't understand that the surveys were not intended as homework, but as "conversation starters" between parents and students. In a conversation with one pro-school reporter, we asked how the district would know whether parents discussed sex, politics, or religion with their children and what right it was of the school's to invade the privacy of the family.

We did receive a letter from the Department of Education's legal counsel. He supported our belief that the course violated the state education code, and agreed that the district's position of delaying waiver decisions placed the student and family in an untenable position. However, he was careful to remind us that the DOE decision was not binding upon the district.

A series of editorials, newspaper columns, letters to the editor, and a petition presented to the district combined to establish that HI's content violated family privacy. Public opinion turned increasingly against the district.

Ultimately, the district granted waivers to our children. They now offer unconditional waivers to most parents who request them. The lesson for parents? Don't give in. Fight for your rights!

Tura Avner

Psychosocial Curriculum

As the mother of four children, I have fought with teachers, principals, and school boards over the increased emphasis on psychosocial teaching in the schools.

When my daughter was a sixth grader, the school devoted an entire week to sex education. At the end of the program, just before summer break, teachers brought all of the sixth-grade classes into one room and showed the students movie after movie for three days. Supposedly this was their "graduation present" from the school.

I also challenged my daughter's "death education" class in which the teacher instructed the students to write their own epitaphs. The teacher also required the class to write a short story for English about the most life-changing incident each had ever experienced—such as the death of a relative or a personal near-death experience. My daughter had no story to tell so she created a fictitious one about dying and going to heaven. The teacher pulled my daughter aside and asked her if this had really happened. My daughter lied and told the teacher it really had. The

4

teacher then suggested my daughter visit the school psychologist "just as a person to talk to about this."

My daughter also learned values clarification at her junior high school. The students were to pretend they were in a life-boat—their ship had just sunk. Aboard the life raft were a pregnant woman, a captain, children, a gay man, etc. Since the raft could only hold a certain number of people, the students had to decide who would have to get out—and thus die—in order to avoid sinking the lifeboat. The purpose of this exercise was to determine the students' values.

I regularly attended school board meetings to oppose these psychological programs in the school. I was always told I was the "only one" complaining, or I was passed off as a "troublemaker." Apparently, the board believed these accusations were valid reasons to dismiss my opposition to various programs.

My son was a GATE (Gifted and Talented) student during his entire public school career. During his senior year he received a book titled *General Psychology*. When I questioned him about studying psychology, he insisted that the book was a civics book. To bolster his argument, he showed me his class schedule which did indeed describe the class as a civics course, not a psychology class. As a concerned parent, I discussed the issue with the principal who said, "Psychology is civics." He added, "Psychology teaches civic responsibility." When I tried to read him the definition of psychology, he said, "I'm not going to get into a semantic argument with you." I left frustrated, especially since I had just been asked to tutor high school students who were failing the "civics" section on state assessment tests.

I became concerned one year about New Beginnings, a program created by the director of the county Department of Social Services. The program involved a "waiver-of-confidentiality" agreement between the school districts and the Department of Social Services. I saw this as a dangerous action for a free society since it would allow unknown bureaucrats to perform "services" for children without parental knowledge or consent.

Another year, I attended a seminar titled "Tools to Enhance School Success" presented to forty-five elementary teachers and counselors at a public meeting room. A district administrator approached my friend and me and told us we would have to leave because the training was "for professionals only." I said we would not disturb the meeting and that as taxpayers paying for the seminar, we had a right to observe the teacher training. We sat in the back of the room and quietly took notes.

The director of a psychiatric center led the seminar, and it was based on his book, *Conducting Support Groups for Elementary Children K-6*.[4] The school district paid $2,700 for the two-day training program, plus the hall rental and salaries for substitute teachers.

The speaker began his presentation by saying, "Younger kids don't have their defenses built up yet so you get better results in the groups." He then suggested that education needed to get rid of the term "support groups" because they are really "educational groups," and that "support groups" provide therapy while "educational groups" do not. He continued by saying that confidentiality should be a group rule and elementary kids know how to keep confidences, "Which surprises me," he declared. This speaker went on to say that he would show teachers fun ways to teach "confidentiality" and a "feeling vocabulary" so that kids could "express their feelings."

At about 9:00 a.m., the teachers took a break. Five sheriff's officers entered the seminar, approached us, and asked us to leave. When I asked what law we were violating, one officer said we were "trespassing." When I pointed out that the building was public property, he said he couldn't argue the point but that the paperwork said "trespassing." He said if we refused to leave we faced arrest. I left. My friend, Connie Youngkin, did not leave, and the officers carried her out of the room in her chair, arrested her, and took her to jail. (Connie Youngkin's story appears elsewhere in this book.)

Later, we found out that one of the school board trustees, a college professor and opponent of psychological programs, had wished to attend the seminar, but the district office gave her the wrong day and time, so she missed it. We asked another community member to attend the seminar on the following day, but the seminar was moved to another location, and the district office would not disclose the new location.

In May of that year, the Fresh Start team sponsored another seminar. Held in a room at the county Office of Education, the seminar's focus was about raising what was referred to as the "Protective Factors" and levels of "resiliency" in students. The introduction listed K-4 students who were considered "high risk" by teachers. These included students who were repeated failures in school; potential dropouts; economically disadvantaged students; children of drug or alcohol abusers; victims of physical, sexual, or psychological abuse; students with mental health problems; students who had committed violent or delinquent acts; students experiencing long-term pain due to injury; and those who had attempted suicide.

My first question about this list was: "Since when have teachers been required to handle and report personal problems?" The second was, "How would a teacher gather this information without violating existing laws regarding personal questions about children and their families?"

At approximately 9:00 a.m., we were told there weren't enough binders, and our notebooks were taken from us.

The seminar presented "wellness" as the foundation for the Fresh Start program. It seemed to me that the word "wellness" disguised various psychological programs to be presented in the classroom. "Wellness" was presented in a psychological context, and it soon became apparent that teachers would determine whether or not a child was "well." The presenter said, "Wellness is a way of life...[it] is woven into our mission goals, statement and strategic plans...[and] provides a key to all students being ready to learn."

At one point, teachers received a Resiliency Checklist to use with students, along with the caution, "I wouldn't send this home at all." During a discussion of permission slips, one participant complained about having to ask for them from parents. The presenter said, "We must trust the process," and then mentioned "educational groups" currently in place at the high school level. Someone asked, "Is that a support group sponsored by the school?" The answer was,

"Yes." The presenter went on to say that thirty-five such groups at the local high school were led by facilitators—not counselors.

On May 9, the seminar convened with discussions on "paradigm shifts," "embracing diversity," "parent training," "tracking behavior referrals," "conflict resolution," "peer tutoring," "problem solving techniques," and "suicide prevention" programs. Sample activities included role playing. Participants were told that Fresh Start was designed to "get the kids to monitor their own behavior."

While some of these programs may have been well-intentioned, the overall surreptitious nature of the teacher training had me greatly concerned. Teachers learned psychological programming and social engineering techniques to use on children.

Educators are not qualified to engage in psychological counseling. It is not their function as educators to administer these kinds of programs. To do so could seriously damage children!

Carol Ann Lindsay

"101 Ways to Do It Without Going All the Way"

During our son's sophomore year in high school, he was taught evolution as fact. On a biology test he was asked to write a letter to the editor in which he was either to defend or oppose evolution. In choosing to oppose evolution, he wrote in defense of creation. The teacher wrote this note at the end of the paper: "Hmm! Just a question—Have you read the book you believe in? Full of great truths, some great history, and a lot of ancient beliefs about how things happened. <u>Beware of fanaticism which is based on ignorance.</u>"

One day, while my husband and I waited in the school office to talk to the counselor, we noticed the physical education teacher copying documents. When someone asked her when she would be finished, she said she had to get the papers copied to hand out to her class that day. Since our son attended her class, we wondered why a gym teacher would hand out papers to her students, so we took a look at what she was copying. The paper was called "101 Ways to Do It Without Going All the Way."

This particular teacher is openly lesbian. Many students and parents report that she has promoted her lifestyle to students.

After taking her class, some of the students were said to be "confused" about their own sexuality.

For my son's final exam, he received a copy of *Health: Study Guide*. This "guide" asked students to list their "personal thoughts" and wanted to know how the class had "changed any views" they may have had towards "health, values or personal wellness." The guide stated that "academic knowledge is secondary to the personal knowledge" the students had gained.

When our state's new assessment test came along, we questioned the intrusive nature of the questions. Finally, we submitted forms to opt our son out of the test. The school refused to allow us this right. We immediately withdrew him from the public school system. He now attends a private school and his education and grades have improved dramatically.

Our local district has since sent us flyers with the slogan: "Remember, it takes an entire village to raise a child." Our district has applied for a grant to bring social services onto the school grounds and officials even refer to some of their programs as "An extended family for the youth." Who invited them?

Steve and Karen Anderson

How Do You Feel About Math?

When my oldest son was in third grade, the teacher tried to convince us that "all the research showed" that a literature-based curriculum was the best thing for our children. Four years later, I went back to that teacher and asked her if she still believed in the literature-based curriculum, also known as integrated thematic teaching, and more commonly referred to as whole language. She admitted that after three years, students—now in fifth and sixth grade—were doing miserably. She said the program was a failure and that they wouldn't use it again. Yet in the same district, another school was implementing the same experimental program.

When my son was in seventh grade, he told me about a "stupid" exercise they had done in math class. He explained that they were divided into groups and told to write in their "own words" how they "felt" about the problem that had just been discussed. My son

9

wrote that he thought it was a "stupid waste of time." Since his "own words" were not good enough, the teacher twice tore up and threw away his paper. Finally he gave up and copied, with the rest of his group, what the teacher had written on the board.

Because this seemed like an unusual exercise for a math class, I contacted the principal to find out what they were doing. He informed me that he gave his teachers considerable freedom in their classrooms. He then showed me the math framework from which this exercise was taken. Once I started reading and asking questions, I learned that the district had not approved this form of math. Not only was my son's teacher using a math curriculum without authorization or proven research, but the principal was condoning it and even approving it by virtue of his "hands off" policy. It was nothing less than an experiment and a phenomenal waste of class time.

When my youngest son was in sixth grade, I heard that all the students would be grouped together in math. In a "back-to-school night" for parents, I questioned his teacher. She said, "Yes, we are grouping students because by the time they get to junior high, there's just too wide a gap in levels of performance. Some perform at an eighth-grade level while others are struggling at the fourth-grade level." I couldn't believe my ears! She wanted to slow all students down to the level of the slowest learner.

I immediately called the principal and stated strongly that math should be taught and is learned better in traditional grade/ability-level groups. Since my son was advanced in math, I certainly expected him to learn at his level of ability. The following week, all the students took math tests to determine their level. I figured all was well.

Since parents weren't invited into the classroom anymore, I didn't notice how my son's love of math was dying. When his first report card arrived, we weren't thrilled to find that he was just getting by in math. He didn't even like math any longer.

I decided to make a surprise visit to my son's class. The day after we received his report card, I went to school and practically had to force my way into his classroom. Immediately I noticed that, despite the fact that the students had taken proficiency entrance exams, they were all together in one classroom. There was no division according to ability. This directly contradicted the stated purpose for the entrance exams. In addition, the teacher was incompetently teaching sixth graders that wrong math answers were okay. I guess he didn't want to undermine their self-esteem. I actually witnessed him encouraging students to applaud a girl who gave a wrong answer. It was unbelievable! No wonder my son was beginning to hate math!

Earlier, this teacher had told my son to stop tutoring another boy in how to arrive at a correct answer. When the teacher used the calculator, he too gave the wrong answer, and yet he had the gall to tell my son that he was wrong! I had had enough. That was the end of my child's being subjected to that incompetent teacher. We pulled him out of that class but the teacher is still there.

The district appointed me to our math textbook adoption committee because of my involvement in curricula research and in helping to defeat our state assessment test. It was unbelievable to watch as adults willingly became indoctrinated with the mantra, "all the research shows," without asking for evidence. I felt like I had entered the Twilight Zone of academia. Most of the people on each district's committee were teachers, with a sprinkling of parents. Only a few of these parents and very few teachers ever challenged the *status quo* at any of our meetings.

Initially, I wanted to find out if there were others who believed as I did about math, namely that rote memorization is vital and that knowledge is cumulative. I was satisfied that sanity prevailed among members of the committee—but not for long. It was fascinating to watch as persuasive tactics were put "to the test." It wasn't long before these well-intentioned and intelligent people accepted theories as fact, and then embraced them. At each district meeting, fewer and fewer members were able to withstand the messages [indoctrination] and "buzzwords," including "empowered learners," "critical thinkers," "in-depth projects," "group learning," "peer tutoring," "teacher as facilitator or coach," and so on.

At one meeting, I asked the assistant to the county superintendent: "Do you really believe rote memorization is unnecessary and that calculators are perfectly acceptable for elementary school classes in lieu of memorization?" I was dumbfounded when she replied,

"Calculation practice is like phonics—not all that necessary!" Need I say more? This is what they call "New New Math."

At another meeting I asked the president of publishing house Silver-Burdett, which had been excluded from the math adoption list because of their failure to conform to math frameworks (written by "New New Math" advocates), how other publishers could, with any integrity, publish materials in conformance with our state's math framework. He responded by saying, "I agree with you. In fact, we lost $1.5 million because, after testing our material that originally complied with the framework, we determined that it was a failure." They went back to the drawing board and produced a math textbook designed to teach math.

The publishers of the Quest 2000 textbook series sent an author to address our committee. This publisher had adhered so closely to the state's math framework that one teacher expressed concern over the lack of assessment benchmarks. The author responded by saying, "We had to put in assessments for the program under the table, otherwise we wouldn't have gotten on the state's adoption list." When asked by the same teacher how students could learn without drill and practice, the author responded again by saying, "We put them in under the table."

Where is the integrity? Where is the research? I was appalled to learn there is neither. In fact, I learned there were no records kept of failed or successful curricula, textbooks, or tests. I discovered this by accident when I suggested that we take the Saxon math publishers up on their offer of free textbooks for any district that would keep a thorough record to either substantiate or negate their curricula. The answer was, "Yes, we used Saxon in the past, but heard that there were teachers who didn't like it."

When I asked if anyone had kept records, the response was, "No." I was told that the district had implemented pilot programs using Saxon but no research was done and no documentation accompanied or followed these pilot programs. I next tried to introduce Saxon textbooks at a school board meeting. As I sat down, one teacher actually hissed at me! Both of my sons are now in private school.

Anne Gluch

Whole Language & a Zero-Retention Policy

We have two children in public school. But I fear that my son is another victim of whole language. At eleven years old, he couldn't write a legible letter or report. His writing skills were poor, and his spelling was atrocious!

Over the years, my husband and I kept in constant touch with his teachers, cooperating with them in every possible way. In an effort to improve our son's spelling, I helped in the classroom and had him tutored. I was very upset with the decision to include sixth graders in middle school because I felt that children our son's age were too immature to handle the additional stress.

At the end of fifth grade, our son's report card was so bad that I was determined to hold him back a year. The principal of his school told me that was impossible. After speaking with the principal, other parents, and school board members, I discovered that there was zero retention at our school. The policy was to pass children through the system regardless of their capabilities. I was determined to keep him back. I talked to more people, including the school board members, who were nice but patronizing. I then decided to have him tested by an independent testing firm to find out if he was capable of fifth-grade work. His scores were good and he showed that he could do the work, so my husband and I decided, with reservations, to let him continue.

The next three months were terrible! He grew more and more disruptive in class and fell behind. His attitude was—if I may use his own words—"I suck; kick me hard!" He said he didn't care anymore—he hated school.

This is where we are today, and we are beside ourselves. For six years I have talked to teachers and heard all sorts of soothing things such as: "He'll get it together; it takes time." "Some kids just have a hard time with spelling." Of course, they ask the standard questions, "Does he get enough sleep?" "Have a place to study?" "How much TV does he watch?" "Has he been tested for A.D.D.?" Because he is adopted, I have heard such helpful statements as, "There are drug babies out there, you know, who have problems with learning." "Does he know he's adopted?" And my personal favorite: "Have you talked with him about how important education is and that you love him?"

I could go on and on, but my point is, we are caring parents who want the best for our children. We both work full-time but our home is stable. My husband is a wonderful, caring father, and we try to be supportive of our sons. We spend quite a bit of time with them, limit their TV, and yes, we have told our children they are adopted.

What's wrong with this picture? If it isn't our home life, it must be the school's method of teaching. I have progressed from a "cooperative parent" to one who is ready to sue the system for fraud, negligence, and malpractice! Yes, I am angry, frustrated, disillusioned, and frightened. My son is in danger of falling through the cracks. He is no longer motivated and believes he is stupid.

The system isn't capable of teaching children who learn at a different pace than the majority. The child who doesn't fit the prescribed mold is simply passed through the system and grows up to be an illiterate adult, further burdening an already overloaded welfare or prison system. But, of course, we must have zero retention! My son's teachers, and the principal, have been conscientious and caring, but they are handicapped by faulty curricula and teaching methods.

I feel vulnerable, inadequate, and helpless. My frustration only increases with the patronizing attitudes displayed by some teachers toward parents or when I, or other parents, are labeled "uncooperative" or "antagonistic." This only makes the tough job of parenting more difficult.

Susan Schnekenburger

Evolution Brainwashing

In high school, my son was required to take a science course for graduation. I explained to the principal that since he had already taken Origin (all about evolution) at one public school, he didn't want to take it again. Origin is in direct opposition to our religious beliefs, and our family felt that taking the course once was enough. Against my stated objection, they placed my son in Origin anyway.

The school placed him and his girlfriend in the same class, thinking he would more easily accept it. He didn't and refused to go to school for three days.

The principal called to ask why he wasn't in school. I told him that my son was upset because he had already taken Origin and didn't want to take it again. The principal replied, "There are things that he needs to do in this world whether he wants to or not." I told him this wasn't his concern and explained that my son was holding down a job and attending school full time even though it was a struggle because of his learning disabilities. I told him I didn't believe it was the school's responsibility to teach my son a "lesson" that he had learned long ago.

At this point, the principal switched gears and said, "I don't see where he has taken Origin before." I explained that whether it was called Origin or something else, the subject was the same—evolution—and that if he thought he would change my son's beliefs by having him take the same course several times, it wasn't going to happen.

The school finally allowed our son to opt out of the "required" course. It was interesting that the only other elective open to my son was Dream Interpretation. Knowing how important Dream Interpretation would be for his future employment, you can imagine how disappointed we were that the class was full.

David Sherrick

EDITORS' NOTE: *The following is a statement made by Mr. Sherrick's son:*

Because of my learning disabilities, I always attended special day classes in public schools. In an attempt to be mainstreamed, I attended the charter school at the end of my junior year and all of my senior year.

One day between classes, I asked the administrator, "Do I have enough credits to graduate?" He responded, "Unpucker your butt; don't worry about it." He said this out loud and in front of everyone in the "break" room. I was very embarrassed and angered by his statement.

My parents and I thought the charter school would be equipped to handle learning disabilities. They fell short. The teachers at the charter school had no special teaching skills or even time for the kids.

At my graduation ceremony, one of the teachers gave a speech. Throughout the entire speech he said, "G--damn it." Since my grandmother and parents were in the audience, along with numerous young children, I was once again embarrassed. This particular teacher consistently used profanity in the classroom.

All I wanted was an education and a diploma. I got the diploma.

Interactive Math Program (IMP)

We are a family of four living in a small town. Our two teenage children are the third generation in our family to attend local schools. My husband and I have always been very involved in our children's lives, coaching baseball and basketball teams or serving on various youth sports boards. Our children were always good students, and all seemed well as they approached high school with goals of attending the nearby university.

When our son began high school, the freshmen and their parents were introduced to a new math curriculum, Interactive Math Program (IMP). We were told our youngsters were lucky to have the opportunity to enroll in this new college-track math program that would fully prepare them for college math. We parents were warned not to be concerned about the fact that there were no books, or that students worked in groups. We were also told that there would be no individual classes in algebra, geometry, trigonometry, or calculus. The contents of those former classes would be combined in IMP, and in four years our children would acquire all of the desired math skills—and then some.

I admit I inwardly questioned the concept of math being taught in a group situation with no books, but, well, this was the new generation. They must have improved their teaching methods, right?

Our son received good math grades all through high school. The first red flag for us came at the end of his junior year when he registered to take the SAT college entrance exam. He received a sample book so that he could practice the types of math problems that he would encounter on the SAT. When he looked up at us with a funny expression and said, "I've never seen problems like this before," we knew we were in trouble.

Immediately we did what so many other families do today; we purchased books and video aids to help our son study and prepare for the SAT. By memorizing "like" problems, he was able to get a high enough score to be accepted at a university.

Our next shock came when he took an assessment test at the college. He was assessed at above average in reading and comprehension skills but significantly below grade level in math. We were very disappointed to find that he would have to spend a year in remedial math before he would be able to take a college math class—a whole year wasted!

My disappointment turned to anger and then to rage when I began talking to other local graduates. Almost without exception, they and their parents reported the same situation. Our brightest graduates were entering college without the math skills to succeed, and worst of all they were unaware of their deficiency until they arrived.

As my son began his college career (and his first remedial math class), I began meeting with other parents in our school district who had had similar experiences. We decided that even though it was too late for many of our own children, we owed it to our community to make our teachers, administrators, school board members, and neighbors aware of the situation. In fairness to the teachers and administrators, I think they really believed in their new math curriculum. We were sure they would be as concerned as we were, and that together we could remedy the situation.

Imagine our surprise when we not only met with resistance, but also animosity. It became obvious to us that the educators in our community believed in the new math curriculum and could not care less how our kids were doing in college. On one occasion, we brought several graduates to the school board meeting to tell their stories to the board. These were some of the top students from my son's graduation class. Without exception, they were struggling in college because of a lack of basic math skills. (Some have since lost scholarships because they could not maintain high grades in classes that required math skills!) Our presentation alarmed the school board and prompted them to schedule a three-hour special session on Saturday morning to discuss the problem.

Because my husband was a member of the school board, he helped us understand how effective short, factual presentations were. Our parent group arrived at the special Saturday session armed with so much factual, incriminating information that we were sure we would change the trend. We had even called our local private schools and documented the math curricula they used. We had evidence that demonstrated the ever-widening gap between the more traditional curricula used in these private schools and the new math curriculum used in our public schools. We just knew we would win the day!

We didn't count on the meeting being manipulated by the teachers and administrators, all of whom were "new math" proponents. The parents had approximately twenty minutes to present their findings while the teachers were given a total of two hours and twenty minutes![5] We listened as we were told to leave the business of educating our children to the professionals and that if our children were struggling in college it was the fault of something other than poor curriculum!

Eventually, through parents talking to other parents, the word spread about Interactive Math Program results. Parents of students entering ninth grade refused to enroll their children in IMP, and this year, enrollment is up in the traditional high school math classes. During this time, our daughter entered her high school junior year. She too had started in IMP as a freshman—after all, we wanted only the best for both our children. By that time, we were aware of our son's problems in college, but our daughter was already two years into the program. A special feature about IMP is that once enrolled, a student can't change courses. In order to apply to a four-year college, a student needs three years of math—either IMP or traditional. She was committed to one more year of IMP whether she was learning anything or not.

We panicked. We finally came up with the idea of enrolling her in the Kumon Math tutoring program. This program assesses a student's math skills and a starting point is found, regardless of age. The whole program is based on the fact that math should be taught in a sequential manner with no forward movement until the current skill is mastered. By moving in small sequential steps, through practice and memorization, the student begins to understand new concepts more easily. It sounded good!

Our daughter came home from her Kumon Math lesson the first day with a long face and explained that she was starting at a second grade level. After years of using calculators and being taught conceptual math theory, she could not even add and subtract accurately with reasonable speed.

With Kumon, our daughter can practice at her own speed and spends one hour every day learning traditional math. By next year, she should enter college near grade level!

My husband and I laugh about the fact that we now are paying for her to take the same math curriculum we learned for free in public education a generation ago. On second thought—maybe it isn't so funny.

Debbie Arnold

Math & Cooperative/Group Learning

When our son was in the fifth grade, we joined other parents who fought against the implementation of Mathland. This is a curriculum that uses "manipulatives" instead of a textbook, and is heavy into "fuzzy" math that doesn't consider computational methodologies important. Many of the teachers were appalled at the lack of tests with the Mathland curriculum. Math without tests? No wonder the kids liked it! Luckily, our son's teacher had a 1970s math textbook and supplemented her students' math knowledge from the old text.

Our son was also subjected to cooperative learning and group grades. Learning generally comes easily for him. He rarely has to study and was reading well before he entered school. Grades are important to him. The only reason we tell you this is to point out how ineffective and motivation-killing group grades are.

Our son's cooperative group consisted of three boys. (Can you imagine three nine-year-old boys working together on anything?) They were assigned a group project. Everyone was supposed to do his part. When the grades were given, our son's group received a "C." Our son has never received a "C" and was terribly upset. He asked if he could approach the teacher about re-doing the assignment.

When asked about this possibility, the teacher said, "Of course, as long as the other boys agree. If they agree, you may do so." The other boys were satisfied with their "C"s and said no. As a result, our motivated fifth grader learned that individual willingness to work hard to achieve a higher standard depended on whether others were willing to let him do it!

What a sad commentary on the old axiom, "Work hard and achieve great things." Apparently not in today's schools!

Shellie Mayne

GATE Math—The Triumph of Feelings over Math Skills

Our son is a sixth-grade GATE (gifted and talented) student. He is assessed as gifted in all academic areas, but is particularly adept at math and science.

We became concerned when we noticed that his math assignments rewarded correct answers with below-failing grades and counted feelings as 10 percent of his total "math" grade. When we questioned the math teacher, we discovered that only two points—or 20 percent—of the grade depended on a mathematically correct answer (which is 30 percent below an "F" or failing grade). The rest of the grading scale was as follows: 1) three points (30 percent) subjectively graded on how effectively the student restated the problem, 2) four points (40 percent) subjectively graded on the student's reasoning and written summary of how he/she came to a solution, and 3) one point (10 percent) was awarded based on how the student felt about the problem. (It was interesting to note that whether or not the correct solution was given as a result of the student's reasoning, full points could be given for any creative reasoning the teacher liked.)

With the above grading system, it was easy to see that a student who never gave a correct answer could always get a "B" in "math," while a student who computed the mathematically correct answer could receive an "F." Also, since 80 percent of the grading was subjective, the teacher could downgrade a student whose feelings he/she did not consider "correct."

We still fail to understand how any student can be graded on his/her "feelings" in an objective subject such as math, unless, of course, our education system is intent on promoting "politically correct" feelings. This frightens us. We now know that students who espouse the right feelings receive more points than students who give the right "mathematical" answers. This was the case with every one of our son's assignments.

At one point, our son wrote on an assignment that he was bored with math problems that asked about his feelings. The teacher naturally did not like his answer and gave him a zero. However, the teacher changed his mind and gave our son two out of seven points on the subjective portion of the material (that part of the assignment that actually dealt with numbers). The teacher then had the audacity to tell us that he didn't believe that our son's response to the feelings question in any way affected his overall grade. The result? Our son gave the correct math answer but failed the assignment.

We were aghast at this type of math curriculum and talked to both the teacher and the principal. We were met with hostile defensiveness by the principal and told that this is the national education trend and that assessment tests in math are going to be given and graded this way—it is called "authentic assessment" or OBE (outcome based education). Under this new education reform, subjective "readers" will evaluate a student's feelings and thinking (grade the "tests") with little regard for correct math or factual answers. We were told that the teacher is preparing students for this type of testing by incorporating these assignments into math.

Unless the school system is attempting to cover its own failure to raise disastrous academic scores, we strongly suggest a return to objective, concrete measures of solid academics. It is terrifying to think that the current "trend" will fail all those brilliant mathematical and scientific minds unless they respond with socially correct answers.

These "assessments" will allow people who cannot add, subtract, multiply, or divide, but who can talk their way out of a paper bag, to become the so-called mathematicians, engineers, and scientists of tomorrow. They will build bridges which will look pretty on paper but collapse when used. People may die because the engineers of the future will not know the mathematical equations that will give correct load and stress factors.

Jonathan and Donna Sorek

Math Renaissance

Throughout our children's elementary school years, we supplemented their math curriculum by reinforcing basic computational skills such as addition, subtraction, multiplication, division, fractions, and decimals. As the years progressed, the learning gap widened between our children and the majority of students who were pushed through without these basic skills.

Several weeks after our oldest son entered sixth grade we noticed his daily class work and homework consisted of nothing more than a review of basic computation. My wife monitored the math class each Friday as a volunteer and expressed our concern to the math teacher that no new material was being presented. We were assured that the "review" would not last much longer. Sadly, the lessons in simple arithmetic continued for more than six weeks. A review of fourth- and fifth-grade material (i.e., coloring checkerboards to study the concept of fractions) was scheduled to continue until Christmas.

In early November, we met with the principal. He acknowledged that the students were repeating basic math computation, but stated that their skills were typical of beginning sixth graders and that every student was forced to "review" regardless of math skill level. The principal assured us that a new program, Math Renaissance, would begin soon and that a "math night" would be held to explain the program.

At the subsequent "math night" meeting, we learned that the new program consisted of "life activities" students would perform using "higher order thinking skills." The program's focus was "developing" the ability of students to work in groups. Further, the teacher functioned as a "facilitator," answering questions only after students asked other members of their groups. As the numerous games and activities were demonstrated, it became increasingly clear the program contained little substance. One student would be held accountable for mathematical understanding, while the others kept busy with cutting, coloring, and pasting.

We contacted our local school board members and expressed our concerns about Math Renaissance. They refused to replace the curriculum. We learned that: 1) grant money was attached; 2) the program was on the state approved list; and 3) the school district received money for books, materials, and, most importantly, teacher training, which amounted to an initial twelve days of meetings the first year and eight days annually thereafter. No wonder the program had the support of both teachers and administrators.

Near the close of the school year it became apparent that Math Renaissance would not cover genuine sixth-grade mathematics. We decided to initiate our own math program. In May, we sent a letter to the principal stating: "After monitoring the Math Renaissance curriculum, we are convinced there is very little instruction that will enhance our son's math skills. The program has been a pitiful year of socializing, creative writing, simple art, and childish games. While the program's goals are admirable, there is little hope of attaining them with grammar school manipulatives." We requested that our son not be scheduled for seventh-grade math and purchased materials for homeschooling him in this subject.

On the first day of the new school year, we found that our request had not been approved. The principal said there was nothing he could do and suggested we speak to the district superintendent. We drove to her office that afternoon where we heard the following excuses for denying our request for partial homeschooling: "It's illegal" (it isn't). "Children have to attend school the full day" (they don't). "No one's doing it" (other districts do it). And finally, "There's no policy for it" (or against it). Still, we refused to leave her office until our request was granted. After more than an hour, she relented.

The following year, we made the same request for our now eighth grader and another son who was entering sixth grade. Again, we were told that our request could not be honored, which led to another trip to the superintendent's office. This time we were told: "Removing children from math class would cost the district money. An alternative method, such as independent study using school materials or a teacher as a sort of mentor, should be considered." We declined, and after another lengthy discussion, our request was once again approved.

Our oldest son entered high school as a freshman the following year. However, he did not enter the freshman algebra program known as CPM1 (college prep math) because he scored 100 percent on the ninth-grade algebra waiver exam. His comment: "It was beyond easy, Dad." He then successfully completed the waiver for tenth-grade CPM2 (geometry), missing only one question. He was the only freshman in the junior-level math (algebra 2), and ranked first in his class.

We attribute his math ability to hard work and the Saxon math book, which is based on the traditional math approach. The text contains no fancy pictures, and the material is down-to-earth, pencil-on-paper work—no group projects, facilitators, cutting, coloring, or pasting. It teaches math the same way that the creators of our modern-day technology learned it. And it works!

Sadly, the students in our district who were forced to participate in Math Renaissance during three full years of middle school did not fare as well as our son. Over 50 percent received a failing grade in the first semester of ninth-grade algebra. Further, during a two-month remedial program, more than 50 percent of these students were still unable to achieve a passing grade.

We believed that with our dramatic success we could convince the administration and school board members to adopt textbooks and materials focusing on basic skills and individual achievement. We presented our case, displayed our materials, and provided statistics from school districts that have achieved tremendous results using Saxon math. We argued that our state trails the nation in math skills, not because we have the worst teachers or the worst parents, but because we have the worst curriculum.

Unfortunately, the overriding concern of administrators is money. In pursuit of grant dollars and state funding, the board voted three to two to approve yet another math curriculum aligned with "New New Math" frameworks—called Mathland—for elementary school children. Despite the success of Saxon math in other states and because state education bureaucrats refused to place it on our state-approved list, the district would have to pay for Saxon textbooks out of the general fund. They were unwilling to do so, and therefore, accepted Mathland and the money that accompanies it. It is clear to us that the real price will be paid by another generation of young adults unprepared for a future that demands higher levels of mathematical knowledge.

Gary Tomak

EDITORS' NOTE: *As a result of Mr. Tomak's experience with his sons' schools, he ran for a position on his local school board. He failed the first time, but true to his tenacious nature, Mr. Tomak ran again and was elected. He strongly urges concerned parents to fight for what they believe in and encourages them to get involved as the decision-makers.*

Scaring Children Away from Math

When our daughter was in third grade at the local elementary school, she suddenly began having nightmares. Normally a cheerful, easygoing young girl, she began acting fearful at bedtime. One night she became very upset. Shortly after we put the children to bed, she got up and asked us if the doors were locked. We told her they were and that she should go back to bed. We thought she was just trying to delay bedtime. Incidentally, we live in a rural, low-crime area.

Shortly thereafter, she got up again. This time she wanted to check to see if the doors and windows were locked. She was extremely upset and crying. Over an hour later, she was finally able to tell us that she was afraid someone would break into our house and kidnap her or steal things, and that her dad would not wake up, or that we would have another car accident. (We had been involved in an accident approximately five months earlier. She had been asleep in the car at the time.)

We stayed with her until she fell asleep—well after 11:00 p.m. She had trouble sleeping for the next week or so and needed continual reassurance. Obviously, something was drastically wrong, but we didn't know what it was.

A few days later I was at the school; her teacher mentioned to me how excited she was about a new math and reading program that really involved the children. She talked about the week's activities that had included reading scary stories and answering questions about things people are afraid of, and doing math graphs about things the children are afraid of at bedtime. The program even offered suggestions if the kids couldn't think of anything. Some of the scary things listed in a dialogue box included: "getting killed," "Freddy Krueger," "murderers," "my dead brother," "maggots," "vampires," "monsters with big eyes," etc.

I was astonished, and told the teacher about our daughter's fearful bedtimes. She asked why I felt the program wasn't a good idea. I spent hours explaining why it is too risky to play psychological games with immature children, even if they did respond to the material. She told me that the state had been pushing schools to stop using textbooks and replace them with new programs that centered on the students' emotions as a means of getting them "involved." She did admit that teachers weren't trained in how to deal with problems that might come up.

One of the programs was called Sorting. It used a technique for teaching math in the second and third grades that was supposed to teach data analysis based on "real data in the classroom." The teacher's manual actually said that, "After trying many topics in many classrooms, we have concluded that the potential sensitivity of a topic is not a reason to avoid it; on the contrary, these are the very topics that most engage student interest." The same paragraph goes on to read, "Keep in mind that students may sometimes want their data to be anonymous." Doesn't that make you wonder what type of "data" they are collecting that would make a child want to keep it anonymous?

The curriculum actually said: "After trying many topics...we have concluded that the potential sensitivity of a topic is not a reason to avoid it; on the contrary, these are the very topics that most engage student interest..."[6] It went on to say, "Teacher Note: Starting to talk about scary things: Students will want to

26

tell stories about their own scary experiences...Inevitably, students' real fears and concerns will emerge in this discussion."[7]

Sorting was not a math curriculum; it was a teaching tool that encouraged teachers to delve into a child's psyche. Teachers might be unaware of it, but trained therapists certainly are aware! We showed a copy of this curriculum to a child psychologist. His comments included the following: "A child cannot grow or learn in a classroom that creates any degree of emotional tension. This is a proven fact. In those cases the child is surviving—not learning or relating. What they learn is how to keep from 'feeling' overwhelmed—not academics."

And yet Sorting encouraged an emotional response. In this case, the teacher created turmoil, fear, and apprehension in our daughter. The teacher wasn't even aware of the harm she was doing!

We were lucky. Our superintendent was very responsive to our concerns and quickly called for the removal of the entire curriculum from every school in our district.

Cheryl Bater

Inventive Spelling and Other Experiments

When we moved, we pulled our two older girls out of the Montessori school they had been attending. We were encouraged by the large sign outside the school in our new neighborhood proclaiming it as a "Distinguished School." We thought that sounded impressive, and believed this would be an exceptional public school. It was only later that we found out that the sign actually meant that it had the greatest number of federally-funded programs.

My husband and I worked hard so that I could stay at home with our children. I decided to volunteer at school. I helped in my children's classrooms two to three days a week (an hour to an hour and a half each time). I chaired or co-chaired several fundraisers and social events. Three years passed before my husband and I began to see the light.

The Home and School Club, for which I was treasurer, was little more than an innovative means for schools to get more money from the community. Many parents think a Home and

School Club is just another name for the PTA. However, parents and teachers do not communicate on educational issues; in fact, parents have little say in how their children are taught. One section of our particular Home and School Club's bylaws actually alludes to the fact that parent members would not interfere with educational issues.

Slowly, I began to notice there was something wrong with my girls' education. Many classes had thirty-four students and only one teacher, even though their contracts called for no more than twenty-seven students per class. Each class included average learners, higher achievers, students with behavioral problems, and an average of seven LEP (Limited English Proficiency) students. The slower and troubled students took far too much of the teachers' time and energy, and the brighter students soon became bored.

I assisted primarily with reading and taught letter sounds in kindergarten through fourth grade. My oldest daughter—a "B" student—and I began arguing about her spelling. Her fourth-grade teacher didn't expect correct spelling as a standard. I did. One week, my daughter came home with graded papers that reflected 90 to 99 percent correct answers. She and I were both so proud! Then I took a closer look—nearly every other word was spelled wrong.

Some teachers did use phonics as the students' introduction to spelling, but most used the "whole language" approach. Unfortunately, my daughters' teachers preferred whole language. My kindergartner didn't know all the alphabet letters and hardly any of the sounds. You can imagine my guilt! All this time I thought I was helping my children by working at the school and helping them with homework. Instead, I had done them a disservice. I should have been gainfully employed so that I could send them to a private school!

The real slap in the face came at a district-wide open forum on the "new math" curriculum series. At this forum, there were four stations where parents could view this new series with people from big business and the school district, as well as parents and teachers, all explaining how wonderful the new math program was.

The attending parents were divided into two groups: English and non-English speaking (Hispanic). The English-speaking parents were not happy and were asking many questions. The Hispanic parents were applauding and appeared very excited—how I wished that I understood Spanish.

When we reached the teachers' station, we waited until the presentation was finished before asking, "If this new math in seventh-grade algebra places kids in groups, does this mean that the brighter children will become the teachers?" The teacher in charge began telling us she stops any student who is giving too much to the group, but she was interrupted by another teacher who announced, "If you have any questions, come back after the last presentation." We started to walk to the next station when I heard the teacher who had started to answer me say to the man who interrupted us, "Gee, you're good!" That's when I realized that they did not want confrontation; they did not want to answer our questions. We never did get any answers that night. I left feeling numb and couldn't sleep.

Following this fiasco, I decided to visit the principal. I threw my child's pack of 90 to 99 percent correct papers on her desk and tried to ask her questions about the spelling standards in our school. "Is it because we are in the computer age and have spell check, or is it because we have so many students in our school who cannot speak, write, or read English that you no longer expect fourth graders to spell correctly?" I asked. She didn't answer me. Instead, what came next is what has happened over and over again to other parents. "What makes you think your daughter is falling through the cracks? We have had children go through our school, our high school, and on to Harvard. Give her some time; she'll catch up," was her reply.

When it is your child, you cannot give it time. Time is what it is all about. That early educational foundation is crucial. It can't wait. "I'm sorry, Mrs. Principal, experiment on some other child. Focus on the ones who bring in more money for the school. That's what you appear to be doing anyway. The Healthy Start grant you just received—you know, the one that targets fifty 'at-risk' (low-income) families—won't it pay you $400,000 to teach those parents how to be better parents so that their children can be better students? What about the students who are already good students? What about the GATE program you dropped? What about the Odyssey of the Mind program? You have all this 'at-risk' money, but you don't have enough parent-volunteers to run a program for your high achievers."

Two weeks after the first forum, we had another. This second forum was not as well advertised as the first, and the only parents who attended were from the Home and School Club. We still didn't get any answers and, in fact, were told that if we had any more questions we should see the principal individually at another time or contact the district representative in charge of school curriculum programs. This is the old "divide and conquer" technique. The principal did say that she thought some of our ideas were good, and suggested that we serve on one of the committees, such as Healthy Start, the next year.

After the forum, I invited representatives from fifteen families to my home. Two school board members also attended, one of whom agreed to accompany one of the parents to present a list of concerns to the principal. When the day arrived, the parent found herself in a "two against one" situation. She was told, "There aren't that many concerned parents." That quote has been driving me crazy ever since. Shouldn't even one parent's concern be important to the principal?

We subsequently requested a copy of our Healthy Start program. It was worse than we thought. The first page convinced us that we had placed our children in an illiterate environment. The program included deception and plans for unproven experimentation. The educational bureaucracy of this nation has no right to proclaim itself a social worker and pry into the homes of its citizens. When will our teachers speak out against it? Do young teachers coming out of college even know how to teach? When are we going to rid ourselves of these deceitful curricula and activities? Where are the good superintendents and school trustees? When are the people in charge going to take an honest look at their own morals and ethics, determine what truly works and what doesn't, recognize what is right and wrong, and say "no" to the money?

My girls now attend private school. And, in fact, none of the board members of the Home and School Club allowed their children to return to this particular elementary school the following year.

At the new school, students begin reading in first grade. There are never more than twenty-four students per class. The classrooms are tiny—some without windows—and the children play on a blacktop parking lot. There is no lunch program—I pack my daughters' lunches. And yes, I've had to go back to work to pay the tuition (but my taxes still pay for those innovative public school programs). Is it worth it? You bet! My children are growing faster than ever intellectually. They are achieving academically. The important issue isn't the size of the school, or the dollars invested, but the content—what is taught and how it is taught—by teachers who believe in solid academics and are allowed to teach them.

It isn't the school's responsibility to mother my children or serve as social director for the federal government. I haven't run away. I'm still fighting the district and the state. If public schools ever return to educational excellence, our children will return to public schools.

Keith and Kim Sparacio

As educators nationwide chase after federal dollars, parents increasingly battle schools that embrace math scores in which feelings count, "Emotional Quotients," and courses titled "Human Interaction" and "New Beginnings." Moms and dads who simply want their children to acquire the basic skills to succeed in college and beyond often find themselves in the unwanted role of community activist, taking on a system that presumes it has ultimate authority.

CHAPTER TWO

FROM BIZARRE TO RIDICULOUS

EVEN THE MOST *diligent parent often finds it difficult to antici-pate and monitor everything their child may encounter in today's classroom. The classroom situations contained in this chapter could never have been foreseen by the parents.*

When we accompanied a group of parents on a visit to their school superintendent several years ago to voice their displeasure over some inappropriate assignments, we were met with glib responses and condescension. The parents wanted to know why the school considered obscene language appropriate. We were told quite blatantly that it is imperative in today's society to keep young minds engaged. To do so, the superintendent said, the schools had to use contemporary subject matter, which often included crude language. He thought that was quite appropriate.

Luckily the parents weren't appeased. They demanded to know why the school lowered themselves to the gutter level and why the school didn't set a higher standard that would serve as an example. When the superintendent asked what the parents would suggest, they were ready. They wanted a return of the classics. They wanted classroom discussions raised to a level that didn't include crude sex and vulgar language. They demanded that they be informed of any questionable material. They knew and quoted state and federal laws that protected their rights.

Pornographic and obscene literature has become commonplace in today's public schools and such literature is often referred to as "authentic literature." The theory is that if we want our children to succeed in life, they need exposure to literature that relates to alleged "everyday" or "authentic" situations. So out with the classics and in with books that focus on drug addicts, pedophiles, gang life, violence, etc.[1]

Often when parents object to something going on at a school, they hear, "You are the only parent to complain." The idea, of course, is to intimidate parents into staying quiet. The parents mentioned above didn't allow the school to bully them into complaisance; they banded together, and they gathered strength from each other. That is a good strategy for others to follow. While it may sound old-fashioned, there is truth in the saying, "There is strength in numbers." (One method used to silence complaining parents is to call them "book-burners." Again, don't let anyone intimidate you or prevent you from doing what is right for your child just because they may call you names.)

Classroom assignments sometimes have nothing to do with academics but instead delve into the private lives of children and their families. For instance, one curriculum for elementary students asks the children to sit in a "talking ring" and pass the "wise person's hat."[2] When the hat comes to each child, he or she is expected to share his or her problems while the other students are told they may have to "go into the realms of imaginations to find answers." Not only does this violate the privacy of the student, but one can only wonder how elementary students can solve each other's so-called personal problems. Some experts say this type of exercise can actually create a psychologically stressful condition for the child, because it could cause undue pressure to think up a problem even if there is no problem at home. This particular curriculum also tells the children to go home and get "Mom and Dad" to tell them their problems so that the children can "share them with the class the next day."

As the following stories will show, vigilance on the part of parents has never been so important.

Plays Containing Foul Language

Our daughter's ninth-grade drama class was given an assignment to act out a skit. She and a friend hurriedly chose from the box of available plays a book containing a piece entitled *The Homesteaders*, by Nina Shengold. My daughter pointed it out to the teacher; he acknowledged that he knew the play and copied it for her to bring home.

After reading the play at home, our daughter showed it to us. While she expressed surprise over the content, we were outraged!

Following are excerpts of actual language found in the contested play. The setting is a discussion between the fourteen-year-old daughter (Laurel) of a divorced man and his twenty-four-year-old girlfriend (Jake). In places where only the first letter is shown, the entire word was used.

> LAUREL: You're a whore. You're screwing my father... Is he good in bed?
>
> Ritsy-titsy tourist s...
>
> It's gross. F... that... Screws her.
>
> He's got a big dick.
>
> How old were you the first time? Did it hurt?... Francine told me it kills the first time.
>
> Double-D tits.
>
> JAKE: You want some bourbon? How about a joint?
>
> LAUREL: What else is there to do in junior high school? (She lights up.)
>
> JAKE: Oh, do they date?
>
> LAUREL: Date, god. Nobody dates.
>
> JAKE: Well what do you call it?
>
> LAUREL: F _ _ _ _ _ g.

We discussed talking with the teacher, but our daughter insisted that she talk with him first.

The next day she told him that she did not want to use the selected play and he responded by saying that she should have read it before choosing it; however, he would allow her to choose another just this once—but it would be her "last chance" to change a skit.

When I heard about the teacher's response to our daughter, I called to express my belief that the play was inappropriate. He defended it by explaining that the students found plays with more adult themes more interesting than the old "Winnie-the-Pooh" type plays that had previously been used. He never said he was sorry or that he would remove the play from the class. He did say he would give any student offended by the materials an opportunity to leave the class to do an alternate activity. We wondered how the students could know ahead of time which skits they would find offensive until they were actually performed by the other groups in class, or whether they might feel too much peer pressure to leave during the performance(s).

The teacher mentioned that my wife had signed a permission slip which mentioned the use of mature material. When asked, my wife said she vaguely remembered a note, but had no idea that she was giving permission for this type of material—after all, what parent would ever dream that a teacher would make an obscene play available to fourteen-year-old students? Such a "permission slip" is no justification for this kind of material.

When we showed the play to the principal, she was visibly surprised. However, she had little to say except that perhaps the play was within state-approved guidelines. Another parent was in the office at the time complaining about the same class for the same reason. The principal admitted she had received yet another complaint the day before. When we suggested that the teacher be reviewed, the principal replied that she didn't see any reason to do so, because he was a good teacher with eight years' experience. She did say she would talk to him.

My wife showed the principal the district's sexual harassment policy and pointed out the specific areas that had been violated. She then asked that our daughter be removed from the drama class. The principal said that it was too late and our daughter would receive an "F" if removed.

Four days after giving this assignment, some of our daughter's friends told her that the teacher asked the students to hand in their scripts so he could remove the ones with more questionable content. According to these students, he mentioned to the class that he was in trouble because some parents were making a big deal out of certain plays, and he felt "betrayed" by the student(s) who had brought the scripts to their parents' attention. He told two of the students in particular that he couldn't believe they had shown their script to their parents. Word of the incident spread among the students, and our daughter was later approached by friends who asked why she had shown her script to her parents—after all, it was "just a play." She felt embarrassed to be considered the source of the "problem" by her peers. Former students indicated the play(s) in question had been used in previous years.

For a week, our daughter spent time either in the library or in a room near the counseling office by herself. Only after we again intervened was she finally assigned to another class.

As far as we're concerned, the teacher violated the parents' trust. We send our children to school for an education, not for exposure to materials of an obscene and extremely negative nature. We are concerned that he admitted no wrongdoing. Instead, he placed the blame for the problem on the students who talked to their parents. Evidently, he believes that children should not discuss classroom conduct with parents!

Raymond and Karan Perkins

"Birth" Class

The twelfth-grade honors English teacher at my high school told all the students in my class to imagine giving birth to a baby. She turned out the lights and had us get on the floor in groups of three. One girl in each group was told to imagine that she was in labor and about to give birth, another student was to be the husband or partner, and the third student in each group was to be the doctor.

Some of the boys had their hands on the girls' stomachs. Some of the boys positioned themselves in front of the girls' legs as if they were about to "catch the baby." Students acting as delivery partners shouted to the "mothers," "Push, push!" The student-doctors said, "The baby's coming; here it comes." The other girl in my group and I told the boy in our threesome not to even think about acting this out with us.

Our teacher called this one of her "real life experience" activities. She was obviously a "hands-on" teacher. She gave the boys an open door to put their hands on the girls in a very provocative manner. She even got on the floor with us and acted out her part. This was definitely a "real life experience." The girls in my class experienced sexual harassment and a violation of their personal modesty. I believe the boys were desensitized regarding how they treat women. All of this took place under the direction, and with the permission and participation, of our teacher.

Heather Fay, Student

Heart Talks

As a ninth grader, my daughter was in a program called Heart Talks. The children sat in a circle and passed a velvet heart from one child to the other. The child holding the heart shared his/her feelings with the other students in the class. The teacher instructed them to keep everything they heard confidential, even not to tell their parents.

Students who did not want to participate sat outside the circle. However, most of them participated rather than be ostracized.

I thought my daughter was in this class to learn English. I had no idea she would attend group therapy sessions conducted by her English teacher. I had not asked this teacher to serve as my daughter's therapist.

When I voiced my concerns about this experimental activity to the principal, she told me that the teacher was trained to conduct these classes. The superintendent said Heart Talks was a state program designed to motivate students for creative writing projects. However, my daughter said that they never did any writing projects in conjunction with these sessions. Instead, they spent the time sharing their personal feelings and thoughts. At least one of the sessions grew so personal that some of the children were brought to tears.

Even the teacher used this opportunity to share her personal feelings. On one occasion, she vented her frustrations to the class about their behavior, because they had asked her if they could read some positive books instead of so many stories about death. Another time she described in detail how she had met her daughter before she was born. It seemed to me that this teacher might have benefited from some therapy herself.

Another curriculum used in my daughter's class dealt with what was called "The Holistic Model of Self-Esteem & Well Being." It explored such topics as intuition, thoughts, emotions, and imagination. In this bizarre exercise, students were instructed to use imagery or "mental rehearsal" to access their wisdom. The curriculum also referred to Heart Talks, Reflective Listening and Total Truth as aids.

These exercises were clearly psychological in nature. My daughter's teacher made exposing their personal feelings to a group seem like a normal thing for kids to do. But what if they could not find closure? To whom could they talk if they had concerns? Teachers are not trained psychologists equipped to deal with painful emotions that can surface in sessions like Heart Talks. No brief "in-service" training session could have prepared this teacher for the possible consequences of her pseudo psychology. Of course, the classes were off-limits to parents per the teacher's instructions. I would never have known about these Heart Talks if my daughter had not ignored her teacher's instructions and eventually told me about them.

Susen Fay

Dangerous Film about Alcoholism

Quite by accident, my wife and I became aware of a program at my ten-year-old daughter's school. We had always cautioned her to answer any personal or private questions asked by teachers with a polite, "You will have to talk to my parents."

This program began with a film instructing students to always carry a quarter with them. The characters in the film used the quarter to phone a grandparent for a ride when their father was drunk and they did not want to ride in the car with him. After the film, the students were instructed to write down anything that troubled them along these lines.

Anyone who comes from a home in which alcohol is abused, as I did, will immediately recognize that bypassing the abusing parent in this situation is a sure way to be beaten within inches of your life. A child in this predicament might actually be in less danger riding with the inebriated parent than defying him.

That evening, the parent of another student informed us about the day's events. Our daughter confirmed the story when we questioned her. The scary thing was that she did not even recognize this situation as one we had warned her about.

The next morning, I called the school and informed the principal that my children were never to participate in any such program again. (We had not received prior notice of this lesson.) She concurred that the incident was in poor judgment.

I discovered that evening that after my conversation with the principal, my daughter was removed from class and counseled by two teachers. This "counseling session" took place in a room with just the three of them and some refreshments. The reason given for this counseling session was that, after the film, my daughter had written that she worried because her grandmother smokes. This is none of the school's business!

The school violated my rights as a parent, my child's right to privacy, and since she was removed from class during regular hours, my child's right to an education. Taxpayers should be outraged that schools continuously waste time and money training teachers to engage in psychological therapy—and that substitute teachers must be hired to fill in during this wasted training.

In a subsequent meeting with the assistant superintendent, principal and three teachers, we could not effectively communicate. They just could not understand what we were concerned about!

My children are now, and will remain, in private school.

Alan and Jana Fletcher

X-Rated Film

The movie *Damned in the USA* was shown to our daughter's Advanced Placement English class. The theme of the movie was censorship. The controversial material shown ranged from Serrano's *Piss Christ*, which depicts the crucified Christ submerged in urine (the teacher's comment was, "Aren't the colors beautiful?"), to sexually explicit photos by Robert Mapplethorpe, some of which included small children's genitals and adults in perverted sexual positions. The latter included one man urinating into the mouth of another man and a close-up of a disgusting practice called "fisting." The photos included a close-up shot of the tip of a penis on which was drawn a caricature of U.S. Senator Jesse Helms that appeared to be talking. The movie also featured a scene of a man with a fully erect penis standing sideways with his arm extended holding a gun and a semen ejaculation caught in still motion. Another scene showed a very young girl with her legs apart and exposing her vagina. How sad.

What was the educational value of this movie? Its misuse and the teacher's accompanying sexual innuendoes are not a censorship matter. We are concerned with the protection of minors.

During the past few years, students have complained of the explicit sexual nature of many poems and stories used in this class. When discussing sexuality, the teacher chose to describe intercourse "with either sex as 'slimy and hairy.'" He also told students that if others disagree with their sexual preference they should tell them to "f___ off." He used the word.

When we first heard about the *Damned in the USA* film, we asked to see it. The school denied parents the right to view it. We pursued the matter further, and the school finally arranged a viewing. When we asked the superintendent if the material and its presentation was appropriate, he said that it was an Advanced Placement class and that the parents had signed permission slips. However, the permission slips were signed months earlier, and the movie was not listed on the slip. The parents trusted that the teacher was following a school-approved curriculum.

We were not satisfied with the cover-up of the situation. Even after parents sent written complaints to the principal and the superintendent, this teacher saw fit to read a story he had written titled "Too Late." The story began with a man late for school and stopped at a traffic light. It then described in detail two girls crossing the street. The teacher wrote about the man in the car watching a tall brunette with her large breasts moving "deliciously" as she walked, and how he enjoyed watching the blonde with small breasts whose nipples showed through her white tank top. The man then noticed another man watering his lawn as the girls passed. The story described how the hose, held in a "cocked manner began spurting erratically."

41

This story made several students uncomfortable, especially the two girls who had earlier expressed their feelings of shock about *Damned in the USA*. These girls felt violated because they fit the descriptions of the two girls in the story. We requested—in writing and in numerous phone calls—to see this story, but were not allowed to do so.

We want to know why the students in his class know that the teacher had one testicle removed. He told them that this type of surgery can cause difficulty in achieving an erection. Why would he insert an ice pack down the front of his pants in the presence of his students? Was he looking for a reaction? Was he acting in a professional manner?

Why should an English class place so much emphasis on curriculum that focuses so heavily on sexual and homosexual content? Why does an English class include discussions of homosexuality, and ask such questions as, "What's wrong with homosexual sex?" This is not a sex education class; it is an English class.

We were very upset that the principal said that the class violated no state education codes. The school defended the teacher, and we had to seek legal counsel to resolve this matter. Why are parents forced to take such extreme measures to protect their children from pornography in the classroom?

Mr. & Mrs. Peter Mills

Witches

My daughter's third-grade teacher rented videos as "treats" and "rewards." Against my instructions not to show violent or age-inappropriate movies to my daughter, on the last day of school, the teacher decided to show the graphic movie *Witches*. This was a realistic depiction of a coven of witches (disguised as beautiful women) plotting to capture, poison, and transform children.

All summer, my daughter fretted over these impressions. She was too frightened to go into public restrooms or even churches alone. Just as we thought she had recovered from the frightening imagery of *Witches*, she and her new classmates were faced with another mental assault.

This time it was her fourth-grade teacher who used a grotesque film (recommended for seventh grade and up), from the district's media department. When I asked to view the film after my daughter's class had seen it, the teacher giggled and said that she enjoyed showing the film because she knew how the young kids "just love blood and gore."

Briefly, the film *Bear Skinner* is based on the original foreign version written by the Brothers Grimm. It was not, however, the same American version the children had read in class. It told a story about a man who prospers by making a pact with an evil character. The movie displayed the real-life, bloody skinning of a helpless bear; a close-up view of maggots and worms crawling out of the man's sores; and the many "deals" the man makes with the devil. These included an agreement not to say *The Lord's Prayer* for seven years, a girl exchanged for rent money, and slowly-narrated scenes revealing the method two girls used to commit suicide. Their reason? They had decided that they weren't pretty enough to live. The teacher asked my daughter to put herself in the story and write a modern version of the plot, which declared in the end that "two souls were gained (in hell) for the price of one."

My daughter's nightmares reflected these characters and caused her to awaken me during the night to calm her down. Her body actually trembled, and she cried in fear.

When I complained, the principal patronized me; the teacher ignored me. After a long, hard struggle to persuade the school board to discuss the movie and the use of other inappropriate and R-rated movies, our superintendent told board members that, even if they wanted to do something about the situation, they couldn't. He said, "...not [to] make access to all material for all students would violate their First Amendment rights."

After four years of homeschooling and private schooling, our family was forced financially to return to public education. Please help us clean up this assault on our children. I stand with other parents who do not want to go through this again.

UPDATE: Since the above incident, other matters throughout the district surfaced; consequently the new superintendent implemented changes that included new accountability measures for the use of unauthorized material. Parental consent forms are now sent out. However, the question remains, "Is this movie still used in public education?"

Kathy Villalobos

Journals

My husband and I have complained about several issues at school and fought the "New New Math" craze. Luckily other parents are taking up that battle. But we are more upset about some of the things other parents may not even realize are happening. For instance, "journaling" is the rage in schools today. How many parents have asked to see their child's journal? We became concerned when we saw some of the topics students were asked to write about. We objected to the personal nature of the questions and wondered why students couldn't keep journals about academic subjects, such as historical figures, etc.

Our son was asked, "What are stupid rules at home that you can't do or have to do?" Other journal assignments included writing about the student's "worst thing," "scariest moment," and "things I hate."

One of the art classes at our son's school sponsored a field trip to a tattoo parlor! They passed two art galleries along the way, but apparently the teacher didn't think art galleries were relevant.

Our school also allowed a really shocking performance by "mimes" for approximately 250 eleven-to-twelve-year-olds. The characters repeatedly used the "F" word and phrases like "lick my b___." The play centered around the Zapatista Indian uprising, and in addition to crude language, a large overhead screen showed dead bodies and graphically depicted farm animals defecating.

Though neither the principal nor teachers had previewed the play, they allowed it to continue for over two hours. During the intermission the principal and teachers decided to allow the students to make their own decisions as to whether to stay for the second half.

Parents were outraged when they heard about the play. The principal's only response was that he didn't think to ask about the language or content and that he wished he had handled it differently. The playwright's comment was, "But I think it's pretty mild compared to what kids see on television." What she failed to understand was that at home parents have the right to turn off the TV and to monitor what their children view. Parents were not warned about what their children would see at school that day.

As a nation, we wonder why so many of our children are depressed, why they fight against authority and aren't learning anything. We know there are good teachers. But we also know from experience that there are teachers who don't show good judgment, and we know there is a shift away from core academic curricula. The only way to change the lack of quality education is for parents to get involved and demand changes.

Don and Lyn Booth

Reading vs. Feelings

Our daughter's fourth-grade class places a heavy emphasis on feelings and attitudes as evidenced by the curriculum used in her classroom called Reading Response. The teacher reads part of a book to the class and then asks students to put their "feelings" about the book in writing. The curriculum pays little, if any, attention to content, punctuation, or spelling in these written exercises. Grading a student's feelings is not only highly subjective but time-consuming as well. With SAT scores continuing to drop, it is obvious we need to get down to business and work on real academics.

The exercise entitled "I Am" is also cause for concern. In this exercise, students complete sentences that describe "their" imaginary sounds, sights, touches, and feelings. The practice of "conjuring" up images conflicts with our spiritual beliefs. We consider it to be a form of occultism. In addition, the "I Am" exercise asks students to divulge personal information, including what they worry about, cry about, and dream about. In our opinion, this is a blatant invasion of privacy.

We are also concerned that instead of individual grades being given for individual work, students are now being placed in groups and given "group grades." The fourth-grade Tribe Report is only one example of this new emphasis on "group learning." For the Tribe Report, our daughter worked in a "group" of three students. While she received an "A" for her individual effort, her final grade was brought down to a "C" because of the inferior work of the other two group members. We're told that group work has important applications in the workplace, however, employees that don't produce can be fired; our child didn't have the option of firing her "tribe" members. In the real world, individual achievement is far more important than group work.

Shortly before the spring break, I had a parent-teacher conference with my daughter's teacher. She appeared more serious than usual and after going over some of my daughter's work, commented, "Your daughter is doing okay." When I asked her about the areas in which improvement was needed, the teacher said, "She is creatively blocked; have you noticed?" I replied that I had not. I then asked if she was saying that my daughter was blocked, because I had refused to allow her to participate in a classroom Indian ritual which I considered inappropriate. The teacher would not reply to my question directly, but persisted in her theory that my daughter was "creatively blocked."

I left that meeting totally dumbfounded. I had sat next to this woman and her husband during church and social events. I almost felt that she had been "brainwashed" by the educational material she was bombarded with during in-service training sessions—many of those took place during the year. I also feared that I would somehow be labeled as the "creative blocker" of my own child. I wondered what the next label might be. If they could do this to an educated woman and business owner, what would they do to a naive parent who was not "in the know"? The thought was frightening. I never brought my daughter back to that school. We homeschooled the rest of that year and the following year. We then sent her to a private school, which she still attends.

It is apparent that academics are no longer the primary focus of today's public education system. The following quote from our former superintendent, in our school newsletter, shows what educators consider important for today's student:

> The skills employers most desired were behavioral [and] social
> skills; [the] least important "skills" were academic basics like
> math, science, computer literacy and foreign language.

We were dismayed that the fourth-grade science textbook referred to the "theory of evolution" as fact. We believe that the law should be followed and that parents should have the right to aid in the selection of textbooks.

Until our education system is held accountable for its finished product (a well-educated graduate), I will not vote for any bond issues, I will not place my daughter in the system's hands, and I will not support it in any way other than with my legally required property tax payments. I cringe at the thought of all those tax dollars and what a private school could do with the same amount of funds.

Name Withheld by Request

A Student Speaks

I have always enjoyed school, because it broadens my range of knowledge and will be a key factor in my future success. I have always thought of school as a place where I could learn useful and helpful skills. I never expected it would be a place where attempts would be made to burden my mind.

I recently read an article by one of our state representatives in which he challenged high school students to be pure. He described their high school years as "the most volatile time of their lives and offering a panorama of choices." I strongly believe that the representative's statement about teenage development is clear and concise. But if we, as a society, believe his statement, then why is our public school system subjecting its students to material which may oppose their morals, religious beliefs, or perhaps even affect their development?

During my senior year, I came to realize that our teachers have too much freedom in choosing the literature for students to read. On the first day of school I was excited and overwhelmed with a sense of responsibility, because twelfth grade is a time for college preparation. But as I entered my English 4 essay course, I immediately became bewildered. Posted on the walls were many issues of *Rolling Stone* magazine. I was astonished that several of the covers portrayed women in provocative attire. I wondered why an English teacher would advertise graphic magazines which had no relevance to an English literature class.

After completing tests, this teacher gave us the opportunity to view back issues of *Rolling Stone* and other similar magazines. Since I knew about the contents of these magazines, I was appalled that a teacher would promote such material during school time.

At the beginning of the school year, this teacher worked hard to win kids over to his side. He used his sense of humor to effectively accomplish this goal. I noticed that humor is a strong emotion and that it can be used to manipulate and persuade unsuspecting minds. I was intrigued and entertained by his manner of teaching, but once I learned he had another motive for his teaching style, I prayed to God for guidance.

I observed his obscene behavior throughout the year. I noticed that as the school year progressed, he not only used humor, but also his position of authority as a teacher, to his advantage. After winning the kids over, he used profanity, obscene gestures, and rude comments during class. The students did not complain, because he had already established rapport with them. They were his "friends."

It seemed that every chance he got he elaborated upon an immoral or obscene topic, both in the literature he chose for us to read and through class discussions. The students' impression of *Canterbury Tales* was negative, because we spent so much time focusing on lewd and lustful thoughts. For example, he elaborated extensively on a sexual scene.

When one girl questioned him about this scene in class, he described in detail with a smile, using descriptive body terms, how men viewed women in a sexual and lustful manner. He really had fun with her comment. He seemed preoccupied with keeping the students' minds on coarse thoughts.

During one class, he acted out various scenes which involved putting on different jackets, etc. Near the end of the period he turned his back to the students, unzipped his pants to tuck in his shirt, and then turned toward us with his pants still unzipped. While facing the class, he buttoned the top button and emphasized pulling up his zipper. In my opinion, it was totally inappropriate behavior in a class that included girls.

When one student refused to participate in his crude agenda, the teacher "flipped off" the student. While all the kids laughed, they were astonished at the teacher's behavior. They waited to see what the student's response would be. I knew the boy quite well, and I was certain he felt cornered, because he knew the whole class was waiting for his response. Finally, he returned the gesture and "flipped off" the teacher. Later, he told me he was very upset at his own action and at having been placed in a position of responding to such crude behavior by a teacher.

When this teacher assigned a book called *Grendl* for extra credit, I chose not to read it after another student showed me a sadistic and evil scene. I could easily see that the book was violent, and I didn't want to read it.

The teacher copied and distributed an article called "Blacamen the Good" during class. The main character was a man who prided himself on knowing everything about religion, etc. Yet he chose to become involved in Black Magic because it gave him power. In one scene he worshipped an evil god.

After "Blacamen the Good" was distributed, the same boy who earlier had "flipped off" the teacher objected to being inundated with this type of material and to repeatedly being subjected to the obscene behavior described in the selected reading assignments. As a result of the student's complaint, and because he tried to alert the school administration about the problem, he was removed from our honors class and placed in a remedial English class for the remainder of the school year. Amazingly, he was told that he would still be responsible for all the work in the college preparatory class.

When his concerned parents questioned the school faculty about the reason for their son's dismissal from the class, the administration responded, "Your son is having a personality conflict with the teacher." School authorities told the student he was "an angry young man—a troublemaker."

Never did the administration acknowledge to the student or his parents that their concerns about the teacher's behavior and reading material were legitimate. The administration effectively silenced potential complaints by other students with its actions toward this one student. Because of the way their fellow student was treated by the teacher and school administrators, the other students in this "honors" class—seniors who needed high G.P.A.s for college—feared the consequences if they spoke out. They were intimidated because it was obvious that the teacher was in complete control. The students got the message as to what would happen to anyone who complained.

After my friend was removed from class, the teacher told us to write our views about pornography. Prompted by his manner while making the assignment, one male student commented, "Hey, you must have looked at this stuff a lot in college." The teacher just gave him a knowing look. He was sly; he never admitted to anything.

This teacher manipulated the school system. He taught the way he wanted to teach, and selected a haphazard collection of various essays for us to read. There was no doubt in any of our minds that he was intent on promoting lustful thoughts and undermining good thoughts. Discussions always seemed to contain sexual overtones, on a demeaning and dirty level—and he made good seem "stupid."

Even at the end of the year, this teacher wasn't finished persecuting the "errant" student. On the last day of school, he wrote a poem, explicitly pinpointing the ousted student by writing, "There was one idiot in the class, but we kicked his dumb a__ out."

The student, of course, was not there to defend himself.

Joe Ranalla, Student

EDITORS' NOTE: The parents of the boy disciplined for speaking out filed numerous complaints with the school and the district. No action was taken. They later learned that their son had been labeled a "troublemaker" to school board members and other parents. The boy and his parents were ignored, scoffed at, and denigrated by school administrators. This maligned student had already won acceptance into the Naval Academy at Annapolis—hardly the accomplishment of a "troublemaker."

As a result of the emotional trauma the boy suffered, however, he did not attend Annapolis after graduating. He enrolled in another college.

Excerpt from *Grendl* by John Gardner

I slammed into the bedroom. She sat up screaming, and I laughed. I snatched her foot, and now her unqueenly shrieks were deafening, exactly like the squeals of a pig. No one would defend her...I could have jerked her from the bed and stove in her golden-haired head against the wall. They watched in horror...and I caught the other foot and pulled her naked legs apart as if to split her. "Gods, gods!" she screamed. I waited to see if the gods would come, but not a sign of them. I laughed. She called to her brothers...they hung back. I decided to kill her. I firmly committed myself to killing her, slowly, horribly. I would begin by holding her over the fire and cooking the ugly hole between her legs. I laughed harder at that. They were all screaming now, hooting and yowling to their dead-stick gods. I would kill her, yes! I would squeeze out her feces between my fists...

Library Books/Junior High School

I attended a local organization's annual membership kick-off drive for English teachers. A school librarian conducted a general session designed to show us how to lead "book talks" to stimulate young people's interest in reading books. We were to begin telling the story and then stop at a critical point saying, "If you want to know what happens you'll have to read the book." She then provided copies of the books for students to check out.

An avid reader myself, I was curious enough about the five previewed books that I requested them from the library and read them. I was shocked and disgusted at the content and would not recommend them for young people. Common occurrences in the books include lying to parents, deception, and/or concealing what should have been shared. The books featured a lot of death, and for the most part, depicted parents as unconcerned, uncaring, uninvolved, impotent, or nonexistent.

Some of the objectionable portions follow. Beware—they contain material about the spirit world and material I consider pornographic. What happened to all the classics? Remember, these are school library books that schools encourage students to read.

Thousand Pieces of Gold by Ruthanne Lum McCunn. Lalu, a young teenage girl in China, is sold by her father to a bandit. The bandit takes her to his group of ruffians and has the fifty men draw numbers for the order in which they will rape her. The author writes:

> Lalu struggled, but against his bulk she was helpless. The sharp points from the earrings hidden in her waistband dug into her belly and she felt a strange hardness swell and press against her thigh. "Get off," she gasped. "And lose the chance to eat a virgin?" he grinned, his callused fingers tearing at her flesh. "...I say we draw lots again." "And lose my low number? Never." Ding laughed scornfully. "You're just afraid that by the time you get her she'll be like a mushy old sweet potato, too much for someone like you with testicles the size of a gnat."

The book continues with Lalu being sold to an American who runs a bar in Oregon. He rapes her repeatedly:

> His skin, stretched taut over fragile bones, was the color and texture of old wax, and his mouth gaped wide, drooling spittle onto Lalu whom he clasped tightly, his long, brown stained nails scraping her flesh raw. He blamed Lalu for his lack of arousal. Her feet were so big and her hands so coarse he thought he was in bed with a man. And her ignorance was not to be believed. Did he have to tell her everything? Finally his loins stirred weakly and he mounted her. And in the stain of blood that proved his victory, Lalu saw the death of yet another dream.

Something Upstairs by Avi. Kenny's family moved into a two-hundred-year-old house in Rhode Island where he often is awakened by noises, and eventually sees a hand, arm, upper body, and finally the whole ghostly body of a slave boy emerge from the floor. Kenny befriends the ghost and travels back in time with him to help the slave escape his haunting destiny. Kenny meets evil white slave traders and appears doomed to entrapment in the spirit world, but finally escapes and breaks the bondage for himself and the slave boy by murdering a man.

Izzy, Willy Nilly by Cynthia Voight. Though Izzy is just fifteen, she has a 1:00 a.m. curfew on a first date with a boy she doesn't really know or like. They attend a party where her date drinks lots of alcohol and later are involved in a serious car accident which results in the amputation of Izzy's leg. While in the hospital, she is subjected to tremendous peer pressure to protect Marco by telling the police that he wasn't drunk. She agrees to lie to the police and her parents by saying that she doesn't remember what happened.

During his introduction to my daughter's junior "honors" English class, the teacher complained vociferously about parents who attempt to censor what is taught. He told the class he didn't want to hear any complaints from parents about objectionable course material. He then distributed a two-page poem set in the 1960s, in Berkeley, California. It contained themes about drugs, sex, homosexuality, cursing, and anti-American attitudes. This high school has a policy that prohibits any schedule changes due to conflicts between parents and teachers. My daughter no longer attends this school.

It is far easier to "rant and rail" against the liberal tendencies in today's public education than to actually commit yourself to changing them—especially when that commitment means using your time. Yet it is so important for parents to get involved. When I was part of a literature selection committee for a high school, we desperately sought parent volunteers to read books that were being considered for the recommended reading list. We wanted parent comments about the appropriateness of the books and were authorized to enlist additional volunteers. A friend and I tried to recruit numerous parents to commit to read just four to ten books, but not one agreed to help.

This apathy resulted in our concerns being considered as "those of a small minority," and our input carried little weight in the final selection process. Because we couldn't find other parents to help us, the district now requires high school students to read books describing the rape of virgins, spousal abuse, suicide as a peaceful solution to problems, extramarital affairs, transvestites, the occult, prison rape, and murder.

Today, parents dare not assume that books their children read are okay just because they are approved by the school or sent home by the teacher. Parents need to monitor what their children bring home. They may be surprised or even shocked.

Name Withheld by Request

The Giver

A year ago, I learned that my seventh-grade daughter's English teacher was reading *The Giver* by Lois Lowry aloud in class. I was shocked when a friend read me a portion of the book.

The following day, I checked out the library edition of *The Giver* to determine if it was age-appropriate for my daughter. The inside cover claims the story "is told with deceptive simplicity." This was a "red flag" for me.

Chapter one of the book says that a "newchild" (infant) in the nurturing center is not growing as fast as he should, and the "Committee of Elders" in this controlled community decides it must be "released from the community" by lethal injection.

This futuristic society allows only two children per family, one male and one female, and mandates two daily rituals: "Dream-telling" in the morning and "The Telling of Feelings" at night. Jonas, the main character, shares a dream with his parents in which he and Fiona, a school friend, are in the bathing room at the "House of the Old." Jonas wants Fiona to take off her clothes, because he wants to bathe her. He describes his dream as a "wanting" and says, "I wanted it so terribly; I could feel it all through me." His mother tells him these are his "first stirrings" and explains that these "stirrings" must be reported so that treatment can begin. The "stirrings" then disappear thanks to drugs.

When twins are born in this Orwellian death-obsessed society, one must be "released." A set of male twins is brought in and weighed. When the nurturer, Jonas' father, determines that one twin weighs more than the other, he takes out a syringe and a small bottle, fills the syringe, and to Jonas' surprise, begins very carefully to direct the needle into a vein in the newchild's forehead, "puncturing the place where the fragile skin pulsed... He pushed the plunger slowly, injecting the liquid into the scalp vein until the syringe was empty... The newchild squirmed, and wailed faintly." Then, "...the newchild, no longer crying, moved his arms and legs in a jerking motion and then he went limp...The little twin lay motionless."

Jonas thinks: "He killed it! My father killed it!" Then he watches as his father picks up a carton from the floor and lifts the limp body into it. Jonas sees his father open a door in the wall, load the carton containing the body into the chute and give it a shove. Trash! "Bye-bye, little guy," says his father.

In my opinion, *The Giver* devalues human life through its promotion of murder, suicide, infanticide, and euthanasia. The book provides an avenue for children to consider killing themselves, and the content violates four different state education codes. Why wasn't the school district restrained from using this book in the future? Furthermore, the book encourages children to keep secrets from their parents, to be rude, and to lie—three rules that qualify someone to become "The Receiver of Memories."

After reading the book, I went before the school board with my concerns. Two of the board members asked to have the book removed until "age appropriateness" could be determined. The book states that it is for "young adults," however, I do not consider ages eight to twelve young adult. In my opinion, sixteen to eighteen is a young adult. And no matter the age, I still don't think it's appropriate in a classroom setting. The book was not banned, but I thank the two members for speaking out.

In fact, at that December board meeting, teachers, a children's bookstore owner, and other parents also spoke out both for and against the book. When concerned parents confronted the administration and the teachers, no one would acknowledge that he or she had brought the book into the school. No one in authority accepted any responsibility whatsoever. In all, eighteen parents supported our position.

Following that meeting, the principal did mail an "opt-out" form to parents, but he lied by saying that "a parent" had challenged the book. Eight children were subsequently "opted-out," and we learned that the book was also being used in the third-, fourth-, and sixth-grade classes.

Finally, the assistant superintendent of public instruction convened an eight-member review panel to read the book and listen to parents' and teachers' concerns. The makeup of the panel was as follows: 1) a librarian, 2) two teachers, 3) a principal, 4) the assistant superintendent, and 5) two community members chosen by the PTA. Their own policy stated that seven members should be chosen and, when appropriate, one member should be a student. Obviously, they did not follow board policy in forming the panel. Why was a student not chosen?

The result of this panel? The book was put back in the classroom at the seventh-grade level. The "positive opt-in" (meaning the student couldn't participate unless the parent said "yes") that we requested was not even mentioned. In fact, during this controversy, a new policy was created.

During this four-month controversy, I had an hour-long telephone conversation with the assistant superintendent who actually told me, the parent, that, "I feel I own these children." She based this statement on the fact that she had been in education for twenty-five years. I was shocked that she would say this to a parent. My husband and I found her sense of proprietorship appalling. Our daughter did not return to public school the following year.

Sally Bowman

Rain God

As I stood before our district's board of trustees, I read this passage from the book *Rain God*, by Arturo Islas.[3] (I warn you it is very graphic. However, this is what the students read. And I decided to include the language just as it was presented in the book to serve as a warning to parents and to encourage them to carefully monitor what their children are being assigned in class.)

> When he forced her to the couch she knew she had won. Men were easy to deal with sexually. Without a word and very quickly she took off her clothes, and he was at her. Her knowledge of these mysteries helped her say several times without meaning it, "Hurt me, Miguel, hurt me." She moaned as if indeed he were and, in that way, gave him the illusion that he was in control once again...

> "What is the name of the son of a bitch who killed my father? I'll kill him myself since you men can't think about anything but your balls." And to the district attorney: "How many times have you sucked a cock, you prissy fool, or gotten some whore to suck yours?"

It was not easy reading this aloud. I have never used such profane language as appeared in this book, but I felt I had every right to read it. My son's eleventh-grade American literature class was required to read the entire book aloud in class, without my permission, and without my knowledge.

I have spent many years teaching my son alternatives to profanity and slang, but now the school that I trusted to teach proper English required students to read aloud a very different vocabulary than I would ever allow in my home. My son was supposed to learn American literature; this was not the type of literature I thought he would read.

When asked why this book was selected, the teacher said many Mexican-American students in our area could identify with the story. Since the book associated profanity, superstitions, and unethical behavior with the Mexican-American lifestyle, I certainly hoped the teacher was mistaken.

When I complained about the book to the principal, he explained that he had no control over reading material chosen by teachers. He said that in the future, if I didn't want my child reading a particular book in class, I could request that he go to the library by himself with alternate reading material. *Rain God* took almost two months to read and study in my son's class. If I had requested that he go to the library, he would have spent two months there with no teacher.

I filed a sexual harassment complaint so that an official investigation would be conducted. Several days later, my son told me that he had gone to the library while other students performed their skits from the book. When he'd asked his teacher why he had to leave, the teacher told him that some of the students might say a bad word. This was ridiculous. My objections were not with the students or what they might say. My objections were with the teacher's choice in reading material that was read aloud in class. Now, the spotlight was put on my son because I complained.

Students in my son's class asked him why he had to spend the class time in the library, and he told them that it was probably because his mother didn't like the book they were reading. I immediately received a call from the administration telling me that my son was discussing the situation with other students. They told me that I should make him stop.

I spoke to my son and he agreed, but it was very difficult for him not to answer questions from his friends about leaving the classroom. Days later, I received a call from my son's counselor telling me that the teacher felt "uncomfortable" having my son in his class and that they would have to remove him. Subsequently, my son was called out of class without any explanation and then sent back to get his books. Obviously, this caused a lot of talk among the other students—they thought he was in trouble. The change could have been made the following day, which would have been less noticeable to the students. Apparently, the school had very little regard for a student's emotional needs.

Our school had no formal policy for previewing reading material aside from a complaint form for parents to complete. Since I had never been notified of the books that would be used, there was no way for me to know I might have a reason to review any of the material. I only became aware of the book after reading some odd study questions in my son's notebook, including: "Who was Mama Chona's bastard son?" "What is a seance?" and "How did they exorcise the devil from their house?" I was concerned about the nature of the questions and the context in which they were asked. They delved into areas that included a family's belief system, and I felt the teacher should not discuss these issues without considering the parents' wishes.

I also wanted to find out how books were approved for use in the classroom and soon learned that no procedures or guidelines existed for teachers selecting reading material. I also learned that *Rain God* had been used for three years but that the book never came home with students, because there weren't enough copies. Therefore, parents did not have a chance to review the book, and according to the administration, there was no specific policy for ordering books, so no one really knew who had approved the purchase.

It took many visits to the administration and the school board, along with the help of many parents, to finally force the district to address the matter. This process took four months. I work full-time but took the necessary time off to pursue the issue.

Teachers fought us by invoking "constitutional rights" in an effort to justify their curricular choices. According to them, parents opposing *Rain God* were attempting to censor reading material at the school. I only requested, however, that the school remove the book as curriculum. If teachers and administrators felt the book was so important, they could put several copies in the library where students (and parents) could choose whether or not to read it. There was never a question of censorship—the issue was the use of an inappropriate curricular supplement without parental notification or permission.

Because of our efforts, the board did create a new policy regarding *Rain God* and a process for selecting supplemental reading material in the future. It was decided that *Rain God* would only be used in twelfth-grade classes and would not be read aloud in class. The school has been instructed to provide a list of books (syllabus) at the beginning of every school year. The problem is that the list is sent home with the students and, therefore, often doesn't reach parents. There is no form to be signed and returned, so there is no assurance that parents ever receive the list. I should note that *Rain God* is on our state's "suggested reading list," recommended for children in ninth through twelfth grades. Yet this book is not appropriate for high school students!

In another change, a curriculum committee will now decide whether schools can use books not on the "suggested" list. The problem is that only three parents serve on this committee, and since they are in the minority, school officials and teachers can easily outvote them.

During this episode, I requested a review of the teacher's credentials by the state's professional standards office. I based my request on the fact that state law requires written parental permission for sex education. The state requested comments from both the teacher and me, and decided that there was not enough evidence to continue the investigation. The administration summarily dismissed the sexual harassment complaint I originally submitted to the school.

The scales of justice are supposed to be balanced on both sides of an argument. In schools, those scales tip in favor of teachers and administrators. Parents have very few rights regarding the material their children learn. Teachers who work with minors have a closed classroom and a captive audience. The children do not feel they can leave the classroom, because they think they might get in trouble, disappoint the teacher, or be ridiculed by either the teacher or their peers. Over the last three years, no other student questioned *Rain God*; and no parents questioned it because parents did not know their children read it.

Our schools should have the best curricula. American literature should include time-tested literature with the best vocabulary. After all, students will use the language they read and hear. Language taught in the classroom should be the language students are expected to use in everyday life. Our school has a "no profanity" rule on campus. Students are punished for violating this rule. But in the classroom, there are no hard and fast rules regarding what is taught. "Profanity is a gray area," one administrator told me. Of course school officials and teachers don't see a gray area when disciplining students for using profanity. The students required to read profanities aloud in class would be punished if they used the same language on campus after they left the classroom.

Paula Goff

Socialism in the Classroom

At one time I had great faith in our public school system. I thought America was best among nations at educating her children—especially in our district. However, my convictions have changed. The following events do not reflect my opinions; they are actual classroom experiences. I helped in the classroom every week, so I witnessed these events!

I wanted to believe it was only an isolated incident when my youngest child did not learn to read in kindergarten and when the first-grade teacher always read to the class without their participation.

The curriculum for my second grader included literature about witches, and some sort of subliminal music played in the background when the children read. During the Christmas play, Santa

Claus was hypnotized. For the older children, the sex-ed class discussed dildoes. The children no longer sat individually in rows of desks but in chaotic clusters of four. During some tests, children stood their books upright in front of them if they weren't supposed to cheat; during other tests, cheating was allowed, and books could lay flat on the tables. My daughter sometimes got confused—she didn't know when she could cheat and when she couldn't.

Children received party voter-registration cards to fill out and turn in to the teachers. (I thought party affiliation in America was a private matter.) In my ten-year-old son's drug curriculum, "Here's looking at you 2000," the students role-played drug addicts. The science teacher told them, "When you drink too much alcohol you'll feel [good] and want to have sex with somebody." My child was shocked, feeling that the teacher was encouraging drinking and sex.

When the school added "journaling" to my children's curriculum, I at first thought it sounded like a great idea, a chance for the children to be creative writers. However, the teachers began prompting them with very sensitive questions: "Does your family get along?" "What are your parents' occupations?" "Have you been blamed for something you didn't do?"

One child's class wrote their own obituaries after having been "done in" by a family member! My nine-year-old had to answer the question: "Have you ever thought of going behind your parent's back? If no, make it up." My children were not graded on sentence structure, punctuation, or spelling (I never saw any red marks for these); rather they were graded on such powerful nonsense as political correctness, a teacher's whim, or length of their babble. These prompts tended to undermine and belittle parental authority and beliefs, and most distressing, seemed to attack the "trust" of the home.

My sixth grader chose a book called *Sixth Grade Secrets* from the suggested reading list. Unfortunately, she neglected to read the book until the night before her "report" was due. Shortly after she began reading, she came to me with the book and said, "Mom, I can't read this book anymore; it's not appropriate for me." I have to admit that, on one hand, I was proud of the fact that she used the word "appropriate." On the other hand, I was concerned about the content of a book that would elicit this type of response from a sixth grader. She and I sat down to read it together. I wanted to know what she considered inappropriate.

Sixth Grade Secrets told the story of children who formed gangs. One gang called the "Pig Gang" discussed an initiation exercise that included boys stealing girls' panties and parading them around on sticks. The panties were referred to as "treasures." When a girl in the story went to the principal for help, he admonished her by saying that she should keep her underwear on under her skirt because that's where it belonged. While none of the panties were stolen off the girls' bodies, the girls were upset; yet the principal in the story didn't support them. The messages conveyed were of a sexual nature.

I called our school's principal the next morning about the book, and she told me to have my daughter report only on the portion she had read and to return the book to her. After much thought I chose not to return the book and instead copied many of the pages and turned those in to the principal. I told her I had decided to keep the book; she didn't argue.

The assignment for this "book report" was to make a postcard. That's right—not a written or oral report—but a postcard. My daughter drew a stamp with a pair of underpants hanging on a stick and girls reaching up in an attempt to retrieve their underwear. What kind of book and classroom assignment is that?

It's not unusual for book reports to omit written or oral reports. When one of my children was in fourth grade, the students made "mobiles, pictorials, or collages" for their book reports. Schools today encourage children to use pictures instead of words!

The following years grew worse; spelling was omitted in my fourth grader's class; math became an "open-ended" problem of the week (basically, no right or wrong answers); science projects became "invention conventions" (nonscientific: creativity without knowledge).

After opting one child out of PG-13 and R-rated movies, I faced harassment and intimidation by the classroom teacher and the principal. Then the school harassed and discriminated against my child after we opted out of a class that spent three months studying euthanasia and infanticide in a core book called *The Giver*. Other reading material included: *My Sister's Killer*, *The Loser*, and the depressing *Caleb's Brother*. The assignments accompanying these books asked students to relate the story to events in their own lives by writing about their memories and feelings. These stories focused on death, depression, gangs, drugs, murder, suicide, and other negative and frightening topics.

My "A" student began receiving lower and lower grades on these assignments. My child's spelling, punctuation, and thought processes were good but he had very individual beliefs, feelings, and memories. After reading *The Loser* and writing against gang violence, stating, "It takes a stronger man not to fight," my child was kept after class and told that unless the "correct" memories, feelings, and responses were written, his assignments would no longer be graded. He was told: "Someone at home must be keeping you from your true feelings." He received an "F" for that report.

At this point we contacted a law firm. The attorney stopped the actions of the teachers, restored my student's grades, and protected his right to express individual thoughts and beliefs free of the teacher's political influence, discrimination, intimidation, and harassment.

As to the required "journaling," the attorney and I were informed by the assistant superintendent, principal, teacher, and their counsel that it was "dialectical" journaling. I researched "dialectical," and learned that it is oral argumentation based on theses, antitheses, and syntheses, and widely practiced by Karl Marx. He used this form of argumentation to change the thinking of an entire society! I am appalled and ashamed that our once great country is teaching this in public schools! Marxism in America!

It is no wonder that America is in crisis. Something must be done—or is it too late? I have placed my children in private school, but our hearts are gripped with despair every time we see a yellow school bus. Isn't anyone listening?

Name Withheld by Request

Julie of the Wolves

When my eleven-year-old daughter was exposed to the book *Julie of the Wolves* by Jean Craighead George (required reading for her sixth-grade class), I appeared before the local school board and testified before our state legislature in an attempt to expose the inappropriateness of the book. Over one hundred parents signed a petition requesting that the book be removed from the "required" reading list. It all fell on deaf ears.

My daughter wrote her own letter and asked me to read it to the elected officials. Below is her letter:

The two things I love more than anything else in the world are reading and playing the piano. The thing that makes me love reading books is that I turn the book into a movie. As I read books, a movie is going on in my head. (It's like getting into a movie theater for free!) When I read the "rape scene" in *Julie of the Wolves* I was thrown back! My mind was racing, saying, "Stop! R-rated movie!" Of course, it was a school assignment and I had to read it! And now it's been permanently imprinted in my mind. I could give you a detailed description of what I "saw," but it hurts my mind to go back through that subject because of how much I disagree with what happened.

I accidentally watch stuff like that on TV commercials and I hear it flipping through radio stations. But when I read it at school—it's going too far. School is supposed to be a safe place from the outside world. You're not supposed to find any of what I found in the book in school!

I have many other friends at different schools that will have to read *Julie of the Wolves* this year. My brothers and sister will have to read it when they get to sixth grade. I don't want them to read the book and have R-rated thoughts like I did. When Julie doesn't tell anyone what happened to her, it bugged me. When nothing happened to the guy who attacked her, it bugged me. When Julie tried to run away from her problem, it bugged me. Those three things go completely against what my mom is teaching me. I thought something was wrong when I read it in fifth grade and I still think something is wrong with reading it in sixth grade. How can you say reading something that bad is acceptable? I don't understand. If there is another book that teaches the same concepts without the bad part, why not read it instead of *Julie of the Wolves*?

Will our children suffer if this book is not taught at the schools? And who will complain because it has been taken off the core reading list? If it stays, our children will suffer the consequences of how it might affect them. And the complaining will be by parents to the schools requesting that their children not read this book. My child will be properly educated despite this book, not because of it.

Name Withheld by Request

Reading Material with Explicit Sex Acts and Vulgar Language

Below is a copy of a letter I sent to the principal at my daughter's high school. Identifying names have been removed.

Dear Ms. [principal]:

I was appalled by my daughter's English reading material at [the school]. [My daughter] is a sophomore in _____'s class. I had heard about her reading material last week when she brought it to my attention that the "F" word and the Spanish word P_t_were being used. I do not allow foul language to be used in my home. I admit I did ignore her concerns last week, but last night when she mentioned to me that a young male student jokingly asked her about the color and shape of her breast I was quite angry. Now, I understand after reading page 128 (copy enclosed) why this young man might have been sexually aroused.

I asked my daughter if this was a sex education class or did she belong to a gang related class (which would have made me more concerned since I know [my daughter] is a clean cut student who has never been in trouble). [She] confirmed to me this was her English class. My concern now is when English reading material is purchased through the [the] school district is anyone reading it? If this type of reading material is allowed in the district then I have a great concern about how my tax dollars are being spent. Most important, the wrong message is being sent to young students that this is allowable/acceptable, which I believe could lead to problems, including unwanted pregnancies.

I am Hispanic and I am embarrassed that your English teacher is promoting *Always Running* by Luis J. Rodriquez. I have glanced at this material and I have reiterated to my daughter that this type of reading material will not enhance her education to the college level. I hope you get my message. I am requesting that you pull this book from your English reading material. I am against future young freshmen reading this garbage at school.

Also, I would like to make our government officials aware of where our money is being spent and the quality of education (poor) being given to our young students.

Sincerely,

Sarah Gama

After I sent the above letter, I spoke with the principal on the telephone and made an appointment to meet with her. The principal greeted me but directed me to meet with the assistant vice principal and the English teacher. I wanted to tape record the meeting but they refused.

During this meeting they tried to justify the use of *Always Running* by saying the book was necessary to counter widespread gang activity at the school. This didn't impress me for three reasons: 1) I have never heard of any gang problems at my daughter's school. 2) Even if there is a gang problem—how can a book with blatant pornographic language help alleviate the problem? 3) The school's "Student and Parent Information Handbook" discusses penalties for students who express themselves with obscenities in writing, pictures, etc. If students are held accountable for obscene language, why isn't a teacher or school held accountable?

Neither the assistant vice principal nor the teacher had an explanation that addressed my concerns. They informed me that I could not tell them what to use in class. The only resolution we were able to reach was that while the other students read and discussed *Always Running*, my daughter read another book. Of course, she still sat in class listening to the discussion.

Since I wasn't notified before this book was used, nor given the choice of refusing permission for my daughter to read it, I've often wondered how many other parents remain unaware of this book. To the best of my knowledge, *Always Running* is still being used.

FOLLOWING ARE EXCERPTS FROM THE BOOK: (Warning, the material is sexually graphic.)

Always Running: La Vida Loca: Gang Days in L.A.
by Luis J. Rodriquez

Page 105: "She brushed up to me and pulled off her blouse. Erect nipples confronted me on firm breasts. I kissed them...I was too f_ _ _ _ _ up to care.

Page 128: My tongue drew circles around her nipples, which were on a dark patch over honey-brown skin. My hands rubbed her c_ _ _ from the outside of her pants. Her hips moved in waves, pushing harder and harder into my hand. She groped for my zipper, tugged and slid it down. Her fingers kneaded the top of my penis, hard and wet with anticipation...oh baby, lick me.

...Then she held on to my penis with both hands...she pulled at her pants...I looked down and saw the tuft of wild hair at the crotch, her legs spread and nearing my shoulders, inviting me to enter...then pressed me down. The penis sank into the bristle of pubis...

Sarah Gama

Arguing they only want to "keep minds engaged" with "authentic literature," schools frequently expose students to bizarre, grotesque, and obscene material that meets "state-approved" guidelines but shocks—intentionally, after all—even the most jaded sensibilities. Desperate parents end up in drawn-out battles against intransigent superintendents who feel they "own these children" and must protect teachers who enjoy "a closed classroom and a captive audience."

CHAPTER THREE

SELF-ESTEEM TRUMPS LEARNING

THE LATEST TREND *in education is to praise students. Unfortunately, that praise is sometimes not warranted and students earn good grades for sub-par performance. Sadly, students aren't fooled when they receive false praise for poor performance or sloppy work. Eventually, they understand that the praise is empty, and they view commendation with disdain. Today's testing presents two problems. One is the feel-good idea of promoting "self-esteem," while the other is lawmakers who believe they can legislate quality education and use testing as the vehicle to prove their success.*

Neither idea works. Self-esteem is not awarded; it is earned by accomplishment. For instance, several years ago a high school teacher said that one of her students turned in an excellent report. When the teacher handed the assignment back to the girl, the teacher said she commended the student on her work and the girl just looked at her and said, "Yeah, right. That's what they always say." The teacher was surprised by the response and asked the girl to explain what she meant. The student replied that teachers always say everything is really good, but they say it to everyone, all the time. The girl said, "Do they think we're dumb? We know they just say it to make us feel good. It doesn't mean anything."[1]

Empty praise is worthless. The only people misled by the deception are not the students, but parents and legislators. To parents, a good grade means a job well done. After all, good grades were earned when they went to school. To legislators, good grades on mandatory tests prove that they have legislated quality education and they can give themselves the proverbial "pat-on-the-back for a job well done." They're deceiving themselves, and denying the very students they think they are helping a real education.

Federal and state laws have crippled education. Schools are under tremendous pressure to produce good grades. As a result, teachers have reported that some schools actually call teachers in to warn them they must produce good grades on the mandatory state and federal tests in order to prevent their schools from retaliation and/or takeover.

For instance, one of the major problems with the national Leave No Child Behind federal law is that it mandates a "teach to the test" model. This does not enhance learning; it merely forces teachers to ensure that students do well on tests. What, you may say, is wrong with that? See below.

Teachers know that teaching to the test does not produce well-educated students. It merely produces high test scores on the limited subject matter covered in the test. For instance, in testimony before the Arkansas Joint Interim Education Committee, two Arkansas teachers, Debbie Pelley and Iris Stevens, warned against "teaching the test." Pelley testified that teachers were being told, "If it is not on the test, don't teach it." She said the "test is becoming the entire curriculum rather than a sampling of the curriculum." She then explained that if she wants her students to learn one hundred math concepts, she will cover those one hundred concepts but may only include ten of them on a test. However, in order to do well on her test, students will need to understand all one hundred concepts. Under the new "teach to the test" model, however, she says students will score high on a test but will only know ten of the needed concepts.[2]

Isn't it time for state and federal governments to allow educators to do their jobs and educate children? Isn't it time to teach children that good grades aren't given, they are earned? And along the way, allow our students to experience the real sense of accomplishment.

Group Grades

One day about three years ago, our daughter came home from her fourth-grade class upset. She complained that one of her classmates "caused the rest of her group to get a grade of 'C' on a class project instead of an 'A'."

Curious, my wife and I asked her to explain her frustration. She described how her teacher had divided the class into groups of four. Each group, she explained, "had at least one smart kid, one kinda-dumb kid and two average kids." Each of the groups was given a project and told to work together to solve the problem. The efforts of the group as a whole would result in one grade for the whole group.

Our daughter's group became frustrated when one of the students decided he didn't want to participate in the group's discussion; he didn't want to do his part of the project assignment. Apparently, he assumed the rest of the students would do the work for him, and that he would actually get a better grade than he normally would get if he acted alone.

The project required several days of work, including homework, report writing, and an oral presentation. The other students didn't pay much attention to the one student's lack of participation until it was too late. (Remember, these were fourth graders.) All of the reports and oral presentations were due on the final day of the project. It was then that the recalcitrant student announced to the group that he didn't do his report and wasn't prepared to give his oral presentation. His announcement left the remaining students in a predicament, faced with the urgency of persuading him at the last minute to do "something," otherwise the whole group would suffer. Their efforts failed, and as a result, the entire group received a lower grade.

Our daughter asked, "Why should I try hard to do good if one kid is going to ruin it?" Good question.

We made an appointment to meet with our daughter's teacher to express our concerns. To our dismay, the teacher actually agreed with our protest of group grading, but stated that all the teachers implemented such practices as part of the daily curriculum.

The good news is that in response to our complaint (and probably the complaints of other parents), our daughter's teacher gained permission to grade on an individual basis as opposed to group grading. Furthermore, the next time we visited the classroom, we were happy to see that the students' desks no longer stood in groups of four but had been rearranged into traditional rows.

We learned a valuable lesson. It pays to be vigilant and to express concerns. We also learned that teachers are not always the enemy. Often, they are forced to implement practices they don't approve of or wish to follow. By voicing our concerns, we were able to give our daughter's teacher some ammunition to help her return to teaching practices that have proven effective.

John and Theresa Bell

Creative Spelling

I'm angry, very angry. Our son is six years old and in second grade. Last year I fumed because he brought home written work with every word misspelled and then told me it was "creative spelling." According to "creative spelling," children must learn two, three, or even four different ways to spell before learning the correct way. These formative years should be spent learning how to spell words correctly the first time!

My wife and I arranged to meet with the teacher to discuss what we consider ineffectual teaching. Our son's teacher told us that she never corrects a student's spelling errors in front of the other children but does tell them when they do good work. I pointed out that SAT scores prove that this teaching method has failed. She said, "SAT scores are global scores that have nothing to do with your child."

She then pulled out a small stack of current teaching methodologies and began reciting them to us. At this point, I asked that we discuss our immediate concerns and not get distracted by lectures. She said she was answering me and that we had a total of thirty minutes. We felt she was wasting what little time she had allotted us by avoiding a discussion of our son's spelling.

We told her that we wanted our son to learn how to spell, and we wanted him corrected in class. She stated she would not do that because it would damage his self-esteem. I tried explaining that when we were children, our teachers didn't harm our self-esteem by teaching us how to spell, read, and write. I reminded her that our SAT scores were "over the moon" compared with today's scores. I also reminded her that the current SAT has been referred to as "SAT Light" due to its increased time limit, allowed use of calculators, and the elimination of difficult sections. She was obviously uncomfortable; she said she was aware of the changes and thereafter quickly changed the subject whenever the SAT was mentioned.

The teacher repeatedly stressed how important it is to "create self-esteem." (In truth, if teachers would revert to standard teaching methods that work, self-esteem would come naturally.) Why can't teachers admit that self-esteem is not created by people telling children, "You're great!" and then, when those children graduate from high school—or even college—they suddenly realize how they've been cheated? Why can't teachers acknowledge that an important part of learning is the self-confidence that comes from the struggle to understand new concepts and gain new knowledge? This struggle includes both sides of reality: 1) approval when one does well; 2) disapproval (and correction) when one does poorly.

When I asked the teacher what was wrong with reverting to a "tried and true" method, she said those methods were no good. I responded by saying that if she wasn't willing to use methods that actually taught children how to read, spell, and write, we would be forced to remove our child from public school. Unflinching (was I surprised?), she said that was my prerogative.

Mine is a common story, but until it affected my child, the rumors, the talk show conversations, even the written articles were always about "someone else's" child. I strongly suggest that every parent take the time to meet with his or her child's teacher—whether it's about spelling or math, etc., and tell that teacher: "I want Johnny to learn to read the first time (or learn to calculate real math)." The teacher's response is likely to both shock and bewilder the parent.

John and Jo Jo Dulaney

EDITORS' NOTE: Shortly after the above conversation, the Dulaneys removed their son from public school. For the last two years he has been enrolled in a private school.

Today, Mr. Dulaney says this about his son's current school: "He has flourished in every way. He is taught the curriculum of a scholar; he is taught the love and power of God, the difference between right and wrong, and the classic 3 Rs. His school believes that students will rise to the level of expectation under inspection and that true self-confidence comes from achievement, not empty praise for doing nothing. With parental permission, poor behavior may be corrected with corporal punishment, therefore, students are generally well behaved; they don't curse or have violent ex-

changes. The atmosphere needed for the art and business of education is created and maintained; learning comes naturally in such a climate."

Assessment Testing

I have three sons and have not viewed education through the same eyes since I first discovered the contents of California's Learning Assessment System (CLAS)[3] that was implemented in the late 1990s. We were told it was the new way to test and was superior to all other testing techniques. This nonacademic assessment was given to my fourth grader in June 1999. Since that time I've become an activist, fighting against psychological, mentally abusive, and subjective values-oriented tests. California was one of the first states to implement these new "assessments" for children. Be warned—"assessments" have little or nothing to do with academic achievement. The emphasis is on a child's attitudes, values, and behaviors.

The assessment testing featured hateful, violent, anti-God, anti-marriage, anti-white, and pro-feminist story "prompts." These stories described abusive father figures and mothers who often wished for their husbands' deaths. In addition, they suggested politically correct themes and mysticism that reflected New Age religion. The stories had a common thread of hopelessness, helplessness, and often, death.

The administration stated that these writing prompts or stories were selected to elicit an emotional response from the students. But they sent terrible messages to our youth. For instance, my son heard, "There are no right or wrong answers." After one story, he made new school rules and discussed them in a group (cooperative learning). The group listed the new rules on paper. These rules could be as benign as allowing "gum chewing," or stretched to the extreme, such as allowing a child to bring a gun to school to shoot the teacher or someone else.

Any discussion like this imprints itself on a child's mind. Yet teachers and administrators cry out, "Why don't children have good values and respect us?" I would say that if our children aren't taking authority seriously, it is primarily because of this type of garbage. These concepts teach them that it isn't important to respect teachers or others. Children are learning a value system without values in school. Maybe this is the reason so many of our youth kill each other and why the suicide rate is increasing among children under ten. Yes, under ten. CNN documented that the "under age ten group" is the fastest growing suicide group in the nation.

I was present when one mother informed a district administrative employee of the hateful, violent, anti-God, anti-marriage, anti-white, and pro-feminist test stories. The employee's response was, "Don't tell me that; I'll have to turn you in." I'd like to know what kind of fascism is going on in our education system.

The information form each student filled out before taking the assessment took forty to fifty minutes. What kind of questions did they ask my fourth-grade son that took fifty minutes? Teachers told me the test included spelling, grammar, and punctuation, but if you read the scoring rubric, you would see that the only things the students received grades on were their attitudes, opinions, and persuasive writing.

The assessment prompts used in CLAS tore down traditional family values. It and its related teaching techniques did not constitute critical thinking, but educational malpractice![4]

Patrice Lynes

EDITORS' NOTE: Parents and even legislators were prohibited from viewing the tests. Only after some courageous teachers made copies and clandestinely passed them to parents and legislators was the true nature of the "prompts" revealed. When it was leaked that copies were "out," those who had them were threatened with imprisonment.

Frustrated Parents

We would like to present yet another example of the sad state of education in our state. Our son showed us a copy of a test that was given to his fifth-grade class. (We had another example but the teacher conveniently "lost it.")

Some of the uncorrected test errors included: Colonrol for Colonial, piorod for period, religus fredom for religious freedom, boarders for borders, servent for servant and england not capitalized. Yet an "A" was awarded for a 100 percent "perfect" paper.

Could that be because the teacher didn't know the correct answers either, or just didn't want to bother? The spelling errors example only highlights the inadequacies in our current system; it certainly wasn't an isolated instance. We encountered similar problems in five different school districts.

How can we expect our children to learn to spell when they aren't taught properly by their teachers? How do you respond to a child who, when you try to correct him, informs you that, "The teacher says it's perfect"? Is it any wonder that we graduate functional illiterates from our high schools, thereby necessitating remedial classes in our colleges? Everyone shares the same feeling of helplessness to affect change. And school officials always say, "You are the only one who has complained." What are frustrated parents to do? The system is an abysmal failure and a total waste of taxpayer dollars. We thought perhaps media involvement would help, but they appear to be duped by the system and don't understand the reality of current practices.

It's little wonder that teachers and unions fight teacher competency testing and the voucher system. They spent millions of dollars spreading lies and using scare tactics to defeat the last voucher initiative. They seem mystified as to the reasons why people vote against school bond issues.

In the final analysis, the big losers are our children who are expected to become responsible, productive citizens with a totally inadequate education. If the schools would concentrate on solid, basic academic education instead of so much social engineering, our children would be far better prepared for the future. Something must be done to fix this completely broken system!

Dawn and Amie Luke
Dana and Carl Patterson

Whether it's getting away with "creative spelling" or handing out good grades like candy, children soon catch on to empty praise. Today's educators, nevertheless, seem bent on muddling academic achievement with programs designed to build "self-esteem." Exasperated parents, meanwhile, simply want their children "to learn how to spell."

Psychological Molestation

CHAPTER FOUR

SCHOOLS: SCARING KIDS TO DEATH

THE NUMBER OF CLASSES *about death, dying, and suicide is growing. Yet, as with sex education, parents don't always know that schools bury these topics in courses such as family life, health, or "career decision-making." It isn't unusual for children in elementary school to report classroom assignments in which they write epitaphs for their own tombstones. Some children have had the dubious honor of going on field trips to the cemetery or to the mortuary.*

The theory behind this morbid focus is obscure, and most parents have no idea what "Death Education" is all about. It's a dangerous psychobabble theory, which holds that exposing students to death and dying is psychologically healthy. But as many psychologists will testify, it may also have the opposite effect. In any case, there is absolutely no justification for schools to engage in this.

Verification that these practices are common was dramatically demonstrated for us while on a speaking tour in the Midwest. When the topic of death education and tombstone exercises came up, several people began to shake their heads; they couldn't believe what they were hearing. Finally, a woman stood up and walked into a nearby third-grade classroom. When she returned, she asked us to accompany her to the classroom. We did and sure enough—there were the children's tombstones hanging from the classroom walls. (The children in this classroom were surrounded with symbols of death all day long.)

While some teachers encourage children to discuss suicide and what it would be like to die, other teachers do not agree with this new trend, as A'lyce Baldarelli, a California educator, points out in her story included in this chapter.

Parents are often left in the dark about these exercises. Such was the case with the parents of Stephen Nalepa—they found out too late to save their son. On March 24, 1990, in Canton, Michigan, eight-year-old Stephen hung himself with a belt. The Detroit News *reported that the day before, Stephen had viewed the film* Nobody's Useless *in his second-grade class at school.*[1]

The parents sued, and in an affidavit for that lawsuit, Dr. David Shaffer, Director of Child Psychiatry at Columbia University's College of Physicians and Surgeons, said:

> It is my professional opinion that the death of Stephen Nalepa on or about March 24, 1990 resulted because he viewed the film *Nobody's Useless* the previous day... [Stephen's death] would not have occurred had he not viewed the film...It is my professional opinion that prior to viewing the film *Nobody's Useless,* Stephen Nalepa was not suicidal, and that his death constituted an act of imitation.[2]

In 1992 it came to light that another second grader had attempted suicide after viewing the same film two years before Stephen's death. In that case, the boy's mother, Mary Jane Egan, said she went to the school in 1988 to tell them about the film and what her son had done. Mrs. Egan's affidavit included this statement: "I went to Gallimore School and told the principal...what Jimmy had done at home. [The principal] said that Jimmy's actions could not possibly be connected to the movie, and she said I was making far too much of the situation." The principal and school board felt Nobody's Useless *was an excellent film and did not consider Mrs. Egan's complaint valid.*[3]

"One of the reasons why the news media have tended to play down teen suicides is because of the copy-cat effect," Samuel Blumenfeld reported in his education newsletter. "It is widely known that even adults are subject to the copy-cat effect. But children are forever imitating others in their games and play. For educators to pretend that such imitation is so rare that no cautions need be taken to protect children from their own imitative tendencies is to suggest that other motives were involved in their lapse of ordinary caution."[4]

Older students, too, are affected when presented with suicide-laced curriculum. One high school student said that after listening to a week-long suicide prevention class, she was depressed for weeks and found herself thinking about suicide whenever she encountered difficulties or problems. She finally asked several of her friends if they had experienced any of the same thoughts. They admitted that after the class, they, too were depressed for several weeks, and found themselves thinking about suicide, which they had never before considered an option. (See story included later in this chapter.)

Another high schooler, already besieged with suicidal thoughts, may have been troubled by classroom discussions about Ordinary People, *a book that deals with a teenage boy's suicide and its effects on his family. Afterwards, the fifteen-year-old boy committed suicide. (Mrs. Barron tells the details surrounding her son's death later in this chapter.)*

Why do elementary-age children—or even teenagers—need to be bombarded with vivid reminders of death? How depressing! Why isn't the focus on good things in life, on happy things? Why don't schools try to encourage positive thoughts and dwell on uplifting literature and exercises? Why is so much time spent on death, rape, dysfunctional families, drugs, and other dismal subjects?

Rather than helping students, this concentration on depressing topics can increase problems. Real Sex Education Facts reports on its Web site that: "Frederick Wortham, a psychiatrist who treats troubled children who have done terrible things, tells us that a child's mind is like a bank—what goes into it comes back ten years later with interest."[5]

In light of Dr. Wortham's observation, parents should beware the content of today's classroom material. Whether it is graphic sex, thoughts of death and dying, or other depressing and negative thoughts, parents should be asking: What are today's schools depositing in children's minds?

In response to growing concerns over the misuse of psychological activities, including death education by unlicensed psychologists—specifically teachers—California passed legislation in 1996 to prohibit such practices by anyone other than a licensed or credentialed psychologist.[6] *Yet in a two-part Los Angeles Channel 13 news interview, the district's suicide prevention curriculum director—fully aware of the new law—said that Los Angeles Unified School District would continue with its death education practice because that was the only way students would get the information. A sixth-grade teacher who also appeared on the program said that he was still teaching suicide prevention in his life skills class.*

During the interview the teacher said that he always notifies parents by sending home permission slips, but when the television camera focused on the actual slip the teacher sent home, there was no mention of suicide or death education listed. The reporter asked about the omissions, and the teacher replied that they were listed in the syllabus.[7] (Parents, how many of you have ever looked at your child's teacher's syllabus? Maybe you should!)

No one doubts that teachers and others who engage in these practices believe they help students; however, they may compound the problem. As Steven Atkinson, M.F.C.C. said, "Depressed children who may be suicidal need in-depth specialized counseling and treatment. They should be referred to professionals. Students who are not troubled don't need the information; in fact, classroom discussions may actually increase the child's vulnerability to suicide."[8] Dr. David Shaffer reiterated that opinion, saying that "curriculum-based suicide awareness programs disturb some high-risk students."[9]

Life Skills/Death

As I sat in on one of our school's weekly department meetings, I wondered with dismay how I was going to avoid teaching the latest life skills curriculum.

I worked in a special high school "at-risk" program. This meant that we were exempt from many, if not all, of the rules applicable to a "regular" program at the high school. And we definitely broke—I mean didn't have to follow—education codes governing parental notification about certain subjects being taught or discussed and school board policies regarding movie ratings when it came to showing movies in class, etc.

The setup for the "School within a School" (SWAS) program was as follows: There were four teachers in the program. Each teacher had one grade level of "at-risk" students. The freshmen's and sophomores' teachers had the kids for four of the six periods of the school day. The juniors' and seniors' teachers had the students for the two remaining periods.

I was the freshmen's teacher. I taught English, life science, world history, and life skills. It was the life skills class I was concerned about. You see, they wanted us to treat these classes as group therapy sessions. Each week a "theme" was chosen for the group therapy/life skills classes. The theme might be divorce, child abuse, rape/date rape, sexual activity, suicide, or death.

One week the subject was death. The department head had stacks of handouts and worksheets—all about death. The handouts included a questionnaire called "Thought Provokers." It asked the students what they thought about death; funerals; the fear of death; choosing the time, place, and circumstances of "your" death; the belief in life after death; how much do "I" think about death; whether "I" think about another person's death more than "my" own. It also asked students if they had ever entertained thoughts of suicide and if so to share those feelings with the group.

There was also a study sheet entitled *Stages of Grieving*, and a reading assignment called *Life after Death: The Growing Evidence* by Mary Ann O'Roark. This article discussed near-death experiences in which a glowing circle of light surrounded people and described the joy and love during these near-death experiences. The introduction said that there were hundreds of stories like those described in the article. I chose not to use the information from the article. If a troubled or impressionable student hears that kind of garbage, he may think death is the answer to his current problem. After all, he'll come back—remember these are presented as "near-death" experiences. To teach this in a classroom sends a message I'm not prepared to promulgate.

Friday was "movie day." The SWAS classes watched a video that pertained to the subject of the week. One week the subject was rape, so the movie chosen was *The Accused*. For "death" week, the other teachers were discussing what videos about death to show the students.

The whole time, I'm sarcastically thinking, *sure, why not. Let's focus all of our attention on death while we are working with students who have given up on life and are "at-risk." Why not show them the video* Faces of Death, *or an uplifting video about someone dying by suicide or in a car crash or a drive-by shooting or a terminal illness? Oh yes, this is my job as a teacher.*

Why did they want me to dwell on death for five days while teaching thirteen- and fourteen-year-olds? These kids are so easily depressed. They give up so easily because they have settled into a pattern of failures that they can't seem to overcome. Why couldn't I teach them skills that would make them success-ful...reading, writing, historical successes, scientific successes? Why must I dwell on death and when the bell rings, expect them to go to their physical education class and emotionally and men-tally turn off the impressions, mental pictures, and emotional baggage that death education may have left with them?

Well, I didn't! I did not teach death education or about suicide and funerals. I don't remember what I taught. I do remember the notes from the vice principal saying that I needed to learn how to improve in leading group discussions. I remember the note on my evaluation about how I needed to learn to work with my depart-ment more when it came to the life skills class. I do remember that instead of teaching about death, I taught my students subjects that would help them cope and be successful in life!

A'lyce Baldarelli, Teacher

My Son's Suicide

When my son came to live with me, we went to his school and consulted with the school counselor to set up a schedule we felt would best suit his needs. While he was out of the room, I ex-pressed my concerns to the counselor about my son's emotional state and his ability to handle a standard academic program. I asked the counselor to keep an eye and ear open and to let me know if there were any problems.

One week after my son moved in, he asked some questions about suicide. I was surprised, but answered his questions calmly. I asked if he wanted to talk to a counselor or psycholo-gist; he said "no." We dropped the subject. The following week, he again brought up the topic of suicide, and again, I answered his questions. This time, however, I said that I knew someone whose teenager had worked with a therapist in a local program and asked if he would like to look into it with me. He agreed, provided that he wouldn't have to go into a treatment facility.

The following week, we had an appointment with a counselor at the facility. The counselor met with both of us and then my son met separately with another counselor. We took a tour of the facility and, before leaving, my son agreed to enroll in the outpatient program. We left with the names of a psychiatrist recommended by the facility and one with whom my friend was familiar.

During this period, I was in contact with the school counselor and shared my concerns about my son. I kept the counselor informed about what was happening, and he assured me he would apprise my son's teachers.

A week later, after reading some of his papers from school—writing assignments about death, nightmares, and worse experiences—I decided that my son was not doing as well as he had indicated. I convinced him that, for his own sake, he should join an inpatient counseling program and I contacted the psychiatrist, who concurred. Before making the change, we spoke with the school counselor to make certain my son would not lose credits while he was in the hospital. The counselor assured us he would work with the hospital staff—he had done so for other students—and no credits would be lost.

My son was out of school for approximately three and a half weeks. When he returned to school, we were again assured that the staff had been advised of his situation.

One week later, I was shocked to learn that the text being studied in my son's English class was Ordinary People, a story about teenage suicide and death. I spoke with the counselor and questioned the appropriateness of this book in light of our recent experience. The counselor agreed and said he would follow up with the teacher, then get back to me.

The following week, we were summoned to a meeting with the counselor and my son's teachers. At that meeting, we were informed that my son would not receive credit for the missed grading period, because the counselor had not followed up with the hospital staff to coordinate the instructional program. We were surprised, because my son had been required to complete his academic work while hospitalized.

His English instructor then informed me that *Ordinary People* was part of the curriculum for that grade level, and suicide was a topic covered every year. She said she didn't see any problem with it. I said that in light of my son's recent history, I found it inappropriate. She looked at me with a blank stare. She obviously had no idea what I was talking about! It was apparent that the counselor had never spoken with any of the teachers about my son's three-and-a-half-week absence! However, my son's teacher just waved that off. She then said the class would complete *Ordinary People* in another week anyway, so it wouldn't make any difference—there was no cause for alarm.

In fact, both the broken promise and the classroom subject matter were of great concern to me. After all, what does a broken promise indicate to an emotionally fragile adolescent? And how valid is it to handle psychologically sensitive topics—such as teenage suicide—in a classroom setting by an untrained professional?

One week later, my son was dead. He committed suicide.

The morning he died, I called the school and asked that his friends be told what had happened. I suggested that the counselor spend whatever time necessary to allow them to express their feelings and also asked that their parents be informed.

Two weeks later, one of my son's friends called and asked if she and a friend could talk with me. During their visit, I learned that the school had never told them about my son. They assumed he had gone back to the hospital. When they accidentally heard from a teacher about his death, they were quite shaken. Crying, they had gone to the counseling office to speak with the counselor. They were told the counselor was busy and that they would not be able to speak with him that day.

Several weeks passed before I was able to speak with the counselor. In tears, he apologized to me for all that had happened. He said he had noticed that my son looked depressed a day or two prior to his death. He said he had intended to talk with my son, but never found the time.

I understand and share the growing concern over the rising rate of teen suicide—not only in our state, but across the country. But more than that, I am concerned about how the problem is being addressed. What makes administrators or individuals working on curriculum at the state and local levels believe that an educator, untrained in the field of psychology, is qualified to handle such a potentially explosive topic as suicide? What guidelines are there for dealing with at-risk students, or even how to recognize one?

As a parent who knows the devastating loss of a child by suicide, I know school is not the correct setting for dealing with the issue. Placing the life of an at-risk student in the hands of an untrained professional can spell disaster. Even in the hands of trained professionals, there are no guarantees. And once a child is gone, there is no way to recover or make up for the loss.

Joy Barron

Write an Obituary

Our daughter received an assignment to write her own obituary. Especially disturbing to us were instructions which included the scenario that a family member caused her death. One of the examples cited by the teacher was that of a sibling who was jealous of certain talents and therefore committed the murder. You can imagine my dismay when I read my daughter's obituary. She wrote that her sister was jealous over her ability to play tennis and thus beat her over the head with a tennis racquet until she was dead! Not only was the assignment totally inappropriate, but to impose a violent focus—by a family member no less—was totally unacceptable! I've always instructed my kids to celebrate and be joyous about the special talents God gave each one of them. As a parent, I felt sabotaged!

In addition to the murder scenario, I have a lot of questions about the inclusion of "death education" in the classroom. First of all, who has trained teachers to deal with a subject that is so psychologically sensitive? I am constantly appalled at the increasingly popular presence of these potentially dangerous curricula in classrooms throughout the country. Sometimes I wonder if it isn't the reason teenage suicides are climbing, and that suicide among younger children is becoming more common. Maybe today's teachers show students how to avoid difficulties by leaving this world.

I have one thought for teachers who go along with the program. Maybe your concentration on death, dying, cemeteries, etc., is encouraging children to kill themselves. Think about it.

Valerie Moore

Honors Class & Death Education

As a high school senior, our son enrolled in honors classes. Approximately three months into the school year, he came home after school one day and said, "Mom, you've got to get me out of the honors English class." Since he had never asked to be removed from a class before, this took me completely by surprise. Of course I wanted to know why. He said, "Because I know suicide is wrong, but I find myself thinking about it all the time. All we read about or talk about in our class is death. The teacher even talks about the 'nobility of death.' The whole class is begging him to give us more positive things to read, but he won't assign anything else."

Imagine my shock and horror! My husband and I began reading the assigned material from the class. While some of the authors were quite well known, the selections must have represented the "dregs" of their work. In our opinion, the material assigned was in some cases pornographic, provocative, degrading, and depraved. We certainly didn't find the assignments in keeping with standards that promote happiness and wholesomeness.

One book was titled *The Lottery*. The plot included a scene in which townspeople congregate around a couple and force the couple's child to cast the "first stone." The mother was subsequently killed. Another assigned book, called *The Baby-sitter*, was about a teenage girl who fantasized about having sex with the toddler in her care! Can anyone tell me of what educational value these stories could be to anyone, especially impressionable young people?

In addition to the negative impact of the curriculum on our child, we were shocked and disappointed at the way our district treated us—both as parents and as taxpaying citizens.

I grew up in our town. Our family is well known, liked, and respected. My husband and I are a loving couple, committed to our family and involved in our community. I've known the superintendent since I was a teenager. When I attended the local schools, parents with questions were treated with the utmost respect and their concerns were taken seriously. Yet my husband and I soon learned that the world has turned upside-down. Behind the scenes, my hometown changed. It is no longer the same safe haven I knew as a child.

After reading the "literature" from our son's class, my husband called the teacher, who very abrasively called him a liar. We learned that this teacher was head of the English department and very popular with the administration. He did guest teaching at our other local high school.

Because we didn't receive a favorable response from the teacher, we went to see the principal. We questioned the appropriateness of the curriculum and said that if the direction of the class did not change, we would have to remove our son. Initially, the principal pleasantly and diplomatically promised to look into the situation. At a second meeting the following week, he said the class was under the control of the teacher and would not change. He also said he would look for an alternate class for our son.

We next made an appointment with the superintendent. At that meeting, I requested that the superintendent read the material offered in our son's class. He promised to look into it and we set another appointment for the following week.

In the meantime, our son had no assigned English class and, in fact, was called out of another class by the principal, the teacher, and a counselor. They summoned him to the office where he was literally "drilled" for at least an hour. They asked him questions including: "Why did you complain to your parents?" "Why are you dissatisfied with the class?" "What exactly did you say to your parents?" and "You really do like the class, don't you?"

To some extent, this grilling created an estrangement between us and our son. We were viewed as creating a "hassle" by putting our son "on the spot." We believed the school was punishing our son by using intimidation in the hope that he would change his story.

We felt powerless and violated. Without our knowledge or permission, the school put our son through the "third degree." There was no way we could undo the damage, and we were beginning to feel emotionally drained by the whole experience. Of course, as we later learned, the tactics used against us were designed to wear us down; to get rid of us. (These tactics are often used against parents who "complain.")

During our next meeting, the superintendent told us the class was "fine" but that, under the law, the district was required to provide our son an alternate English class. However, the school was not required to offer another honors English class. He explained that there was only one other English class available, and beyond that, he could only offer independent home study with a supervisory teacher. My husband objected to this solution and suggested that the school choose literature that was more positive. The superintendent responded by saying that they were required by the state to present the material in question and had no choice. (We later learned he lied to us. The state does not mandate this material; teachers and schools can choose from a suggested list containing many wholesome and acceptable selections.)

I asked the superintendent, "Have you read this assigned material?" He said, "I don't have to—I have my experts that read the material for me." "And who are they?" I asked. "The teacher in the classroom," he answered. I then asked, "Do you mean to tell me we came all this way, went through all the channels to meet with you over such a serious problem, and you haven't even shown us the respect of looking at the material? Whether you agree with us or not, shouldn't you at least be familiar with the material under discussion?" His response was merely to say that he had the one alternate English class to offer us. This was his only resolution for the problem.

When I visited the only other English class, I asked the teacher about her approach to the same type of material. She said: "I like the students to get in touch with their feelings, so I have them bring in symbols when reading a certain piece to represent their feelings. For example, I tell them to 'bring in your symbol of hatred.'" I thought, "Oh no, here we go again." I asked our son to visit the class and give us his impression. The day he visited, the students brought in their symbols of death for the teacher and then discussed—guess what?—death. Suffice it to say, that was the end of that class.

By this time, much of the school year had passed, and our son was in jeopardy of losing an entire year of English credit. The only remaining alternative for him was to enter the "independent study" program. He was assigned a teacher and given an initial assignment. However, when he tried to meet with her again, he couldn't find her. Without telling us, he spent days looking for her. The office was of little help. I finally contacted the school, only to learn that the teacher had gone on extended leave to get married; no other teacher had been assigned to our son. He had "fallen through the cracks" bureaucratically—or had he? The administration knew before our son was assigned to this particular teacher that she would be leaving to get married. According to the school, there was no one else available. By this time, it was virtually too late for our son to complete a year's worth of English credit. He lost his entire senior year of English. Was this another punishment for our temerity in interfering?

I believe we came up against something sinister that was much too big for one set of parents to deal with alone. I later learned there were other parents who had also expressed concern. At the time, I wasn't able to articulate what was happening in the school, nor did I even understand it. I did know that our education system was headed in a very damaging direction. As a result of our experience, I wanted to learn more about what was happening and began doing research. I discovered that our son was exposed to death education and that similar curricula are prevalent in public schools all over the country.

Death education is only part of a systematic effort to change the values of our children and establish a new approach to education. There is a "push" for students to learn about and come to "terms" with death as a "realistic" part of life. Whenever there is a suicide at school, common practice is to discuss it in every class. Even my son's math class included suicide discussions. It isn't uncommon for students to be referred to counselors to deal with their "psychological trauma" without notifying parents or requesting their permission.

Every time a young person commits suicide, families and other influences are blamed. Yet have we ever thought to look into what is being taught in the classroom? Maybe we should. Perhaps some of our vulnerable children could be saved if we stop the insanity of death education and return to teaching absolute values. Death curricula should be replaced with that which offers hopeful encouragement, joy, and solid academics.

My hope is that by telling our story, other parents who find themselves and their children in similar circumstances will be strengthened by the fact that they aren't alone. Sharing our experience also gives us the satisfaction of continuing to "fight on" and, hopefully, to ultimately be able to undo the damage that our district and those across the country are doing to parents and children by furthering this inappropriate social agenda.

Name Withheld by Request

Health/Suicide

During my daughter's ninth-grade health class, her teacher said, "Suicide is a permanent solution to a temporary problem." The students were then shown a movie about a child who committed suicide. My daughter told me the movie was very depressing and put a dark cloud over the rest of the day. She said that suicide would always linger in the back of her mind and admitted that she could not honestly say that she would never commit suicide. She felt that, after the presentation, suicide would always nag at her consciousness during the toughest situations in her life. Many of her friends admitted they felt the same way. Prior to taking this mandatory health class, my daughter never thought about suicide.

The morning after the class, I spoke with the teacher and told her I disagreed with her approach to teaching the suicide issue. When I questioned her about the class, she immediately became defensive and responded by saying that my daughter could have a medical examination without my permission or knowledge. (She apparently believed this inappropriate response justified her teaching a class about suicide without parental knowledge or permission.) I then informed her that I should have been notified about the suicide prevention class and that had I known, I would have had my daughter removed.

I asked if I could sit in on her class that day. She almost had a fit and said that I couldn't just show up and demand to sit in on a class. I asked her, "What do you have to hide?" She replied, "I knew you would say that." I persisted so she finally told me I would have to receive permission from the administration. I went to the office, got permission, and returned to the class.

The topic that day was drugs. Not once did I hear, "Kids, don't do it." The emphasis was, "Think about your choices."

Name Witheld by Request

In tombstone-adorned classrooms where students write of their own demise, "death education" is joining sex education as a critical issue for parents who recognize the values their schools teach can literally have deadly consequences.

CHAPTER FIVE

OBSCENE CLASSROOMS

PARENTS WORRY *about their children. They worry about their children's safety, health, and education. Parents also trust that schools have the best interests of their children at heart. And finally, most parents believe that today's schools focus on educating their children. And while many schools and teachers work hard to uphold the trust of those parents, others use classrooms to promote their own agendas or liberal bias. The problem is that parents often aren't aware if their children are in one of those classrooms.*

Some of the exercises are abhorrent to parents; others are just silly. For instance, a Pennsylvania mother reported that while her daughter's third-grade class was reading Alexander and the Terrible, Horrible, No Good, Very Bad Day *by Judith Viorst, the students wore pajamas to school. When hearing about the above incident, a California mother replied by saying that not only did her child's school take part in pajama day, they also participated in "cross-dress day." She said some of the male teachers wore dresses in honor of that day.*

Another parent reported that her eleventh-grade student received an assignment apparently designed by the teacher, since it had no formal title. She was upset with the negative connotation of the exercise. "Rearrange the letters in the word PARENTS *and you get* ENTRAPS... *If you take the letters in the word* DIVORCES *and rearrange them, they spell* DISCOVER." *The exercise then asked students: "Parents are supposed to have the answers. Has there been a time when your parents didn't have the answers?"*

In New Jersey, students in one gifted program were given guided imagery instruction from a program called Your Mind's Eye. One of the exercises, called Tranquil Scene, instructed the teacher to have the students close their eyes and relax: "You're standing on a sandy beach... Feel the sand between your toes... See little white fluffy clouds drifting, drifting... See yourself sipping your favorite drink. Taste it... enjoy."[1] While on the surface this may sound harmless, it becomes more significant when at the end of the exercise, the teacher is told to count to ten, "giving the students an opportunity to adjust to returning." The need to "adjust" to a return indicates that for some children, this was an altered-state-consciousness journey. Was this just a fun activity or a hypnotic-like trance? Finally, the teacher is told to make notes about what each student remembered. One can only wonder: why?

The following stories point out some of the classroom exercises in which students are required to participate. And it isn't unusual for teachers in these classrooms to instruct students not to go home and tell their parents.

One manual for a secretive school-based psychological program advises teachers, "As you begin to lead support groups for elementary children, there are a couple of useful suggestions...first of all it is generally prudent not to allow children to take home any work they do in the support group...this will ensure that none of the children's creations will risk becoming the focus for derision or anger..."[2]

It's no wonder they advise against allowing children to take information home since this program has children engaging in "relaxation exercises" sharing intimate information about their families including "chemically dependent family members, divorced parents, or their own self-defeating behaviors."[3]

Today, more than at any time in history, it is important for parents to question their children's teachers about what will be taught during the year, to ask to view the teacher's syllabus (and supplementals), and to file written letters with the schools that opt their children out of assignments with which the parents disagree. It is also important for parents to have open dialogue with their children about what happened in school during the day. Starting these discussions early in the child's life will pave the way for more open dialogue as the child matures.

Profanity

Our problems with the public school system began in the early 1990s when our niece lived with us. She attended summer school at a local school.

My niece's seventh-grade English teacher gave the students permission to use profanity, because she thought students would find it "hard to break habits when you are around your friends."

This teacher also gave students an assignment to bring in a poster that represented themselves. She said, "Do not, however, bring posters that relate to nudity or drugs, such as a naked man lying in marijuana." Did she think this was funny?

The math teacher told twelve-year-old students that they could listen to music with headsets while they worked on math problems. For years, professionals have told us that children should not do their homework in front of television and that music can distract them. How dare this teacher decide to violate common practices without asking parental permission!

At another time, a math teacher at the junior high used classroom time to show MTV. I complained to the vice principal, but then the teacher substituted rap and heavy metal music during class. MTV is readily available to all students during lunch in the student council room. The use of valuable school time for MTV defies common sense.

Another teacher invited a women's group, "Women's Crisis Support," into a seventh-grade coed elective class to discuss rape—including men raping men and women raping women. The discussion covered forced oral or anal sex and penetration by fingers or objects. Needless to say, my child was very embarrassed. This presentation occurred without parental consent and therefore violated our state education code. I immediately went to the principal, but his only response was to allow the group to return, this time with parental consent. I then complained to the superintendent.

During the last week of school, a history teacher showed a PG-13 movie which we would never have shown to our children. I complained to the administration. They agreed not to show the second half of the movie; instead they played a PG movie that showed bare-breasted women sunbathing on the beach. Once again our daughter was embarrassed and asked the teacher, "Excuse me, but would you please fast forward through this?"

On another occasion, our foster daughter came home from school and said she had been involved in a scuffle that others had started. While concerned for her, I also wanted to be sure that I heard the entire story, so the next day I went to the school to talk to the administrator. I told the receptionist why I was there, but the administrator refused to see me. The receptionist played go between—walking in and out of the administrator's office relaying my questions—but the administrator answered none of them. Frustrated, I left. The next day I went back to register my foster son for class, and this time the administrator invited me into the office. I sat down and asked why she refused to talk to me about the scuffle. She actually said, "We don't want the parents involved." To which I replied, "But she is my child." Again she said, "We don't want the parents involved."

To top it off, the ESL (English as a Second Language) aide called our home the last day of school and spoke to our foster daughter. She said, "I will be mailing you a book. Read it over the summer—we will be going over it in eighth grade. Don't show it to your mom; she won't like it." The book, *Always Running* by Luis J. Rodriguez, came in the mail and contained stories about gangs, prejudice, hate, violence, and sex. (This book is discussed in more detail in Chapter Two.) Our foster daughter said she had already read some of the book at school with the teacher and it depressed her. This particular teacher knew of her background, which had consisted of dating gang members. Our foster daughter said to me, "Mom, I want to put that life behind me. I don't want to read about it." With all the great literature out there, why do teachers choose books like these for our children?

We send our children to school to get an education—not to watch MTV, listen to rap and heavy metal music, discuss sexual perversions, use profanity, read obscene material, or have administrators tell us: "We don't want parents involved." I thought the big push today is to encourage parental involvement. Obviously, the schools mean involvement on their terms only.

Ron and Janette Anderson

Time-in Room

For seven months, May through October, our daughter left P.E. once a week to spend time with a "trusting adult" (the school's words) in what the school called a "Time-in" room. According to the school, the purpose of the "room time" was for our daughter to bond with a "trusting adult." Often, our daughter and the "adult" were the only ones in the room.

In December, I denied permission for our daughter to participate in this activity. I even hand-delivered the permission slip to the vice principal's secretary. The permission slip sent home by the school read in part:

> At [our school] we are here to support all of our students through the transitionings of adolescence. Adolescence is one of the most turbulent times in a child's life. This is a time when a child needs lots of support and encouragement. The Time-in Room enables students to have a support system and a connection with a trusting adult while they are at school. A volunteer adult acts as their mentor once a week....This is not counseling, only time to connect on campus with another adult.

Even with our written denial of permission, the school continued to take our daughter out of class without our knowledge.

Initially, we were upset by the middle school usurping our parental authority. Then we grew angry—outraged! We take our parental responsibility very seriously, so seriously that I resigned my job as a public school teacher to stay home to be a parent.

We had denied permission in writing. Who gave the school the right to remove our child from class once a week for a period of seven months? As parents, we believe that we are the adults with whom our child should "bond."

During this period of time, we had problems with our daughter. When the "Time-in" sessions stopped, so did our problems with our child.

The school violated our trust. We hold the principal, vice principal, and the P.E. teacher, who released our child from class, responsible for this gross violation of parental rights.

John and Pat Jorgenson

Medicine Shield

We've experienced many problems with the public school system. However, during our daughter's eighth-grade year, a series of occurrences within a period of a few weeks really alerted us to the change in today's education. We want to use our story to urge other parents to visit their children's classrooms and insist on viewing curricula, surveys, assignments, etc. Some of the content is mandated by state law; some is used because state law allows teachers to bring in supplemental materials that many parents would deem inappropriate. It's imperative that parents monitor today's classrooms.

The first assignment that caught our attention involved something called "The Medicine Shield." It was a social studies project that prompted each student to make his/her own "medicine shield" or "power shield." In a handout explaining the "medicine shield," students learned: "Each shield carries medicine...In times of uncertainty, a Medicine Shield is a source of comfort, a source of protection from fear, and a reminder of the serenity of centered knowingness and connection. To balance the energy of uncertainty, the shield is meditated upon by its maker. As he or she enters the silence, questions of self-mystery are answered."

The teacher asked our daughter to make a shield that included her writing a sacred verse for "herself," then required students to list: "Your past, your moon, the season of your birth into this earthwalk" and "[your] power animal."

It's one thing to teach about different cultures and quite another to enter into the religious practices of that culture. Can you imagine the uproar if a teacher asked the students to read a passage from the Bible and write a prayer? What is the difference? This particular teacher projected a speech by Martin Luther King on the wall as she read it. At one point in the speech, Dr. King thanked God. The teacher paused, skipped that part of the speech, then continued with the rest of the speech.

Our daughter's language arts teacher launched a "gender bias" assignment. While this may sound like a great idea, in actuality, unless a student gave answers that reflected the teacher's idea of "gender bias," he or she was ridiculed in front of the other students. This assignment did not teach tolerance; it directed the students' thinking to what the teacher considered the "politically correct" answer. Gun control was another topic for discussion. The students read a newspaper article that they learned presented both sides of the argument. They then wrote their "own response."

My daughter wrote that she didn't see the article as even-handed and felt it was grossly weighted to the gun control point of view. She also quoted the teacher's own viewpoint, which was, "The right to bear arms isn't really needed today; it was only given to our forefathers who used guns for hunting and other things like that." My daughter went on to say that our Founding Fathers knew the importance of maintaining individual rights because they lived in a time and place where they didn't have rights. She concluded by saying, "I don't like these kinds of assignments. They make people argumentative, and we shouldn't be graded on our points of view, or have to share those points of view with our teachers or our class." I agree.

Valerie Moore

Hypnosis/Developing Understanding of Self and Others (DUSO)

Our startling awareness of the seriousness of the problems in public education came when my husband and I contacted our local school board trustees about banning hypnosis as entertainment in the school district.

We began by helping a local parent whose children were victimized by a psychology-based program called "Developing Understanding of Self and Others" (DUSO). Upon examining the program, we found that it used relaxation techniques to induce hypnosis (an altered state of consciousness). Guided imagery and visualization, designed to change a student's values, were also incorporated into the program. The creators of DUSO confirmed our suspicion that they designed the program to change views and values when they stated in the instructions: "Most children change their views quickly and easily."

When we expressed our concerns to the trustees, they said that since the program had been in use for as long as fifteen years in our area, they didn't understand why we had a problem with it. I was shocked at their statement. Not believing them, I questioned my daughter, who is now twenty-one years old, about the program. To my horror, she recounted that at the age of ten, she took part in a similar exercise while attending a performing arts program. She was told, "Lie down, close your eyes, pretend you are a cloud—floating upward, upward..." She couldn't recall what happened after that, but suddenly it made sense to me. I recall a period of time when she suddenly refused to attend church, spent time fantasizing (talking and making gestures to a small tree as though it were a person), and started doing poorly in school.

Due to extensive research on our part, we now know that other programs, such as "Project Self-Esteem," are currently in use in over two thousand public schools. Many of these programs also employ hypnotic techniques.

Shortly after our encounter with DUSO, my stepdaughter, who lives with her mother, called to tell us that the high school had forced her to attend an assembly. The featured attraction was a hypnotist. My stepdaughter objected, but was told that the assembly was mandatory and that she had no choice. She said that after the second assembly, one girl went to the hospital in an ambulance. The *Los Angeles Times* later reported that after the hypnosis assembly, a girl returned to her class and grew so lethargic that she was unable to stay in her seat. Finally, she became so unresponsive that the school called paramedics, who couldn't rouse her. She was taken to the hospital, where a doctor recognized the symptoms of a hypnotic trance and revived her.[4]

The next day, my husband and I went to the school to find out why the school had unnecessarily subjected our daughter to the practice of hypnosis—a practice "vigorously condemned as entertainment" by both the American Medical Association and the American Psychiatric Association—to which we strongly objected.[5] The school told us that in order to have our daughter excused, we would have had to notify the school twenty-four hours prior to the event. The school also claimed that the assembly was of "educational value."

According to our daughter, the program focused on selected students hypnotized and asked to perform various acts which were very humorous to the audience. The hypnotized students were then told that "they could have anything they wanted." One student wanted "good grades" and was told, "You have it!" Another student asked to be a "good athlete." One girl wanted "to be thin, have lots of boyfriends, and go to the beach a lot this summer." The hypnotist responded each time, "You have it!" When our daughter heard the last request, she remembered thinking, "That sounds good."

After this assembly, much to our surprise, our daughter promptly quit her part-time job, even though she had planned to work during the summer in order to save money for a car. During this time, she also began treatment for nervous stress, including a nervous stomach disorder, and was on medication for nearly a month. Her grades fell and she was subsequently required to attend summer school in order to enter her senior year in the fall. Twice she quit summer school. Later she explained that she "wanted to spend more time at the beach." Needless to say, she didn't graduate with her class. We believe her problems were related to the assembly on hypnosis and that she became hypnotized herself and received a post-hypnotic suggestion that led her to desire the same request as the last student. We believe other students may also have been unknowingly hypnotized.

Mary Potter

Few parents recall hypnosis, "time-in rooms" to bond with an adult, "medicine shields," and "guided imagery" sessions when they were in school. But all this and more—from the silly to the sublime—is prompting parental alarm as schools adopt activities and programs often "designed to change a student's values."

CHAPTER SIX

THE X-RATED CLASSROOM

THE SEX EDUCATION *industry boasts a strange history. At the time of its introduction in the 1950s, no strong demand existed for it. Venereal disease rates were not skyrocketing among our youth, nor did America see any teenage pregnancy crisis. Even our public schools still taught Christian values, and the family unit remained intact compared to today.*

Why, then, did this movement start? Well, it was about revolutionizing society by replacing America's Judeo-Christian values system with an atheistic worldview. The zealots behind this movement didn't really care about the "children" in the way they wanted people to think. Their real goal was to ingratiate the philosophy of the sexual revolution into our culture—and what better way to do this than to target our children?

The major impetus behind this movement was two books by Dr. Alfred Kinsey which argued that children were far more sexual than anyone thought and that a healthy society would accommodate their urges. His work later generated controversy over the methodology used in his research.

Indeed, in 1964, the Kinsey Institute—along with Dr. Mary Calderone, the medical director for Planned Parenthood and a driving force behind the legalization of abortion in the U.S.—formed part of the group that created the Sex Information and Education Council of the United States (SIECUS).[1] They founded SIECUS for the specific purpose of creating sex education curriculum and programs based on Kinsey's bizarre theories.

This movement never had the support of the vast majority of Americans or parents, so its supporters used stealth and deceit to achieve their goals. Thanks to spineless politicians, the main players in this movement, Planned Parenthood and Education Research and Associates (ETR), were able to obtain millions of dollars from federal and state governments to finance sex education programs that treated children like guinea pigs. Due to a largely Christian population that trusted school boards to do what was best for its children, this movement succeeded beyond anyone's wildest imaginations.

Various sex education curricula have endorsed prostitution, anal sex, same-sex marriages, pornography, and incest. Even pedophilia is not off-limits. A study of the sex education leadership by the Institute for Media Education found that a large number of the leaders of the movement are admitted pedophiles, have published in pedophile publications, have publicly advocated sex between children and adults, or are actively involved in the pornography industry.[2]

Indeed, today's children have sex at rates no one would have imagined a decade ago. Naturally, sexual diseases have grown as common as the flu. A 2008 report issued by the Centers for Disease Control found that more than one in four (26 percent) teenage girls between the ages of fourteen and nineteen are infected with four of the most common STDs.[3] Our nation's rush to embrace explicit sex education has not helped our youth. Instead it has enticed them to participate in behaviors that have serious health consequences. In addition to the health risks associated with STDs, hundreds of thousands of minor girls now become pregnant each year, and most will get abortions, compliments of Planned Parenthood's network of abortion mills.[4] And of course, Planned Parenthood's response to the CDC's report was that more "comprehensive sex education" is needed.[5]

So on one hand Planned Parenthood created and funded sex education programs that promoted the "here's how to have sex safely" philosophy, and then on the other hand reaped business from the victims that became pregnant.

Much of the responsibility for this can be attributed to liberal elected officials who are supported and funded by a Political Action Committee of either Planned Parenthood or NARAL (National Abortion Rights Action League).[6] If the local churches didn't pay attention—and most don't—then the school board seats were easy pickings and still are to this day. Unless the church wakes up, there is nothing to stop these zealots from brainwashing our children.

For those who may think the abstinence movement is changing things, don't hold your breath. The abstinence movement has already been largely co-opted by the sexual freedom crowd. All the usual sex education groups have simply repackaged their standard curricula by mentioning that "of course abstinence is the only sure way to avoid STDs, but since we know you will have sex anyway, use a condom." This attitude conveys to youth that it is okay to have sex and that everyone is doing it and schools are even winning government grants to teach this damaging philosophy.

Thanks to the promotion of the homosexual lifestyle, public schools have now introduced a new form of sex education called HIV/AIDS Education. Even the American Red Cross offers sex education that plays into the SIECUS mindset.[7]

Hailed as a well-rounded, unbiased alternative to other controversial curricula, the ten-week course integrates sex education into all aspects of the curriculum, including history, music, and literature (no wonder teachers complain there's no time to teach academics!).

While male-to-male sexual contact is and has always been the most common cause of HIV transmission, the Red Cross over and over again ignores this fact and instead stresses that "worldwide, 75 percent of HIV transmission is through heterosexual contact," as if some bizarre—and debatable—demographic trend in Africa really is relevant to the health of American students.

The Red Cross manual is NOT about avoiding high risk sex but rather about how to engage in high risk sex in an allegedly safer way:

> For oral-anal contact or oral-vaginal contact, barrier protection is also recommended...dental dams (squares of latex) may be purchased...a latex condom cut open to form a sheet of latex may also be used as a barrier over a vaginal or anal opening.[8]

This program comes with flash cards with phrases such as: "Perform Insertive Anal Sex," "Perform Oral Sex on a Male," and "Sharing Sex Toys?"

Sex education and HIV/AIDs education programs share common features, especially their incessant reliance on condoms. Rather than direct students away from sex, these manuals teach how to engage in the riskiest practices imaginable. The American Red Cross manual plays down all risk when it tells teachers in its appendix that:

> Correct and consistent use of latex condoms is highly effective in preventing HIV infection and other sexually transmitted diseases, including gonorrhea, Chlamydia, genital ulcers, and herpes simplex virus infection.[9]

But this is not an accurate statement. The Medical Institute for Sexual Health (MI) says:

Consistent condom use (100%) during vaginal sex reduces your risk for:

- HIV by 85%,
- Gonorrhea by about 50%
- Chlamydia by about 50%
- Herpes by about 50%
- Syphilis by about 50%
- HPV by 50% or less

Few studies have been done to see whether condoms reduce the risk of STIs, including HIV, during oral sex or anal sex. Waiting to have sex until you are in a faithful, lifelong relationship (such as marriage) is the only certain way to avoid being infected sexually.[10]

This risk assessment is clearly not the same as the Red Cross's "highly effective" misinformation. A 2001 study by the National Institute of Health (NIH) greatly questioned the effectiveness of condoms.[11] As comprehensive as the NIH report was, the prestigious National Physicians Center for Family Resources (NPCFR) issued a press release in which they criticized NIH for soft-pedaling their own study results. NPCFR concluded that the promotion of condoms "without providing all the facts regarding the true risk of STD transmission offers the American public a false sense of security. It is, in essence, medical malpractice and cannot be tolerated."[12]

Through suggestion, group pressure, and the overall attitude promulgated in many of today's classrooms, current sex education breaks down personal conviction to abstain from sex and legitimizes youthful inclination toward self-indulgence and rebellion. A book used in several states called Changing Bodies, Changing Lives *apparently believes it is foolish to practice abstinence. "Protecting a girl's virginity to keep her as 'pure undamaged goods' for the person she will eventually belong to, doesn't make much sense," it says.[13] And the book assures kids that:*

It's quite common for kids to have lots of different kinds of sexual feelings and experiences. Some of our early sex play may have been with girls, some with boys, and some with both girls and boys. Unless we were caught and punished, or somehow hurt, most kids enjoy this kind of sex play and exploration. It usually feels good (and sometimes exciting) to have someone touch our body, or to touch someone else's body.[14]

It then goes on to tell teens that it isn't true that "a person is either all heterosexual or all homosexual, and for life...Most people are neither 'all straight' or 'all gay'."[15]

In a section called "Exploring Sex with Someone Else," this book quotes one thirteen-year-old named Matt:

> In my sixth-grade class it seems like we talked about everything. I mean like we talked about rubbers, birth control, VD, everything. The teacher told us a lot of stuff. But then a little later on I saw some people actually doing it, you know, making love, and I thought it was pretty weird looking.[16]

This and other books used in schools across the country often describe sex in explicit and graphic detail. And while there may be much of the information that teens should know, the question again arises: Are parents asked to give permission before these courses are taught, and if they are, do they receive full knowledge of the content before they sign permission slips? According to many parents the answer is no. And without fully disclosing the graphic language contained in these books, the rights of parents to determine what their children learn and when they learn this information are flagrantly violated. And the sad reality is that many parents are never given the option of reviewing controversial sex education curricula; they aren't informed about the content of sex education classes and have no idea about what their children are being taught.

The real tragedy in the way this nation currently conducts sex education occurs when it downplays the risks while appearing to promote unhealthy sexual activity. And it allows teens to believe that the risks are small and to think, "That won't happen to me," rather than correctly concluding, "That could happen to me."

The Condom Lady

My department head was excited. He had scheduled "the condom lady" from the county Department of Education to be a guest speaker.

Because ours was "special program" for "at-risk" students, we didn't have to notify parents about a speaker coming in or about what she would say. (The education code clearly states that if reproductive organs, etc., are discussed, the school must notify parents, inform them about what could occur, and give them the opportunity to prohibit their child from attending such presentations.)

My department head went on to say that the speaker could only make three presentations and had decided to combine the freshman and senior classes. Since I taught freshmen, I strenuously objected to having thirteen- and fourteen-year-olds in the same class with seventeen- and eighteen-year-olds during a discussion about sexual activity.

I even asked if my class could skip the presentation, but was unequivocally told "no." The presentation would include my class. I asked the department if I could contact the speaker myself to ask if she would give four presentations.

I called, and was happy that she agreed with me about keeping the freshmen and seniors apart for her presentation. She agreed to do four presentations. I asked her to please stress abstinence. She said she always did.

The day arrived. The "condom lady" came, but first, before she arrived, I talked to my students about the fact that there is no such thing as "safe sex." I talked about AIDS, herpes, Chlamydia, and other STDs.

It was time. I watched as the speaker set up her visual aids. I saw the birth control pills, the douche kit, the contraceptive foam, the jelly, the IUD, the bag of condoms.

She began her presentation, telling the students that abstinence was best, but she then followed with a thirty-minute presentation that instructed the students on the use of contraceptive foam, an IUD, the best time to douche, and the different types of condoms.

With great delight, she told the kids about the different colored condoms available...why, they could even buy condoms in their school colors. She even described condoms with different flavors—mint, fruit, chocolate—and excitedly showed them striped condoms.

It was all I could do not to stop her, but the department head had told me to let her make her presentation. I had requested that she emphasize abstinence. I had talked to the students before she arrived. I had done all I could without getting myself written up. I did stop her when she offered to allow the students to personally "handle" each of the items she had brought by saying we didn't have time. After she left, I talked to the students again, hoping that what I had to say would dispel some of the lies she had propagated with her "safe sex" message.

I did not tell the students that I had learned more about birth control and colored, flavored condoms than I ever wanted to know. I did tell them there was no safe sex. I told them about condom failure rates, and how they could get AIDS while using an IUD or birth control pills. I told them that abstinence was the only way to stay completely safe.

I want to tell everyone reading this that outside speakers who visit your students' classrooms just might be, and probably are, telling your children more than you want them to know. Insist upon receiving notifications about and invitations to these presentations!

A'lyce Baldarelli, Teacher

Homosexuals Teaching AIDS Awareness

As a high school senior I attended an AIDS awareness presentation through my government/economics class. I prepared this affidavit from notes that I took in order to tell my parents some of the details of the presentation.[17] I didn't think my parents would believe what I was going to tell them. The school sent no notes home and gave no prior notice to my parents to inform them of the content of the presentation, or to give my parents an opportunity to grant or withhold permission for me to attend. I would have stayed home if I had known what was to be presented and discussed. I'm positive my parents would have refused to allow me to attend school that day.

The AIDS awareness presentation occurred in three rotating sessions. Two openly homosexual men with HIV—and maybe full-blown AIDS—conducted one of the sessions. They seemed to be trying to elicit sympathy for their condition, but they did nothing to warn against the lifestyle that is a main cause of AIDS. Instead, they promoted tolerance for, and acceptance of, the type of sex engaged in by gays and lesbians. They kept making jokes and talking about sex in a very crude manner. They named and de-

111

scribed sex acts that I had never heard of and could not have imagined people doing. I felt sickened by what I was hearing, and almost felt like I was being abused or molested.

They used terms like "going down on" and "cum." "Cum" was used both as a noun and as a verb. They talked about condoms a lot. It was like an advertisement for condoms as sex toys rather than as devices used to protect against pregnancy and disease. They talked about the colors and the flavors. They said lamb intestine condoms "are gross." I wondered how anyone could do the things they described doing with their mouths—yet could draw the line at a lamb's intestine condom.

The speakers said that prostitutes put rolled up condoms in their mouths and then when they are "doing the guy" by "giving head" they put it on him with their mouths and the guy doesn't even know. In other words, they were trying to teach us to be proficient in using condoms. They said to use a condom because, "It isn't good for a girl to get a load down her throat. She wouldn't appreciate it."

They put a condom on someone's head to prove it would fit any size penis. They also talked about "cunnilingus," "analingus," and "felatio," which I had never heard of and won't even know if I spelled the words right. I have tried to block out of my mind what these words mean.

They also talked about the use of cellophane. They said there are different colors, but "clear is best because you can see what you want to lick." They said cellophane is also good for use in group sex because, "There are more hands to hold it." In using cellophane, they said the pleasure is more for the partner/recipient.

Some of the discussion about condoms was about the way they are used, the size being changed to contain the "cum," and the tip-nipple where the semen ends up; how to take it off carefully after sex, and to always be sure to tie a knot in it.

They also talked about a girl who was having sex with a guy and noticed warts on his penis and wondered what they were. She apparently felt them with her tongue. There were many references to oral and anal sex, as if everyone is supposed to do it, or is doing it.

The speakers referred to homosexuality in a positive light. They told the students not to feel bad if they have homosexual or same-sex feelings. No one expressed regret about their lifestyle or sexual behaviors. They made it sound like it wasn't the lifestyle that caused AIDS and played down the risk of becoming infected with HIV. The main point was to feel okay about your sexuality and sexual activity, but to try to limit the risk of getting AIDS while still having a great time with all these options for doing sex acts.

Nothing was said about abstinence. On the contrary, when the subject of abstinence came up, the presenter laughed as if to say, "No one is abstinent."

I feel I was abused, molested, and my innocence about sex was lost that day. I still associate certain words and phrases with some of the things described by their perverse slang—like when I used to go to the grocery store with my mom, she might ask me to go pick out the lettuce, and then say, "One head." It seems that when I hear the word "head," I associate it with someone's mouth on a guy's penis. And I don't even have a dirty mind. It's the same way with the word "cum." Or "go down." Those words, whether spoken separately or in a sentence, trigger the memory of what those guys referred to. Their words conjure mental pictures that I can't seem to erase.

I am very upset over this and wish my parents and I had filed suit against the school district. However, I did not want to be ostracized or belittled by my classmates and peers. It even crossed my mind that I might lose my scholarships if we had filed a lawsuit. Many of my classmates knew about my high moral standards. I had, and still have, a good reputation, but I didn't want to be stigmatized because of those standards. I felt alone about the way this presentation made me feel. However, I am sure there must have been others who were just as repulsed but didn't know how to handle it either.

I am still a virgin (by my own moral choice) but I have had a very nice boyfriend for the past two years (also a virgin). I am now confused about what kind of physical behavior would be okay, especially in marriage, and not degrading or perverse like the acts I heard about that day. I am considering getting counsel-

113

ing to sort it all out in my mind, because I have been trying to block most of it out.

Please prevent this from happening to anyone else, and please do whatever can be done to bring to light the kinds of programs that are being put into the schools without parents' knowledge, and for which the schools are receiving funds. Even if those guys had made their presentation for free, the schools still get paid for daily attendance. I didn't go to school that day to hear and see these kinds of things. My trust and my parents' trust was betrayed that day by school administrators and teachers who not only promoted and arranged for the presentation, but allowed it to continue until all seniors had attended.

Jill A. Mead, Student

"Safe Sex" Takes Over Core Subjects

For over two years, we experienced a complete disregard for the students and parents of our local district who wanted their children to hear the abstinence message—with an emphasis on heterosexual, monogamous marriage. We did not want them to learn about "safe sex" or that "promiscuity is okay if you don't get caught or get sick"—a direct quote from the handout given to inquiring parents. Current sex education "saturates and permeates" the school community. One cannot simply opt a student out of a sex education unit and feel safe that all bases are covered.

My ninth grader, not enrolled in sex education, obtained a sexually explicit date rape questionnaire in his music class. Another student wrote the questionnaire as part of a sex education assignment from her instructor in that class. The instructor had approved the handout. However, we didn't approve it; we weren't asked, and our son wasn't asked. When we complained verbally to the principal, he implied that we shouldn't trust the word of a student over that of a teacher, and refused to pursue the issue even though the girl said the teacher assigned it, and the teacher didn't deny it.

After we complained in writing, with copies sent to the superintendent, we received a letter informing us that one word in the handout—"ejaculated"—was inappropriate. Yet no apology was made to us nor was any action taken against the teacher. When we objected to the manner in which the school handled our complaints, we heard lectures about following standard complaint procedures.

When another parent asked the sex education teacher for copies of all materials used in the sex education portion of the class, the teacher did not fully comply with that parent's request. He subsequently sent home an assignment requiring students to go to the drug store to price and rate condoms. The parent was outraged, but again the school took no action. In fact, the school's response was, "There have been no other complaints."

My ninth and tenth graders were exposed to "AIDS Awareness Week" in which statistics about the disease were broadcast every day during announcements. I was unable to obtain a transcript of these announcements despite many requests. In addition, the school had many assemblies dealing with sex. When we declined to allow our son to attend, a teacher refused to give him an alternative assignment. The principal supported the teacher 100 percent.

Both of my sons have been exposed to unwanted discussions about homosexuality, condoms, rape, gay rights, etc. These were couched in terms of "relevancy" to whatever subject was being discussed. And gay rights now "connect" with the issue of civil liberties in American history. Oral composition (required) appears to have no limitations in opening the door for "debate." Biology includes attitudes and beliefs, not just the biological mechanics of sex. Homosexuals are invited on campus to discuss their lifestyle; however, no heterosexual couples successful in maintaining long-term, loving relationships have been asked to share their stories.

The sex education unit is repugnant. It doesn't stress traditional family values, but condones any behavior between consenting participants. Nowhere is statutory rape mentioned, or that a minor cannot consent to sexual activity. The abstinence message is given, yet the demonstrations and role-playing do not reinforce the message. Protection during oral sex is discussed (dental dams), but no mention is made of the dangers of anal sex.

No mention is made of condom failure rates or the known transmission rate of HIV to married partners who use protection. Heterosexuality is not promoted.

As the current education reforms move toward more integrated studies in which the lines become still more blurred between sex education and core academic subjects, I fully anticipate having to be on the defensive more frequently. I am very worried about the "restructuring" effort in education nationwide. Heterogeneous classes are a joke. Group assignments, with group grades, do not teach children individual responsibility or accountability. The move to teach "correct attitudes" for responsible citizens leaves me terrified. (Who defines "correct"?) The move toward interdisciplinary studies is merely an excuse to discuss any objectionable topic at any time. How can we stop this monumental experiment and get back to teaching basics?

Sarah Broadbent

EDITORS' NOTE: Mrs. Broadbent included the following examples:

From an American history class came this notice—

> As a follow up of our Civil Rights unit in which we examined the issue of gay and lesbian rights, I have invited the Lesbian, Gay, Bisexual Speaker's Bureau to speak to your child. The LGBSB is being invited to this U.S. History class not to advocate any particular form of sexuality, but, rather to educate and enlighten students about what being gay or lesbian in the 1990s means with regard to civil liberties...These students only wish to begin educating others about the very real "facts of life." If we are to be a tolerant people who accept and understand difference[s], we must learn to face all our differences.

(Note: Don't you just love being lectured by your child's teacher?)
A handout from the same class included these statements:

> ...teen-agers aren't getting the safe-sex message—either at home or in school...Nobody wants to talk about male-to-male sex in the teen population.

From a handout in a sex education unit titled: How Is HIV Transmission Prevented?

Directions: ...For your own use, assess how well you are protecting yourself from HIV infection.

Notice the subtle message that the child is having sex. Some of the birth control methods listed include: withdrawal, douching, rhythm, birth control pill, abstinence, latex condom and foam, contraceptive foam, contraceptive sponge, and dental dams.

The date rape questionnaire included a statement about how the boy and girl were drinking with friends when someone poured beer over the girl. Everyone was intoxicated. She went upstairs to put on an oversized shirt:

> When dressed, she opened the door and Kurt suddenly walked in and closed the door. He said she looked great in his oversized shirt and how much he liked her...began kissing and fondling her. She protested and felt uneasy...Kurt then pulled up her shirt to fondle her again. She felt great, but didn't think they should go any further *on their first date.* She decided they could touch only above the waist, but that's it. When Kurt started to remove her underpants, she protested very clearly and said she wanted to stop. Kurt got very angry and called her a "tease," and that she wasn't going to stop him now...forced her to have sex until he came (ejaculated) (emphasis added).

Human Sexuality Class—Parents Not Allowed

My daughter informed me that the teacher had issued an open invitation to allow me to sit in on any of her classes. The teacher had already told me that I could sit in on her human sexuality class and also come to hear the speakers on rape and sexual harassment. The following are some notes I took on the human sexuality course:

> Teacher: "Sexuality is a delicate, intimate subject based on culture, family, and religious beliefs. If you can't talk about it, wait. Sex occurs in your mind, not in your pants. We are not animals; we feel love, pain, and emotions. That's what distinguishes us from animals. Wait till you are ready. What's so bad about waiting? Sexuality is a broad subject and involves ethical and moral beliefs."
>
> On sexual orientation: "Homosexuality is still debated...before 1974, homosexuality was considered to be a mental illness...Ten percent [of the population] is homosexual, which means two hundred students at the high school are homosexual. You can go to Rainbow Alliance." The teacher covered bi-

sexuality, trans-sexuality, and heterosexuality. She talked a lot about herself with regard to trans-sexuality and how she would do it. Very odd.

Teacher's comment on sex changes: "…Maybe change the district in which I'm living. It's gruesome surgery. Someone opting for this is very despondent…If you act on your feelings, find out what your feelings are."

On sexual practices: Sexual intercourse was discussed— practices included: vaginal, oral, and anal sex. About abstinence, she said that some people choose it. She described masturbation as being asexual, i.e., not interested in sex. As she passed out a "sex test," one student asked, "What is abstinence?" Another student in the class answered the question. The teacher, however, only referred to "abstinence" once. During a follow-up test, another student asked, "What is abstinence?" The teacher spent less than one minute on the subject!

After the test, the teacher said: "How people act on their feelings is unique to them. You have to respect that feeling. It's a choice of yours." She talked about the biological part of sex but also talked a lot about herself and how she felt about her own body.

On health: "If you're sexually active, have yourself checked. If you want to have a good sex life, check on your health." She then told the students where they could get help. Several local clinics were mentioned. She told them, "Try to go to your parents and trust them." (Don't forget I was sitting in the class taking notes.)

On another day the teacher told the class, "If you have sex, do it with zest and enjoy it!" This comment was made to a class of thirteen- and fourteen-year-olds!

When I arrived for the class on rape, the teacher told me I could not just show up and expect to sit in. I reminded her that she had issued an open invitation and that I expected her to honor that invitation. She realized I wouldn't go away, so she pretended to ask the guest speaker for permission. The speaker had no objections.

I am a very quiet person, but I was taking notes, which seemed to upset the teacher terribly. She called for help. One of the assistant principals showed up near the end of the class. I praised the presentation, conducted by a representative of a local hospital's rape center, and thanked them for letting me sit in, but both the assistant principal and the teacher said I couldn't just show up at class again. Apparently, the teacher had forgotten that it was she who had issued "an open invitation."

At one point, I spoke with the assistant principal about the difference between "opting-in" and "opting-out." He told me that when he teaches racism in his history class, he will not allow students to be opted out by parents! Unfortunately, my son will be in his history class.

The health teacher informed me that since the sexual harassment presentation was a pilot program, I would not be allowed to sit in. (Why does the term "pilot program" change the rules?) I decided to let my daughter attend that class. I found out later why the teacher didn't want me there.

The following story was discussed in the "pilot program":

> Tina and Erica met at camp. Tina had trouble with her boyfriend so Erica told Tina to break up with him. As the summer progressed, the girls became close. One night they kissed each other and had to keep it secret. Tina's boyfriend called again. Erica became jealous and went to Tina's house. Tina had girlfriends there and Erica became very unhappy. She yelled at Tina and threatened to reveal Tina's "gayness." Erica then hit Tina. Later she called to apologize.

If this is not promoting the gay and lesbian agenda, then what do we call it?

This particular health teacher told students: "We are your surrogate parents." Apparently she believes our children belong to her. I take strong objection to her statement. Unfortunately, this seems to be the prevailing attitude in today's educational community.

Are parents going to continue being forced into the background over decisions regarding their own children? Should parents be forced to fight for their rights to determine how and what their children are taught? I think not.

Name Withheld by Request

We're Dying From AIDS, But Having a Good Time

Because I see many young people each year who are at risk for pregnancy or sexually transmitted diseases, I was curious about

119

the sex-education messages given in school. Several other parents and I viewed some sex-ed videos used in the classroom and believed they presented a weak abstinence message.

When I heard that a certain group would give sex-education presentations during assemblies at our local high school, I asked for (and received) permission to attend.

The assembly was held twice, once for freshmen and sophomores, and then for juniors and seniors. I attended the first assembly. Around 150 to 200 students attended, along with a few teachers and eight or ten parents. The following notes represent a partial accounting of that assembly.

JIM, AIDS POSITIVE: Most of the kids he knows have had one or two children of their own as well as multiple abortions. He recognizes the conservative element and wants to work with both sides. He wants what is best for kids. A best friend just died of AIDS on Wednesday. God created you "as a sexual being; learn how to use that awesome gift and use it properly."

SKITS:

EMILY AND ERIN: Statistics show only 1 percent of thirteen-to-nineteen-year-olds have HIV/AIDS but 21 percent of twenty-to-twenty-nine-year-olds have it. The reason? AIDS can take up to ten years to develop. Teens are at risk. Teens experiment with drugs, alcohol, etc. which weaken their resolve. (Discussion ensued about being monogamous, i.e., one boyfriend *at a time.*)

AM I GAY? The first boy wonders whether he is gay or not. One girl is concerned that the first boy may have AIDS and that she might get it. The others say it is no longer a gay disease and that worldwide, 77 percent of those infected are heterosexual. With regards to whether he is gay or not, the general consensus is that it is not a choice he made. He is reassured that the others are "there" for him.

BOY/GIRL: This young couple has been dating a month or so. The boy wants to know when they can have sex. The girl thinks she is ready and has brought along some condoms. He resists using the condoms but she refuses to have sex unless he does. She is concerned about STDs. Her final decision is that unless he wears a condom, she won't have sex with *him.* The implication is that she *would* have sex with another boy *if he* wore a condom.

TRANSMISSION: First was an explanation of how AIDS is *not* transmitted. Then it was discussed how it is transmitted through semen, vaginal secretions, mother's milk, and blood. Various sex acts are mentioned, i.e., anal, vaginal, oral. According to the discussion, 30 to 40 percent of teens practice the first and third kinds of sex in order to prevent pregnancy. Discussion followed about how to prevent HIV transmission—this included abstinence from sex and drugs and proper use of condoms (latex with water based lubricant—non-oxynol 9 can be used but some are allergic to it and can develop a rash). Dental dams, microwaveable Saran wrap, and proper care of needles were also topics of discussion.

CAM, AIDS POSITIVE: HIV positive for eight years. Had a monogamous two-year relationship—got shingles. Two years ago he tested positive for AIDS, but kept it secret. Best friend is also positive. He has already lost thirty-five to forty friends to AIDS. Best advice: "Protect yourselves."

RON, AIDS POSITIVE: "It's criminal that you don't get the information you need. You need to make responsible choices." Stressed that AIDS is not just a gay disease. Was HIV positive for seven years and has had AIDS for two years.

LORELEI, HIV POSITIVE: Is a forty-year-old woman whose husband was a drug addict. They were divorced when she got infected but they had gotten back together. She discovered in December 1987 that she had syphilis and was HIV positive. Said she was pregnant at the time and got an abortion. Was glad she had the choice. Her husband died in July of 1990. She has a ten-year-old daughter who lives with her.

MORE FROM JIM: He states he was from a large Catholic family with eight children. He doesn't like his parents. He began smoking at seven, drinking at nine, was arrested at ten, took dope at twelve, and used hashish at fourteen. He cleaned up through "Interact" and went to college. He reiterates that his family is a "bunch of jerks" and says that all the students have dysfunctional families, and if they don't believe that, "You are in denial." He had a committed relationship, wasn't promiscuous, and didn't sleep around. However, he had a fever for four months. When his lover failed to show any understanding, Jim left. He said he talked to his parents but they weren't compassionate.

What a disturbing day! The young men who were HIV positive or who had AIDS were attractive and appeared healthy. Were they chosen deliberately? What would the message have been if the presenters showed the devastation that accompanies the latter stages of this disease? Surely it would have conveyed a stronger abstinence message!

Pearl Hammerand

Protect the Children and Lose Your Election

While a relatively new member of our county board of education, I attended the first HIV/AIDS Prevention Education Workshop created in response to new state legislation.

The day's agenda consisted primarily of sensitivity training and "values clarification" exercises for the teachers. Under the title of "Community and Social Issues," a young, engaging, AIDS-infected homosexual male from a local AIDS awareness advocacy organization spoke about his life and the disease.

This young man said he quit his job to devote full time to the "cause." He told us that half his friends were dead and that he took twenty medications that cost over $700 per month. He said that by the end of the month he would have no insurance but that he could apply for financial assistance from the county because he had "full-blown AIDS." We learned that this qualification was determined due to "twenty-two occurrences of opportunistic disease infection."

The speaker said he had known he was HIV positive for five years and that "yes" he was still sexually active, but that his past partner still tested negative after four years. His current partner was negative to date. He went on to say that AIDS is a health versus civil rights issue with regard to testing, confidentiality, and anonymity. He also said that he judges each day by "how I feel that day" and that infection statistics are dropping because of education.

During the "Question and Answer" period, I asked him if he had contacted any of the people with whom he had been sexually active before finding out that he was "HIV positive." He said he had contacted some who were still around but that others had left the area and that he had not attempted to find them.

What I found disturbing was that no teacher expressed concern about this answer, but many did ask if he would be willing to speak in their classrooms.

Almost three years later, a newly elected board voted to suspend AIDS Care after they learned that a very graphic presentation by infected homosexuals had been presented. The board discovered that no formal contracts existed, that no prescribed guidelines or boundaries existed for the workshops, and that representatives from this group solicited teachers to gain access to their classrooms. This may never have occurred if the county Schools Office had not given them exposure and reputability.

A workshop that violates the spirit of the law was unacceptable to me, to the majority of the school board members, and to parents. The new law mandated that while junior and senior high schools offer HIV/AIDS education, other state education codes state that sex education must clearly stress abstinence as a preventive measure.

The new board members believed we could not ignore the fact that the mandate to teach HIV/AIDS could not supersede the abstinence requirement. Our state law reads:

> ...course material and instruction shall stress that pupils should abstain from sexual intercourse until they are ready for marriage...and shall teach honor and respect for monogamous heterosexual marriage.[18]

Our board determined that any teacher training should follow those principles. Teachers and even some parents may have preferred the more liberal message of sexual emancipation for teens, but the county board believed public schools were not at liberty to promote it to minor children in direct violation of the law. State statute does not legitimize either heterosexual or homosexual premarital sex for minors.

As a result of our stand, another board member and I were targeted for recall. The charges against me were: I "illegally usurped the power of others...[had] interfered in the operation of schools over which I did not have jurisdiction...[and had done] the foregoing for the purpose of advancing my own radical agenda, without consulting or taking into account the wishes of local school boards, teachers, parents, and students affected by my action."

A homosexual advocacy group and a minister from a very liberal church spearheaded the petition drive against us. The superintendent of schools, responsible for the workshops in question, spoke at the first recall organizational meeting, offering assistance to the advocacy group and discrediting the board.

The recall effort failed for lack of sufficient signatures. However, I was defeated in my re-election attempt. The campaign against me was filled with distortions and mudslinging. And all because I tried to uphold the laws of our state and protect the children under my care.

Wendy Larner

More Time for Genital Mutilation and Less on Basic Skills

On six different occasions during the past four years, our son and daughter have been exposed to lessons on human reproduction without prior parental notice. Two of these lessons forced my eleven-year-old daughter to think about bestiality and the concept of humans copying the sexual behavior of animals.

One lesson required my fifteen-year-old son to consider: 1) a woman dying frightfully in childbirth with the baby's head sticking out of her vagina, and the family's decision to bury the mother and baby in that condition after considering the gruesome alternatives; 2) a husband dying in agony during intercourse because he got stuck inside his wife; and 3) several examples of sexual abuse such as a husband urinating in his wife. Schools should not force my children, or any other children, to think about such horrifyingly negative sexual scenes.

Early in our son's freshman year, he complained about his modern civilization class. Most disturbing was the teacher's graphic and detailed description of an ancient castration technique performed on prisoners of war, which took place during a lesson about democracy.

When I complained, the teacher smiled and justified the lesson. Initially, the vice principal was shocked but soon accepted the teacher's behavior and said that the union lawyer advised him to protect the teacher from our "harassment." No one ever acknowledged that the teacher should have notified parents before describing human reproductive organs. They failed to explain that our children could complete an alternative assignment for this or other inappropriate lessons. (One of those "other" lessons included a teacher who required students to memorize, and sing repeatedly, a song about worshipping man.)

Our son finally withdrew from the class due to our frustration, and as a result, lost his high academic honors status. Because of his withdrawal, the vice principal said our son should attend summer school for two summers to make up the course. Following this episode, the same teacher assigned a book about the mutilation of girls' external sex organs as practiced by some cultures. Our son's classmates complained. The book, *Warrior Marks: Female Genital Mutilation and the Sexual Blinding of Women* by Alice Walker and Pratibha Parmar, was 373 pages long!

I was told that while the book was not purchased with curriculum money, the topic was appropriate for students my son's age. Some parents also considered it a worthwhile assignment. However, many students signed a petition protesting the book and other parents complained that it was, "disturbing, hideous, nasty, gross, horrifying, insulting, and totally inappropriate for teenagers who are in the formative stage sexually."

Some of the information contained in the book included:

1) techniques performed during surgery on the genitals of six-to-twelve-year-old girls without painkillers;

2) ways in which relatives tricked girls into cooperating; and

3) long-term consequences of the mutilations.

The book graphically described the blood and the pain, referred to the thorns and restraints used, and discussed the childbirth complications and diminished sexual pleasure that resulted. The book also made the ridiculous assertion that forced genital mutilation on unwilling immature girls equates with the decision of adult women to have a facelift or liposuction.

The head of the history department told me that mutilation is performed on one-third of all women in the world. The truth is that both the *Encyclopaedia Britannica* and *Warrior Marks* estimate the number to be 4 to 18 percent.

Far too much time was spent on this subject. An extensive search of dictionaries and encyclopedias yielded only one paragraph that even mentioned these practices. If students could read all twenty-nine volumes of the *Encyclopaedia Britannica* during their four years of high school, they would spend less than one minute reading this single paragraph. Yet, students were required to spend at least a week on the subject.

State law requires public school teachers to notify parents at least fifteen days prior to presenting any material on human sexuality. These notices are designed to give parents the opportunity to preview the proposed material and to "opt out" their child if they find the material unacceptable. This procedure was not followed and state law was violated.

When we complained that the assignment was psychologically abusive and an inappropriate use of class time, the history department head justified the topic and the principal refused to return my calls. Finally, I wrote a letter to the principal as he requested. Though we highlighted specific provisions in the education code, we were told that we were mistaken.

Eleven months after my initial complaint, I wrote to the board of education and a few state legislators. District officials falsely insisted that the city's teachers always gave parental notice and followed state law. The principal used our letters as a reason not to talk to us about the issue. Two meetings we had scheduled were canceled without notification, and the agenda of the school Parent-Teacher-Student Association meeting was changed at the last minute to omit our request for a curriculum subcommittee. Some teachers used words such as: "hostile parents," "witch hunts," and "censorship" to intimidate and discredit us.

My son's experience in his honors English class shows how important it is for parents to receive "informed consent" notification. This requires an accurate summary of course content. For this honors English class, parents would have had to review more than two thousand pages of text from thirty authors. At the beginning of the year, for instance, my son's English teacher assigned books that included descriptions of human reproductive organs and processes with no notice to parents. When my husband and I read one of the assignments, we were shocked and sickened.

We persisted and contacted the district's lawyer, who confirmed the teacher should have notified us. As a result, the school has since decided to send letters home to parents along with a list of required reading. The letters simply state, however, that "Instruction materials may be utilized which describe, illustrate, or discuss human reproductive organs and their functions and processes." It then states that parents have the right to review materials and opt out their child. The letters do not explain the graphic nature of the material. Any teacher who teaches the same material every year knows which pages are graphic or explicit—and should either summarize or identify those pages so that parents can review that material specifically.

More importantly, sex education does not belong in English, history, etc. It should be taught in health class after parents have been properly "informed" so that they can give genuine "informed consent."

Ideally, based on the abuses I have seen, sex education should not occur in elementary schools. Middle schools and high schools should concentrate sex education in one course only, and that course should be an elective! This would allow students and parents to decide when and if the student is ready for the course. That way, alternative courses would exist so that students opting out would not be embarrassed, and parents would control what and how much sex education their children receive.

Maybe that's the problem; government thinks they know what's best for my child.

Name Withheld by Request

EDITORS' NOTE: In identical letters sent to this parent and a parents' group who complained about the book on genital mutilation, the district said:

The Committee considered all of your objections to the book and on each point decided that we could not agree with your statements. It is the opinion of the district that the teachers and administrators are following the law regarding parental notification and review...

...the teacher is in the best position to determine how much time is needed to effectively cover a subject...the teacher is in the best position to determine the details of how to teach that part of the curriculum...a teacher is qualified to match materials with the maturity level of the students.

Teaching Sixth Graders to Have Sex

I have two children, aged nine and twelve, and have been a PTA president and member of the school governance team. I tell you this so you understand that I have been active in the schools and have tried to stay informed.

When my daughter was in sixth grade, I reviewed the social health curriculum used at her school, the School of Creative and Performing Arts (SCPA). I also attended a public review of the curriculum at our neighborhood school, where my son was a fourth grader. Both schools used the same curriculum, and school nurses conducted both presentations—not the teachers conducting the classroom instruction.

The social health curriculum (sex-ed) claimed that it taught abstinence when in fact neither the word nor the concept appeared anywhere in the curriculum. The curriculum left any discussion of abstinence entirely up to the instructor—usually the sixth-grade teacher. The sixth-grade curriculum included: 1) abortion as an option, 2) homosexuality as an alternative lifestyle, 3) sexual intercourse as natural when there is "mature love," and 4) a live-birth film showing a full-frontal, vaginal delivery.

When I reviewed the curriculum, I was struck by five questions that appeared on page five. Both nurses had skipped these particular questions in their presentations. These questions and responses were as follows: 1) What is contraception? 2) What is a homosexual? 3) What is masturbation? 4) What are sperm cells? 5) What is a transsexual? The nurse at SCPA was asked directly what she would tell a student if she were pregnant. She answered, "Just as it states in the curriculum, 'Abortion is an option.'"

I was shocked that the school district had approved and intended to distribute to sixth-grade students—ten- and eleven-year-olds—a pamphlet from the Centers for Disease Control (CDC). Pages one and two made references to anal, oral, and vaginal sex. The pamphlet also stated that, in addition to abstinence and having sex with one lifelong partner (not a spouse), there were other ways to help stop the spread of HIV. The advice included using a latex condom and using a spermicide containing non-oxynol 9 with a condom. Remember, this was for sixth graders.

I object to the inaccurate information as well as the content. We now know the HIV virus is smaller than the latex weave in condoms and can cause infection at any day of the month. We know that non-oxynol 9 is an irritant and can promote the spread of HIV. And we know that abstinence is the only real form of "safe sex." The idea that no one should have sex until marriage was never mentioned.

When I went to the principal and expressed concern, I was met with casualness and the response that "this is all on MTV" so what was the problem? I asked that the school send home the CDC brochure in a sealed envelope for parents to review prior to presentation in class and was told, "No" by the school nurse. When I expressed concern about the brochure at my daughter's school, they said that since there were not enough of them to go to all of the students anyway, they would not include it with the resource materials.

I brought up the matter of social health at the governance team—comprised equally of teachers/staff and parents—and was met with uninterest from the teacher/staff members. They told me, "This is the way it is in junior high and high school, and we can't teach abstinence because 'they will do it anyway'."

Michelle Abrams

Hurray for "Intergenerational Sex"

Two days after we signed a permission slip to allow our eleven-year-old daughter to participate in the district's HIV/AIDS prevention program, two speakers from the Committee United Against Violence (CUAV), a gay rights group, visited her sixth-grade class. The classroom teacher had invited them—ostensibly to educate the children about problems with racial violence and hate crimes. Instead, the speakers provided graphic first-person accounts of their own sexual activities.

The presentation traumatized several of the students, but the teacher did not allow them to leave the room. I filed a police report alleging child abuse, and the PTA testified before the Board of Education that the presentation represented child abuse. The director of the school district's Health Programs Department and the deputy superintendent conducted an investigation which we learned corroborated the description of the class provided by my daughter and her classmates. Because of the publicity, and perhaps due to threats of legal action, CUAV was temporarily banned from our schools. Later, the district disclosed that this group was a regular participant in the district's HIV/AIDS prevention program.

Shortly before the statute of limitations ran out on filing suit against the district, my wife, daughter, and I met with the superintendent, who assured us that CUAV would almost certainly not make it through the review process. This process included a review by the Family Life Education Advisory Subcommittee before the program could be reinstated. As a result of these assurances, I did not pursue further legal action.

Imagine our surprise when we learned that almost immediately after the expiration of the "statute of limitations," CUAV was allowed back into our high schools. The reinstatement was based on a privately negotiated "Memorandum of Understanding" (MOU) with our district. This MOU was not reviewed or approved by the Family Life Education Committee. In fact, three members of the committee, parents who were not employed by the district, requested that "in light of past problems," the CUAV curriculum be reviewed. The district told them the committee could not review the program because it had been approved in 1978!

After repeated demands by the three parent-members, the district did produce part of the CUAV curriculum for use in high schools, which contains, among other things, justifications for sadomasochism, "intergenerational" sex, and rationalizations for promiscuity. The three members wrote a long letter to the district criticizing the curriculum and requesting documentation that the curriculum had indeed been approved in accordance with the state education code. They also requested the results of an investigation conducted by the superintendent and deputy superintendent into another incident nearly a year earlier. No one responded to their request.

Subsequently, these parent-members filed a formal public records request for information they believed they were entitled to review, and were in fact required to review, in order to perform the duties for which they were appointed. The requested material was not forthcoming. Since the only recourse left available was expensive legal action, which they could not personally afford, they did not pursue their request.

One member, who represented the PTA, did continue to press the issue. Because of this member's persistence, the school superintendent insisted that the PTA remove that person. The PTA refused. At that point, the president of the school board met with the PTA and threatened that if this member was not removed, the committee would be dissolved. The PTA refused and the committee was disbanded. (The school board president claimed to be one of the founders of CUAV's speaker's bureau.)

Through my efforts to resolve the problems with our district, I met many other parents with similar problems subjected to similar stonewalling. I also met with teachers and other employees concerned about the continuing abuses related to sex education and the promotion of gay issues, conducted under the guise of legitimate and necessary HIV/AIDS education. These individuals have been reluctant to speak out because they fear retribution.

Since the district has refused to deal with these problems, I have communicated with a string of officials at the state Department of Education (DOE) and made four separate requests for assistance. While sympathetic, these officials have taken no action. I believe that the DOE has been negligent in its responsibility to see that HIV/AIDS education in our state is conducted according to law and that taxpayer funds are properly spent.

In addition to breaches of parental consent law and inappropriate classroom presentations, I am concerned about who pays for this abuse of public trust. While no one has admitted paying for the presentations, it appears that CUAV and all related activities are funded, at least in part, with taxpayer dollars.

Quite frankly, after nearly two years, I despair of securing any remedy locally or through the state Department of Education. No wonder parents distrust the "system." It appears the "system" believes parents are to be deceived, derailed, and disdained. If our experience is any indication, parents should not trust their children to the "system," and any parent who does so needs to wake up, ask questions, visit classrooms, and read the curriculum. School today is not what it was when we attended!

Bruce Budnick

From visits by "condom ladies" with bags of tricks to AIDS patients graphically describing homosexual acts, public school students—including sixth graders—are confronted more than ever with the message that since you're going to engage in sex anyway, you might as well learn how to do it "safely." Parents are increasingly on the defensive as academic disciplines integrate and bring "sex education" even to music classes.

Indoctrination

CHAPTER SEVEN

LAND THAT I LOATHE

"MULTICULTURALISM" *is a popular buzz word in today's schools, and there's nothing wrong with learning about other cultures. But that's not what our schools mean by "multiculturalism." The schools' use of "multiculturalism" makes all cultures morally equal. For example, a primitive culture in South America that engages in human sacrifice has the same value as the American culture.*

But it sometimes goes beyond that. Some cultures and religions are promoted in the classrooms and in the textbooks as superior to America's Judeo-Christian culture. The "melting pot" concept has largely disappeared from the schools. No longer do schools stress what unites Americans; rather, schools increasingly teach the evils of our own culture and the moral superiority of other cultures.

In the past, we weren't hyphenated Americans; we were simply Americans, a united people with a single purpose and with pride in our country. People of differing cultures still recognized and honored their own beliefs and customs but proudly considered themselves Americans. Schools taught about different cultures, and, if students in the class wanted to share something about a country other than the United States, they were invited to do so. It wasn't called "multiculturalism"; it was called sharing information and educating children.

Anti-Bias Curriculum

Our state Department of Education recommends *Anti-Bias Curriculum Tools for Empowering Young Children*, published by the National Association for the Education of Young Children in Washington, D.C., for kindergarten through third grade.[1] It is also recommended for preschools across the nation. I was shocked when I first learned about this widely used curriculum for young children.

My two daughters attended a government-sponsored day care. At one point, the center sponsored a meeting for parents to introduce its new *Anti-Bias Curriculum*. A short video was shown but no specifics were given to explain what was planned. One teacher did tell us about an experiment they conducted in my two-year-old's class. She explained how they compared the classic flesh-colored Band-Aid to a black child's hand and discovered that it didn't match. The students then wrote to the company but the company would not change the color. However, the company did send clear Band-Aids to the students.

I doubt that two-year-olds understand the concept of a "company" or that the "company" is allegedly doing something wrong. I do believe that such an experiment would point out to even a two-year-old that he is different and would make him feel awful.

Some of the recommendations in *Anti-Bias Curriculum* include telling innocent little children that Thanksgiving Day is a day of mourning, because the white settlers killed off the Indians and stole their land. One of the teachers argued that they had to present these alternative viewpoints. I then spoke with an American Indian activist from the Red Cloud Society. She was not aware that Thanksgiving Day was considered a day of mourning or that wearing an Indian princess costume was considered a sign of disrespect. She did acknowledge that some American Indians protest Columbus Day and disapprove of some of the usage of Indian names. But it is not necessarily the minority groups that are spreading these destructive ideas.

Two other situations occurred at this school: 1) At Halloween, a four-year-old wanted to dress as an Indian princess, but the school would not allow her to do so. According to them, it would be disrespectful to the American Indian. I believe this little girl wanted to honor a group of people she admired. The mother became so upset that she quit her job and pulled her two children out of the preschool. 2) Another mom told me that her four-year-old reported that in his classroom they talked about having two mommies and two daddies. She asked, "Oh, like us?" (They have a step-family situation.) He said, "No, it wasn't like that."

I noticed that my three-year-old colored and painted people brown but my seven-year-old, who had not spent much time in *Anti-Bias Curriculum*, did not. After looking through the curriculum, I found that the book frequently recommends offering black and brown paints, play dough, etc., and only occasionally offering peach-colored. If the children object and say, "Yuck," then the teacher is supposed to help the child discover his or her feelings and begin conducting activities that foster the child's learning about cultural and physical differences. Don't children naturally prefer bright colors? What are these teachers telling impressionable children?

When I had the chance, I attended the conference for the National Association for the Education of Young Children. The author of the curriculum conducted a workshop entitled "On Becoming an Anti-Bias Educator: Stages of the Journey." She presented it as a three-stage process: Stage I—denial and resistance; Stage II—disequilibrium; and Stage III—reconstruction or activism.

Stage II, she said, is a period of "emotional masturbation" in which a person massages all those feelings and emotions. Stage II ends with the realization that if a person is white, he/she wouldn't know if he/she wanted to be white anymore, and if a minority, the person would want to "reclaim" his/her identity with his/her own group. (I'm extremely concerned about Stage III. I know I don't want radical educators experimenting with my children.)

In discussing the correct "visual/aesthetic environment," *Anti-Bias Curriculum* suggests that images in the classroom should include "gay or lesbian families (families with two mothers or fathers)."[2] Under "book suggestions," *Anti-Bias Curriculum* warns educators to "BEWARE of using only the large number of children's books picturing only families with two parents, and always with one parent of each sex; BEWARE of using the large number of books that assume readers are Christians."[3]

It is certainly convenient to target preschools with this anti-bias program, because parents don't know what is going on and most children don't tell. However, as I stated previously, this particular *Anti-Bias Curriculum* book is also recommended by our state's Department of Education for kindergarten through third grade, and the public schools already promote many of its ideas.

Let me share a conversation I had with my seven-year-old. She said her teacher read a story about Martha Washington and said that Mrs. Washington was gay. The teacher then explained that this "gay" meant "happy" and asked if anyone knew what else the word "gay" meant. Several children raised their hands, and they discussed "gay." I asked my daughter what it meant. She said it was a boy acting like a girl and a girl acting like a boy. When I discussed this with the teacher at the next parent-teacher conference, she said it was just a quick discussion because "one of the children had laughed." However, this was not the impression I had gotten from my second grader.

Anti-Bias Curriculum also teaches acceptance of witches and witchcraft. The educator's goal is to create a good category of witches through activities like having a "witch-healer" table where children can make their own potions, chant, and lay out a black cloth where they can then symbolically throw objects into the "pot."

Not long ago, a teacher from the preschool told me that they weren't allowed to read *Bambi* because it is biased. She didn't know why. However, the teachers were encouraged to read a book about farts so that the children would become comfortable with the use of the word "fart."

I want my children to play and learn with children of other races and to be left alone by these so-called adults. I believe *Anti-Bias Curriculum* creates division and animosity between races. Government and public schools need to return to being wholesome institutions that concentrate on age-appropriate skills and discipline.

Susan Krumpotich

Multiculturalism

Our district promotes Global Studies for Multicultural Understanding. Global Studies was developed to bridge the gap between the varying cultural and socioeconomic groups throughout our school system. In other words the district devised a way to "bus" students to other schools via the use of technology.

As a teacher, I initially thought the idea of students doing reports on computers and talking to pen pals using a video-telecommunications machine ("V-Tel" hookup) was a great idea. However, I soon began to wonder about the political agenda of the multiculturalism program and the amount of time it was taking from academics.

The new program began in the sixth grade at two middle schools. Teachers signed a contract requiring them to teach Global Studies as well as the regular core curriculum. If teachers refused to sign the contract, the district moved them to a different grade level. No one, however, thought to argue or even refuse to sign, because we all felt excited about incorporating new technology into our classrooms. We had been waiting for it for a long time. As the year progressed, however, I became more and more disillusioned with the curriculum.

In implementing Global Studies, teachers first continued using existing core curriculum and gradually integrated Global Studies in order to ease into the new curriculum and not overburden teachers with time-consuming planning. Teachers from our "partner" school used the novelty of the "V-Tel" machine as a way to hook students into using the new multicultural lessons.

As the year progressed, teachers from the two schools soon found they were no longer at the same place in their studies. This made it difficult to blend Global Studies lessons with our partners. As a result of this confusion, the teachers substituted superficial lessons on multicultural understanding. Teachers faced the need to move core curriculum (social studies, math, language, science) to different times in order to teach the affective and/or values education associated with the Global Studies curriculum. It took precedence over core academics.

My argument is that not enough time was spent on core curriculum. Why are teachers being asked to fragment an already beleaguered curriculum with more nonacademic "stuff," especially in areas that counselors or religious leaders, not middle school teachers, are better trained and qualified to teach? Good academic teaching requires a continuous span of time for the linear development of skills and concepts for building a unit. Each time the continuum is interrupted, students lose their focus. Teachers must then take time to review what they previously taught before moving on. Honesty, responsibility, and cooperation are all naturally a part of social studies and literature. These should not be taught as separate subjects.

We all know that state test scores are at their lowest point ever, yet administrators continue to implement more programs not aimed at improving the literacy statistics but focused on "feel good" education. After receiving in-service training on new teaching methods, many teachers go back to their classrooms, close the doors, and continue with what they know works. Talk about being "in the closet." This type of management is oppressive and humiliating to teachers, and more importantly, destructive to the academic growth of students. It is also dangerous because the commonality of curriculum among all students within a district is lost. Inconsistent curriculum will give some students an advantage while others become pawns of experimental education programs. We need to stop inundating curriculum with programs that impede the process of teaching the "3 Rs."

Our sixth-grade class went to a multicultural fair at our "partner" school. The first event was a series of cultural acts performed for the whole student body and, of course, us. About halfway through the presentation, an Aztec folk dance group took the stage, and a woman representing the group approached the microphone. She first said *"Buenos dias!"* After a lukewarm response from the audience, she held out her fist and yelled *"La Raza!"* The host school crowd went wild with applause and cheering while the students from our school sat still. They didn't understand why the others were applauding.

To understand the importance of this issue, it is necessary to know that La Raza is a Latino activist group. The name means "The Race" and stands for "Power to the Hispanic race." It is a phrase commonly used at Hispanic "separatist" rallies that call for revolutionary activism.

This type of exclusion or divisiveness is the basis for multicultural education. Differences are pointed out and emphasized. Multiculturalism doesn't focus on unifying the various cultures represented in our district and imbuing our students with the knowledge of, and pride in, our common culture. Many students have no idea why and how the United States of America was formed or what it means to them personally to live in this country. Yet this information is crucial to understanding their place in the United States. Whether a person came to this country because they were fleeing political persecution or oppression, or because they were searching for a better life economically, these factors need to be explored so a child learns to develop respect for this country and all it encompasses.

I am a first-generation American. My parents emigrated from Ukraine. They came here with their families after being saved from communist work camps by the American Red Cross. The details of their journey were repeated to me as a child so that I would not forget why I am here and how I got here. I am humbled by the American flag and any other symbol representing the USA. This country harbored my people in their time of great need. I am also thankful I never had to live under communist law. America is not perfect but she deserves our respect in return for the compassion so many families have been given!

We should be teaching this history to our students! We should be teaching them why our country is still great and what so many suffered in order to give us all a chance at freedom!

Students do not know how or what to respect unless we teach them to be literate about American culture. E.D. Hirsch, Jr. wrote:

> ...it is our schools which must make sure that our literate traditions are successfully conveyed to every child from every sort of home...only recently have we come to understand that "Jack and Jill" and "George Washington" belong to an alphabet that must be learned by heart, and which is no less essential to higher order literacy skills than the alphabet itself.[4]

This is our means of communication. This is what ties us all together. This is how we are able to compare democracy with socialism, communism, and fascism.

I believe it is the responsibility of parents and private institutions to foster the understanding of the personal traditions, history, art, and literature of a child's heritage. My parents, who did not have much money, paid tuition to a Ukrainian Saturday school so that my sister, my brother, and I could learn about our culture.

This was our "special interest" and we did not ask for public funds to subsidize it. Over a two-year period, our district has received almost $1.4 million a year in state voluntary desegregation money to use computers and the V-Tel, two-way video to link low-income Latino pupils with middle-class white children, and there has been no evidence that such a program increases academic performance. Public funds should be used for public purposes. It is that simple.

This is a time when state funds and test scores are critically low! We must focus on our purpose! Weed out superfluous programs that do not clearly meet the objectives of public education. When the district cannot provide its students with enough supplies such as pencils, paper, glue, scissors, and textbooks because of a budget crunch, how can we rationalize dumping millions of dollars into a program whose main purpose is to socialize children? At our school, each teacher has a minimal budget with which to purchase supplies. Each copy made on the Xerox machine is counted. Some teachers even ask students to share worksheets. Where are our priorities?

Let's not allow special interest groups to manipulate us with emotional propaganda that evokes fear, shame, and guilt and bleed funds from the public pot so that the effectiveness of public education is diminished! Let's require parents and religious groups to take back the responsibility for values education! We must show courage, conviction, and integrity! As Robert Frost wrote in "The Road Not Taken," "...Two roads diverged in a wood, and I—I took the one less traveled, and that has made all the difference."

Laura Pratto

Risk/Multiculturalism

I was first alerted to potential problems in our school over the issue of multiculturalism. As I previewed sixth-grade courses planned for my child, I was disturbed by a course called Intex International Exploration. As I read through the information, it seemed to be a course in political correctness and multiculturalism.

During a meeting, the school principal told us the course was really only a geography class with a few other things "thrown in" to help students be "more accepting" of those of different cultures.[5] After about an hour, the principal, in great frustration, exclaimed, "We should have just called it a geography course!" The inference here, of course, is that no one would be the wiser as to what the real curriculum was. I was not allowed to make a copy of the course outline. The principal indicated there were still changes being made. I requested to see the final draft but never received it.

I don't really blame the principal for defending the Intex course; this particular school is an example of the "expanded middle school concept." Sixth graders are mixed in with seventh and eighth graders, and teachers are given a lot of freedom to develop new and innovative programs. Intex was one of those with which they got carried away, though not necessarily with evil intentions.

However, I didn't want the public school teaching my daughter "political correctness" nor did I want her to participate in the amount of "group work" called for in the course descriptions. We pulled her out of the school and began homeschooling.

The same middle school gave my eighth-grade son a "Risk Survey." I wrote a letter explaining that my son was not to participate and pointed out that the letter the school sent home was confusing. It did not state clearly whether students would only take the survey if the school received a "yes" from the parents or if they would be given the survey unless a "no" response was sent in. It appeared that the letter was merely a gesture and not really meant to inform parents about the nature of the survey questions and ask for their positive "opt in."

I also took exception to the fact that the school claimed the survey was anonymous. The fact that only certain students were targeted to take it indicated that somewhere in a computer certain students were already "tagged" in some way. Furthermore, the first page of the survey asked students for their age, sex, grade, and race. By the time a student answered all the survey questions, any computer could quickly identify him or her.

The principal indicated at a PTA meeting that the survey results would help determine the kinds of "prevention" programs needed. My first thought was: "How many of the students really answer these surveys honestly?" If the student really believed he was anonymous, he might answer in a way that he considered funny. Ask any kid who has taken one of these "surveys": they tend to think they are a joke. That being the case, how can surveys given to students be accurate enough to actually develop expensive new programs? Who is kidding whom?

Second, the vast majority of children have already gone through D.A.R.E. and other classroom drug education units. Enough is enough. Regardless of whether the students smoke, drink alcohol, or carry a weapon, I don't believe there is anything a school can do to change attitudes with additional prevention/awareness programs. The results of numerous in-school prevention/awareness programs, including D.A.R.E., have proven to be insignificant in preventing drug and alcohol use.

It is not the job of the school system to fix all of society's ills. I send my children to school for an education, not for social programs, risk surveys, or "preventive maintenance." As a responsible parent, I am angered that the public school system (and legislators who pass the laws) continue to steal academic time from my children to participate in more government-generated programs.

The public school's emphasis on solving society's problems is also having an adverse effect on teachers.

I used to criticize the teachers as well as the curricula, etc. However, I now volunteer in a classroom on a regular basis and would never have believed what today's teachers experience.

One teacher has five classes with thirty-six students each; two of the classes are GATE (gifted and talented) and three are "regular." The students write book reports and essays, and keep journals on books they read. One hundred and eighty journals have to be reviewed every few weeks. Individual book "conferences" are held with each student. Everything must be checked in, graded, and entered into a computer. A minimum of three times per week, the teacher holds a parent/teacher conference because some parent is unhappy about a child who is not doing well or who has received an "unfair" grade, or because the teacher doesn't like the child, or…

The phone rings constantly with requests for missing homework assignments. Kids make up missed tests every day. And additional time must be spent with "problem" students—at least 10 percent of them—who constantly disrupt class, "mouth off," or harass other students. We're not taking into consideration the time spent dealing with ethnic problems. (I was stunned to discover the prejudices these young kids have and how gangs, drugs, and violence affects what goes on in the classroom—and this is in a good neighborhood!)

As I watch what goes on and how stressful teaching is today, I wonder how much of this is a direct result of laws which intrude into the lives of teachers, students, and parents. How much time is wasted on nonacademic curricula and activities? How much time is spent on disruptive students because teachers and schools are not allowed to kick them out for inappropriate behavior? How much time is wasted because discipline is ignored?

Linda Rice

Multiculturalism

The following are my observations as a substitute teacher and lecturer in some of the elementary, middle, and high schools in my county. My concern is that students in these schools have been so propagandized and politicized by multicultural programs and curriculum, they have been turned into angry youngsters who hate America. Let me give some examples:

> 1) Hispanic students demonstrated against a statewide ballot initiative at a homecoming parade in the stadium by staging their own parade, raising the Mexican flag, and using obscenities in Spanish against the United States, the state, the schools, and their teachers. After marching around the stadium, they demanded to leave the grounds. Several teachers tried to restrain them but without success. (I saw some adults participating but don't know if they were teachers.)

> 2) Many Hispanic students at the fifth- and sixth-grade levels were expressive in their views about Mexico being a better country than the United States; they denounced the United States, its history, our flag, and government, and resented my speaking about what made the United States a great country. They especially resented my explanation of the free enterprise system and the need for personal responsibility in a free republic.

> 3) There was a very strong anti-American feeling among the students. They denounced the U.S. government and the flag,

and demanded that all our western states be given back to Mexico. Many students had no knowledge of American history or cared to hear about the free enterprise system. They expressed anger against capitalism, knew very little English, and most were not interested in learning it.

One teacher resented the fact that I broke up a potential fight by stating, "Oh, that's what they do all the time. It's okay, they'll get over it." I saw gang activities which I reported to the main office and to security. I saw Hispanics using foul language directed towards "Anglo" students as they passed in the hallways and tried to provoke them into fights. There was poor supervision by teachers on campus; lesson plans were poorly prepared; there was little substance to material being presented but lots of magazine cutout projects displayed on blackboards with little writing required.

4) Hispanic high school students in English as a Second Language (ESL) classes resented learning English. They spoke against ESL, American history, and our state's history. They believed the western states would return to Mexico via population growth. They were interested in getting welfare and didn't care if the Mexican government was killing Indians in remote areas of their home country. They didn't seem to value life. They resented saluting the American flag, and most would not do so when asked. Again, there was a lot of anger and gang hand shaking activity with no knowledge of Western civilization. Little English was taught in any of these classes, and virtually no writing or reading in English took place. Forget learning how to communicate in English; the students had very poor communication skills in their own language. One Hispanic high school teacher challenged me to prove that the western states did not belong to Mexico. When informed that the U.S. is the only stable country in the world that has extensively contributed worldwide, he responded, "Cuba has sent troops to Angola!"

5) Another school followed a similar pattern but was far worse. School buildings were called "villages" by students and teachers. Hispanic students were very militant; they used foul language against Anglo students and, once again, strongly expressed the view that Mexico is better than the United States. They gave numerous reasons including: "You took us away from Mexico," and "You took away our culture." In an antagonistic manner they stated: "We are going to take [the states] back with a war and lots of people from Mexico being born here."

In this particular classroom, the entire class seemed angry and displayed gang sign language in the presence of a D.A.R.E. officer. They wanted to know where I lived and what kind of car I drove. They were not interested in learning about capitalism, freedom, democracy, or America's financial contributions to Mexico. They shut up briefly when I told them that the U.S. had forgiven Mexico its debt several times and is currently paying for Mexico's sewage system in the Tijuana border region. The D.A.R.E. officer even tried to explain that I wasn't against them but was trying to inform them of things they needed to know.

Later, while I was alone in the classroom, several students walked by and yelled, "*Viva Mejico, bajo con los Estados Unidos!*" This means, "Long live Mexico, down with the United States!" Students complained to the principal that I was prejudiced against Mexico. The principal and I had an after-school conference in which I gave him extensive information about the Aztlan movement.[6] He knew little about it and thought it was a cultural teaching program. He never responded to the information.

Students at all grade levels—Anglos, Asians, and Hispanics who don't speak Spanish—often come to me after class to thank me for speaking favorably about our flag and our country. They say they never hear it from their teachers. All of them express fear about speaking up for what they believe. They have a difficult time comprehending that a Hispanic teacher (me) "would be on our side." Many seem quite upset about how they are treated in class by their own teachers and peers. There is a lot of resentment among these students.

I now understand why there is so much gang violence in some schools and communities, and why our education standards need to be upgraded—NOW! There is virtually no assimilation of ethnic students into the American culture. Patriotism is out, English language instruction is minimal, and colleges and universities in our state and across our nation undermine the democratic process by teaching "multiculturalism." It must stop if our nation is to survive!

Ruth Flores Harper

"Multicultural" and "Anti-Bias" programs meant to "empower" school-

children and help unite the nation, instead have accentuated differences, stirring division and distorting the U.S. and its history, according to the witness of many parents. One Hispanic parent and teacher no doubt echoes many who fear the current path threatens America's very survival.

CHAPTER EIGHT

PUSHING THE HOMOSEXUAL AGENDA

UNDER THE GUISE *of reducing hate and promoting tolerance, including tolerance for homosexuality, homosexual activists have persuaded legislators across the nation to pass laws designed to shape children's attitudes about homosexuality through curriculum revisions and teacher training. They call these "safe schools."*

There is nothing wrong with tolerance as long as that tolerance applies to everyone and allows for diversity of thought and belief. Yet the reality is that homosexual activists have hijacked the effort to reduce racial prejudice in order to promote their political and cultural agenda.

The most common propaganda strategy used by the homosexuals is to claim that gay students have no rights and need to be protected, but the idea that existing constitutional rights and laws against harassment and violence don't apply to some students based on some behavioral characteristic is preposterous and without legal foundation. A California gay activist lays out the real strategy:

> Once students are protected from discrimination in schools, then curricular inclusion becomes not only possible but almost certain (eventually), as both students and teachers must be taught why not to discriminate.[1]

Over the past ten years, California has passed some of the most liberal "tolerance" laws of any state in the nation. Yet when viewed critically, tolerance in California is no longer about accepting opposing views but instead has devolved into not only "tolerating" but also "celebrating" homosexuality. Those who disagree, including school-age children, are labeled "hateful." The debate is no longer about ending discrimination;

it is about redirecting "hate" toward anyone, especially Christians, who do not agree with the state's idea of discrimination and tolerance.

Teacher and gay activist Jacki Williams held a workshop on promoting the gay agenda to kindergartners at a Gay, Lesbian & Straight Education Network (GLSEN) conference, and she stated that "children that age are developing their superego and that is when the saturation process needs to begin." GLSEN is a multimillion-dollar organization whose sole purpose is the promotion of the homosexual agenda in America's public schools. Kevin Jennings, its co-founder, said, "I can envision a day when straight people say, 'So what if you're promoting homosexuality?'"[2]

California, New York, and Massachusetts are leading the charge to use public schools to promote homosexuality. Increasingly, legislators are dictating the values of individuals. They believe only they have the right value system and any parent—or church—that dares differ with the politically designated "correct" thought process must be crushed. And while legislators have no place in designating themselves as the social, moral, or religious monitors, the reality is that far too many of them are committed to pushing their own agendas and are passing laws that require schools to delve into the personal values of their students and parents. A teacher in Massachusetts said, "We're to use inclusive language, so we can't even say 'mother,' 'father,' 'wife,' or 'husband.' We're supposed to use the generic terms 'parent' or 'partner'."[3] Most parents have no idea what our schools are teaching children about homosexuality. Many of the big-city schools aggressively promote the homosexual lifestyle, and it's only a matter of time before this trend spreads to all schools.

Given the amount of resources spent on drug and alcohol abuse and the public school mantra about "teaching our children to make wise decisions," one would think that promoting a lifestyle that engages in extremely high-risk behavior and which reduces the lifespan of its practitioners by eight to twenty years, on average, would be strictly prohibited.[4] However, it is now obvious that the need to engage in social engineering and undermining societal norms has become more important to our public school leaders than the health considerations of the students.

A primer for "all school principals, educators, and school personnel" called Just the Facts about Sexual Orientation and Youth *declares that its purpose is to help schools better help homosexual youth. Instead, it is a diatribe against "reparative therapy."[5] (Reparative therapy is a method used to help homosexuals who wish to leave the lifestyle. While RT is controversial, it has helped thousands reject homosexuality. Many have married and are happy with their decision.) However, Just the Facts never mentions the success stories or discusses that reparative therapy deals with far deeper emotional needs than just the person's sexuality; it only tells school officials across the country that any such efforts are harmful to students and stresses that schools must be "open and accepting so these young people will feel comfortable sharing their thoughts and concerns." And, of course, it points out that there can be legal consequences for the school that might mention or recommend "these treatments."*

At no time does Just the Facts talk about youth that have successfully left the homosexual lifestyle or mention that these youth are often harassed by homosexuals or suggest that gay youth be "tolerant" of those who have left that lifestyle. Instead, the brochure does nothing but denigrate the programs with which it disagrees![6] Wouldn't the kind and sensitive thing be to explain possible alternatives to youth who may want to change?

The argument here is not with youth who may be homosexual but with the way schools are dealing with this issue. Classrooms are not the place where sexual "identities" should be discussed or promoted. Public funding for public schools should be spent on actually educating children. Protecting all students equally should, of course, be of paramount importance, which means punishing anyone who harms or attempts to harm or harass any student for any reason—not just those that meet certain criteria. Public education should be about education! It is only in the last decade that the agenda of activist legislators and educators has escalated to the point of being able to derail the primary purpose of education. During this same time period academic excellence has plummeted in this country. It is time for the U.S. to return education to its primary purpose. However, in the name of tolerance, our public schools are promoting homosexuality in a variety of ways:[7]

Literature:

• In Massachusetts: Governor Mitt Romney's education department distributed books such as *King and King*, designed to promote acceptance of homosexuality to children as young as kindergarten.

• In California: *Jesse's Dream Skirt*, a story for second and third graders, tells how a little boy dreams of wearing a skirt everywhere he goes. He wears it to school one day and the children laugh. The story ends with all the children in Jesse's class cross-dressing and celebrating.

Days and months designated to celebrate homosexuality: Such days include Gay and Lesbian Pride month, and the annual "Day of Silence" in which students are encouraged not to speak for the entire day, including not participating in classroom discussions. The purpose is to support gays who say they have suffered in silence for so many years by not being able to openly declare their sexuality to the world. Some teachers encourage and participate in this outlandish exercise.

Note: To counter Day of Silence, the Alliance Defense Fund, a pro-family legal firm, now promotes their own "Day of Truth." (For more information, visit dayoftruth.org.)

Speakers: Many schools have assemblies featuring gay speakers.

Proms/dances: Los Angeles and New York school systems sponsor "gay proms" and dances at which even adult homosexuals are invited!

Parades: Boston school officials allow students to attend "gay pride" parades during school time.

Social Studies: Many big-city schools will have lesson plans featuring "famous gays in history." A Los Angeles school actually distributes material claiming Abe Lincoln was a homosexual.

Commissions/Committees: Some states and school districts set up commissions or committees composed of homosexuals to figure out ways to promote homosexuality. San Diego Unified has such a committee, and in Massachusetts, Governor Mitt Romney funded the "Commission on Gay and Lesbian Affairs" for this purpose.

Gay Schools: Some states have publicly-funded gay schools, which cater to gay, lesbian and bisexual youth. Such schools exist in Los Angeles[8] and New York.[9]

"Fistgate": Massachusetts made national news in 2000 when the Gay, Lesbian, & Straight Education Network (GLSEN) sponsored an event in which children as young as fourteen attended. The conference is now referred to as "Fistgate," because it contained references to a homosexual practice called "fisting."

The first two stories in this chapter were submitted by Brian Camenker of MassResistance, Massachusetts' leading pro-family organization. Due to the fact that at the time this book went to press both of these cases were still in litigation, the families involved were unable to submit the stories themselves.

Promoting Homosexuality to Kindergartners

In January 2005, David and Tonia Parker of Lexington, Massachusetts, a Boston suburb, got the surprise of their lives. Their five-year-old son brought home a book from his kindergarten class portraying homosexual relationships as a reading assignment. Titled *Who's in a Family*, it's a picture book for young children that regards a homosexual "family" structure as a morally equal alternative to other family constructs.

Who's in a Family was written specifically to indoctrinate young children. In an interview with National Public Radio, the author of the book, Robert Skutch, said, "The whole purpose of the book was to get the subject [of same-sex parent households] out into the minds and the awareness of children before they are old enough to have been convinced that there's another way of looking at life."[10]

The Parkers were upset and distraught, because they were not informed beforehand that the book would be presented to their son. They immediately complained to the kindergarten teacher and principal. The principal informed them that the school had no obligation to inform parents when it discussed homosexual families and would continue the practice. (Although the state Parental Notification Law includes "human sexuality issues," the school denied that the law applied in this situation, because, they claimed, homosexuality is not a human sexuality issue but a "civil rights" issue.)

Over the next few months, through e-mails and face-to-face meetings, the Parkers continued to request that they be notified when these subjects are brought up with their son and that he be allowed to opt out of discussions. The school continued to deny the requests. A meeting was scheduled April 27, 2005, with David

Parker, the principal, and the school system's director of education to discuss the Parkers' concerns.

At that meeting, David Parker told them that he felt very strongly about his right to be notified and to opt his son out of such discussions. Parker said he would not leave the meeting until they could come to a satisfactory agreement. At first, the director of education agreed to Parker's demands. But the superintendent, via telephone, overruled him. Parker refused to leave the meeting. So the officials called the police.

The Lexington police came to the school, handcuffed Parker, arrested him, and put him in jail overnight. The next day, Parker entered the district court in handcuffs. He was charged with trespassing and banned from all school property.

(Interestingly, several major *pro bono* national conservative legal firms actually turned down Parker's original request for legal help, forcing him to pay his legal expenses out of his own pocket.)

The case became an immediate media sensation, covered in newspapers, radio, and TV, not only in the metropolitan Boston area, but across the country. At one point, *ABC World News Tonight* did a segment on it, and Parker was interviewed on Fox News' *The O'Reilly Factor*, National Public Radio, and others.

But the school became more hardened on the issue. School officials notified the community that they would continue to introduce homosexual-related topics in the elementary schools and that they had no intention of informing parents or allowing them to opt out their children. The new Superintendent of Schools also went on radio shows and even a national television show saying that he supported the decisions and portraying the Parkers as out of the mainstream and even fringe. At this point, the Boston homosexual community became active against the Parkers. The Boston-based homosexual newspaper published vicious attack articles against them. Local homosexual activists organized street demonstrations against the Parkers in Lexington and conducted a letter-writing campaign in the local newspaper. There was a concerted effort to intimidate the Parkers and anyone who agreed with them.

At one demonstration, in which two members of the elected school committee participated along with a Unitarian minister and local liberal activists, it became so hostile that the police would not let Parker come near it out of fear for his personal safety.

Eventually, the trespassing charge against David Parker was dropped and the ban against going on school property was lifted, but only after great personal legal expense. The school continued pushing homosexuality and related issues in the elementary school with great vigor.

In early 2006, at the same elementary school, a second-grade teacher read *King and King*, a book about homosexual romance and "marriage," to her class. Parents Rob and Robin Wirthlin had a similar experience as the Parkers—their son came home talking about men marrying each other. The Wirthlins had no idea what was going on. However, when they complained to the teacher, they were told they had no right to be informed or opt their son out of the class. Like the Parkers, they were furious.

In April 2006, the Parkers and Wirthlins jointly filed a federal civil rights lawsuit against the school system, the town of Lexington, and the individual officials involved. They sought the right to be informed and to opt their elementary-school-aged children out of such programs and discussions. The school system hired a prominent Boston law firm and teamed up with the Massachusetts ACLU, various local and national homosexual activist groups, and others to fight the lawsuit as vigorously as they could and immediately tried to get the case dismissed.

However, the Parkers were determined to stand up for their rights and not back down. The case began to wind its way through the court system. David Parker hired a high-powered Boston legal firm that had experience with First Amendment cases and was sufficiently aggressive to stand up to the axis of power lined up against him. By early 2007, the Parkers had personally paid over $250,000 in legal fees—their life savings. (The Parkers are paying the entire cost themselves.)

It's been a long, rough battle. In February 2007, a liberal federal judge, Mark Wolf, ruled to dismiss the case. Wolf wrote that he believed that in today's world, teaching homosexuality was a school's right and duty—to instill "good citizenship"—whether the parents objected or not. The Parkers appealed, and in December 2007, the case was heard before a federal appeals court. Parker is determined to fight to bring this case to trial, and his lawyers say they're committed to going to the U.S. Supreme Court if necessary.

But it's taking a toll on the Parkers both financially and emotionally. In twenty-first-century America, this is the kind of insanity that happens while everyone else looks the other way. Meanwhile, the school system has pushed the envelope on homosexuality even further in its elementary school, bringing in more aggressive and explicit programs. And the Parkers still refuse to back down. (A chronicle of the entire incident and the ensuing court appearances can be found at www.MassResistance.org.)

Brian Camenker, MassResistance

The Laramie Project

Amy Contrada works for MassResistance, which is well known by Massachusetts' homosexual activist community due to its efforts in fighting pro-homosexual legislation. Amy believes the following incident involving her daughter was precipitated as a result of her job.

Amy's daughter, Claudia, is a seventeen-year-old special-needs student with psychological and emotional issues, as well as learning disabilities. However, she is a very talented singer and actress with a beautiful voice and a fantastic memory for lines and lyrics. She has won awards for her acting and her therapists encouraged Claudia's participation in the school's drama program for the positive effect acting has on her specific needs.

The local high school decided to have its drama club perform *The Laramie Project*, a pro-homosexual, anti-Christian play filled with profanity and violence. During the summer, Mrs. Contrada met with the drama board to beg them to choose a different play, citing Claudia's vulnerabilities. She was coolly rebuffed and the board refused to consider a different play. Amy, along with other parents, also met with the high school principal that summer but their concerns were dismissed, including Amy's deeply personal appeal with regards to her daughter.

156

Finally, given the extreme importance of acting for Claudia, her father reluctantly allowed her to be in the play. The family believed the school had placed them in a no-win situation.

As the tryouts for *The Laramie Project* began, the drama director gave students reading material that normalized homosexuality and demonized those with traditional values as "haters."

Claudia started coming home with stories about how her mother was considered "crazy," a "homophobe," and even "scary," by the other students. "Everybody in the cast knows I have a crazy, bigoted, homophobic mother," she said. Over time, these messages seemed to intensify. Then Claudia's language around the home became aggressive and vulgar just like it is in the play.

Two other issues were also of concern: 1) the drama department sent e-mails to everyone connected to the play with both the students' and parents' e-mail addresses clearly listed. When Amy requested that the addresses be "blind-copied" due to safety concerns, her request and concerns were ignored. 2) Shortly after the cast for the play was announced a twenty-four-year-old homosexual activist from Boston posted a "news item" on his Web site titled "Anti-gay zealot's daughter to star in *Laramie Project*." It was a long and vicious tirade against Amy, which he sent far and wide. The following is a portion of that posting:

> ...Contrada's daughter is clearly a brave, compassionate, and inspiring young woman who is willing to lead in the face of adversity—in this case coming from her own mother...we have seen how [Amy] Contrada's style of homophobic religious terrorism can painfully tear families apart...

> [A comment from another blogger on the site said:] "I can't even imagine the horror of living in a house with that bitch Amy. Poor, poor kid."

Several months before, in May 2007, after Amy had reported on a Youth Pride event as part of her job, the Web site carried the announcement: "Rumor has it that Amy's daughter is supportive of GSA's! We're on it!" The question, of course, is how did the adult male who authored the Web site know about Claudia? Did he have contacts at the school? Had he been forwarded one of the e-mails from the drama department with Claudia's and Amy's e-mail addresses clearly listed?

At the same time, "gay/trans" students at the school were becoming a part of Claudia's short list of personal friends. Also at that time, the Contradas' college-age son began receiving harassing messages from the twenty-four-year-old adult via Facebook. Amy's son ignored the messages but warned his family about the harassment.

A few days after the September posting, a Boston homosexual newspaper published an article about Claudia. The article quoted from the Web site and spread Claudia's name throughout the homosexual community. Another homosexual newspaper, also distributed in Boston, published an article about Claudia, gloating over her "lesbianism."

A chain of local supermarkets was selling tickets for *The Laramie Project* and when customers complained, the company's spokesperson responded by saying that Amy's daughter Claudia was in the play, so that made it okay. (One wonders how the spokesperson knew what was circulating on gay activists' sites.) When Amy confronted the woman on the phone, she was forced to apologize.

Amy has since learned that about this same time, the twenty-four-year-old started befriending Claudia; first via e-mail, then by telephone. He offered to be her "ally" in her struggle against her mother. He persuaded Claudia to admit him as a "friend" on her Facebook account.[11]

Judging from her e-mails at that time, Claudia was very confused but was relishing the positive attention, which she had rarely received from her peers at school. Besides her communication with the older male, Claudia's name was turning up on various homosexual Web sites. Her drama club even began to consider her "cool." Claudia clearly felt special. But her parents also started noticing erratic behavior.

In October, the high school held a school-wide "coming-out day." The message to kids was that "coming out" as a homosexual or transgender was very progressive. The next week was highlighted as a homosexual/transgender "ally" week and the school tied it in with the performance of *The Laramie Project* play.

Claudia was riding high. She suddenly decided to tell everyone that she was "really a lesbian." All of this was clearly known by Claudia's school counselor—who was also the school's gay-straight alliance club advisor and whose office was plastered with pro-gay stickers, a rainbow flag, "coming-out" pamphlets, rainbow "Ally" wristbands, and books such as *Queering Elementary Education*—and other school officials. But to them, this apparently was a "positive" move for Claudia and they never communicated anything about it to her parents.

Claudia is not a lesbian. Her bedroom walls are covered with pictures of boys. Claudia has always had crushes on boys—never girls. Her personal writings and drama skits (from her heart) confirm her heterosexual loves. So when Claudia told Amy and her husband that she was a lesbian, they basically ignored it as another silly idea that Claudia got from the latest school lunacy. They just linked it to the fact that she had always been rejected by the boys she liked. Claudia does not really understand what it means to be a "lesbian." (What kids really do, since confusion at that age is not all that unusual?) For her, it was about getting attention.

Claudia's parents, however, did worry that she was starting to hang out with some kids who appeared to have their own emotional problems stemming from "gay" and "transgender" identity issues.

Claudia's "coming out" was exactly what her new Facebook "friend" was looking for. It is unclear whether he found out from other kids he was in contact with, or whether Claudia mentioned it. But he moved pretty fast. He persuaded her to do an "exclusive interview" with him and promptly published it on his Web site. He encouraged his friends to add comments and then blasted it out to the homosexual community everywhere he could.

Almost immediately, dozens of homosexual Web sites and blogs across the country picked up on the new posting and commented on it. Some of the stuff they printed was pretty vile. Homosexual activists began to contact Claudia via her Facebook account. As for Claudia, she couldn't believe how "popular" she was becoming. She was excited that she was now "famous." Then the big guns began to hit on her.

Claudia began receiving numerous requests and encouragement from homosexual activists and reporters. A locally known lesbian activist asked Claudia to be a featured speaker at the Youth Pride 2008 event; a reporter for a homosexual magazine that has published articles on incestuous sex between brothers, the Pope's penis, and pornographic ads asked for an interview. Another message, from a representative from a well-known university saying she had read Claudia's interview on the Web, asked her to consider attending that college because "we have a vibrant queer community and always have room for more activists." Is this what the homosexual clubs at colleges spend their time doing? Trolling the Web sites to connect with high school kids?

At the same time all this was going on, the older male who started it all wrote to Claudia and said that while he knew lots of people would be trying to contact her that he wouldn't give out her contact information. He said, "I will not give them any contact information. They will have to search you and find you and friend you [Facebook lingo] the same way I did."

Even a reporter from the local newspaper who said she had read Claudia's story on another popular homosexual Web site tried to get an interview with her by using Claudia's Facebook account. The reporter said that in order to respect Claudia's privacy she was willing to meet with her without her parents' knowledge. Unbelievable. (Claudia is a minor and her parents only found out about this by accident!)

Claudia wrote in her Live Journal that was sent to friends: "I'm famous. I'm famous," and then listed all the places where she was being discussed and the requests for interviews. Claudia was excited. She only knew that all these people were paying attention to her. She didn't understand that they were cruelly using her; that they wanted to hurt her family. How could she know?

One friend replied: "I'm proud of you. I'm sorry your mom isn't more understanding...break a leg."

This whole experience would be extremely difficult for any child. But for Claudia, and her family, it was particularly traumatic. After the initial burst of excitement, Claudia was very confused and continued to crave attention. She began spending more of her time with an unstable group of risk-taking "gay/trans" kids. Claudia, now unable to function normally, became more and more involved in destructive, unhealthy behaviors and could not focus on her schoolwork. But rather than being understanding of Claudia's special needs as described earlier, school officials continued their tacit support for Claudia's "progressiveness" and continued their outright hostility toward her parents' concerns. Claudia's pre-existing issues were exacerbated to such a degree that her health professionals and parents finally concluded that for her overall well-being, Claudia needed to leave the high school.

The attacks on the family continued after Claudia went to a private boarding school. A radical homosexual set up a Facebook page attacking Claudia's mother. They called it "In Defense of Claudia Contrada and Her Freedom to Love." Almost a hundred students from the high school and homosexual activists from all over hysterically claimed that Amy was an "abusive" mother who was "destroying her daughter's life." One comment said, "She deserves to burn in hell." The comments posted by friends who were more closely involved with Claudia and which came closer to expressing the truth were instantly removed from the site. The Contradas finally had to threaten legal action against school officials if they didn't have the site taken down immediately. They pointed out that the site was "bullying" one of their students by attacking and "bullying" her mother. The site was down within twenty-four hours of the family's formal complaint.

Some homosexual activists cruelly use other people's children, leaving parents to pick up the pieces. This story isn't all that unique. We've observed for years that some homosexual activists first push their way into schools, then seek out the most vulnerable and emotionally unstable kids, befriend them, give them positive attention, and persuade them to "come out" and adopt a "gay" identity. It happens in schools across the nation. Far too many schools do nothing to prevent it. Whether they are intimidated by fear of lawsuits or being labeled as homophobes, the growing trend is to allow innocent children to be used. This is possibly happening to your own children or their friends. Our hope in writing this is to alert parents that this could be happen-

161

ing in your child's school and to encourage you to talk with your children. Be aware and alert.

Brian Camenker, MassResistance

"Coming Out" Day

My daughter's high school sponsored a "Coming Out Gay & Lesbian Students" panel in the library. I attended the presentation with my daughter and observed the following:

The "permission slip" was not a request for permission. It was a slip that was to be signed if the parents did not want their child to attend the homosexual panel presentation. The information given to parents was neither complete nor accurate. The form stated that the students would have the chance to hear a "...lecture by students from [the school] on gay and lesbian issues."

On the day of the presentation, a teacher stood at the door of the library and asked the more than 150 students who came in, "Do you have your parent's permission?" Naturally, each student said, "Yes," and was then admitted. Many of them had no written authorization whatsoever. Apparently, the school didn't really care whether they had permission or not. The students I saw entering were not stopped or turned away for not having permission slips. In fact, the chairman of the event acknowledged the confusion caused by sending the forms home and announced that those without permission could leave. This created an embarrassing dilemma for some students.

When the panel entered the room, I was very surprised. The event had been billed as a "student" panel discussing homosexuality. There was only one "student" in the group, however; the others were adult gay activists, including a sixty-five-year-old grandmother.

Discussion items included: 1) Places students could go to meet homosexuals in the area, and 2) the "wonderful" and "fulfilling" homosexual lifestyle. ("It is the only thing that has brought fulfillment into my life," one of the panelists claimed. The school said the purpose of holding the panel was "not to promote or condemn" the homosexual lifestyle, yet it was being painted as "courageous, admired," and "wonderful.") 3) The students were told that 10 percent of all students at their high school were homosexuals (over two hundred) and that there was nothing they could ever do to change it. Finally, 4) the sixty-five-year-old gay activist informed the students that she preferred younger women.

The entire presentation consisted of one-sided misinformation. No one represented an opposing view, or mentioned that the viewpoints presented were the opinions of the panel members only. Instead, the school presented the panelists as "experts," and allowed their statements to stand as documented and substantiated fact when they were neither. For example, the 10 percent figure is an urban myth; every reputable study shows that the actual percentage of homosexuals in America is between 2 and 4 percent.

The event created a huge controversy in the school and in the local newspapers. Parents were upset that they were paying for presentations with which they disagree and school representatives appeared to exhibit only arrogance and disdain toward parents' concerns. Schools are not supposed to promote behavior which could have deadly consequences. Homosexuals have much higher rates of sexually transmitted diseases, sterility due to increased sexual behavior, and a higher risk of death due to the transmission of HIV/AIDS.

After the panel discussion, my daughter heard teachers speaking about the "homophobic" pastor across the street, who had published an editorial in the newspaper about the "goings on" at the school. In one of her classes, my daughter defended me publicly and subsequently received an unsatisfactory grade in citizenship. She had previously received three excellent marks and one satisfactory mark that same quarter. This turnabout seemed highly unusual to me; I definitely believe she was discriminated against.

Since schools are so adamant about keeping religion and education separate, shouldn't they follow their own dictates and leave the teaching of morals, values, and personal beliefs to parents and churches? Shouldn't the role of education be to educate students in academics? No wonder today's students suffer academically; too much time is spent exploring areas that have nothing to do with concrete, measurable knowledge such as science, math, history, etc.

Rick Bloom

Gay Propaganda Invades Special Ed.

You can imagine how surprised we were when a gay/lesbian panel addressed a group of fourth-, fifth-, and sixth-grade special education students and a group of fourth-grade regular education students at our local elementary school. This panel consisted of the school district's marriage and family counselor (a gay man), a lesbian high school student (as she described herself), a black bisexual (as he described himself), and a male college student. Because the special education teacher had been called "faggot" by some of the students, the principal, a self-proclaimed lesbian, had arranged for the panel to deal with the issue of "name calling." She, too, was a panel member.

When the fourth-grade regular education teacher raised objections about the appropriateness of the panel and their presentation, the principal told her that the superintendent approved. When I voiced my objections, I was also told—twice—that the superintendent approved. The second time, I asked which superintendent, but the principal declined to identify anyone.

I was concerned for the students too young to comprehend sexuality in general, let alone the particulars about homosexuality. Children that age don't even have hair under their arms; they are about the wonderful business of childhood—or should be. I was also concerned for the parents not informed of the true nature of the discussion, who had no opportunity to preview materials to be presented, who were not given the names and qualifications of the panel members addressing their children, and finally—and most importantly— did not have an opportunity to refuse permission for their children to participate. Parents were not told that their children would be a captive audience for a panel chosen for its sexual orientation and whose topic would be how the sexual orientation of its members affected their lives and their choices.

One parent later remarked, "My child belongs to me, not to her (the principal). These children belong to us, not to the district." I wondered why the principal proceeded with a presentation that she stated could "blow things wide open." Obviously, her perceived success with a similar panel at another school gave her confidence to repeat it at our school.

The fourth-grade regular education teacher spoke at a staff meeting and expressed her complete surprise over the content of the panel discussion. She stated that she was not prepared for what took place: a description, by the lesbian principal, of homosexual practices such as artificial insemination as a means of procreation, families with "two moms" and "two dads," and expressions of affection between gays. This teacher said she believed the panel members "were seeking 'validation and approval' from these ten-year-olds." The principal did not challenge any of this teacher's observations, perceptions, or statements. In closing, the teacher said that she and the principal had "agreed to disagree."

The faculty meeting did not elicit much discussion on the appropriateness of the panel. Their focus was on: 1) honest and open communication between parents and teachers, and 2) the need to inform parents—staff members who were parents were particularly adamant about this point—regarding classes in sex education or sexual orientation. In the following days, however, there was much discussion about the appropriateness of assembling a sex panel to address the issue of "name-calling." Some of these comments ranged from mild disapproval to total disgust—one teacher called it "stupid."

One individual asked, "If I were called 'straight' in a derogatory manner, would they have assembled a panel of 'straights' to discuss 'straight' sexual practices and lifestyles? What about if I were called 'whore' or 'prostitute'?"

As a parent of four children, ages ten, thirteen, fourteen, and seventeen, and as a teacher and counselor, I say that this presentation was inappropriate for eight-, nine-, and ten-year-olds. I also consulted with other experts, including a black psychologist, a Hispanic psychologist and family therapist, a black social worker, a member of the Gay/Lesbian Lutheran Organization, and a member of the Gay/Lesbian Catholic Organization. All of them felt that this was an inappropriate panel discussion for eight-to-ten-year-old children.

While high school students may need to deal with these issues, they must be handled appropriately and with sensitivity. The coarseness of the two students' presentations, in which the statements "hands on butts" and "f----- lesbian" were made, do not increase understanding, acceptance, or a mature awareness of differences. This panel only served to further confuse many of the students in attendance.

Toni McMickin

The Gay Rights Agenda Takes Over an Entire School District

I have been an active parent and community activist for over thirty-five years. I am involved with an inner-city education commission and other parent/school committees. My three children are graduates of our local school system. I tell you this so you know that I fully understand curricula and school policies.

In the mid 1980s, our district adopted a pro-homosexual program called Project 10. This curriculum was sponsored by the Homosexual Issues Committee of our local teachers union and has been used as an advocacy for the homosexual agenda, placing children deemed to be "confused" in touch with outside homosexual organizations. Our Project 10 has been used as a model for such advocacy, and the literature actually urges students to "find their lover at the local gay center."

Instead of academic achievement, we have made "sexual diversity" a priority for students. Our district has adopted numerous programs over the years designed to promote the homosexual agenda. Parents' concerns are not considered for discussion unless they support the "educating for diversity" agenda. For example, a document called "District Bulletin No. 36" (procedures for collecting data and reporting hate crimes) is used to compile data on students and "traditional families who do not respect the homosexual family."

At a monthly parents' collaborative meeting in April 1997, a draft proposal of the district's multicultural awareness curriculum was presented. Presentations were made by a member of the division of instructions and the director of a local gay and lesbian organization. The purpose of the meeting was to inform parents and community members about the district's new classroom curriculum. It was clear that with this new curriculum classrooms would be used to teach all students to respect homosexual unions that included two gay men and/or two lesbians as families. The parents in attendance wanted to know how their children could be taught academics instead of homosexual lifestyles. They received no answers from the speakers. However, many parents were reminded that they should be careful, because opposition to the homosexual agenda could be considered a "hate crime." Even history lessons now contain information about "famous gays in history," such as Abraham Lincoln.

Millions of taxpayer dollars have been spent on week-long training conferences for staff development, which include methods and techniques for teaching homosexual tolerance and other non-academic subjects. Sex clinics are now located on some campuses for the purpose of providing condoms and other "how-to" sex information to students. The district even sponsors a "gay prom," and outside homosexual men are allowed to attend. It is no longer necessary for homosexual child molesters to kidnap children; they can attend their local school's gay dance and find minors who have been told that gay sex is great.

Since the district's adoption of a pro-homosexual agenda, the district has experienced a steady increase in criminal child molestation cases. Student safety has become a major concern for parents. Our children are being used as experimental guinea pigs in the promotion of a private nonacademic agenda. Overall student academic achievement in our district ranks below the norm, and many parents are convinced that as long as the current curriculum integrates such an aggressive homosexual agenda, student academic achievement will not improve.

Parents and the community are requesting a review of all district social programs for moral and academic content. We are in a culture war for the minds of our young people.

Clinton Simmons

Using Obscene Literature to Teach "Tolerance"

Please note that this section contains especially graphic homosexual material as an example of what children in a public middle school have been subjected to. If you do not wish to view it, please skip this section and proceed to the beginning of the following chapter.

I am a twenty-year veteran special education teacher in one of the largest school districts in the nation. Since 1992, my district has used its "Gay and Lesbian Pride Month" to promote homosexuality and disparage persons like me opposed to forcing young children to embrace homosexuality and become mindless advocates for homosexual political concerns.

The proverbial "straw" for me came when homosexual staff members at our school distributed a religious brochure entitled, "Is Homosexuality a Sin?" which affirmed homosexual behavior and stated that God approves of gays and lesbians. This brochure grossly misrepresented the Bible and Christianity and promoted hatred of persons like myself who believe that homosexuality is sinful behavior that can be forgiven and overcome by the power of Jesus Christ.

When I expressed my offense regarding this dishonest brochure to our site administrator, I was told that the school district was powerless to suppress the free speech rights of homosexuals. When I questioned my administrator about *my* rights, she consulted with the district's legal staff, and then advised me that I could express my views on a bulletin board as my homosexual colleagues had done.

I then produced two bulletin boards in opposition to the district's view. My boards suggested that tolerance should be a two-way street, that students should be permitted to consider both sides of controversial issues, and that persons could disagree with one another on controversial issues and still learn and work together and even be friends as I am with my homosexual colleagues.

The homosexuals at my school, who had forced their offensive views upon myself and others for five years unabated, had the audacity to complain that they were offended by my views, and I was ordered to immediately remove my bulletin boards.

In 1998, with the help of civil rights attorney Rick Nelson from the Orlando-based American Liberties Institute, I sued the district in federal district court for viewpoint discrimination.

Viewpoint discrimination is a civil rights concept based on the fact that when the government opens its property (such as the public schools' bulletin boards and displays) for speech on a specific subject matter (homosexuality) for a specific time (June) and designates specific speakers (teachers), it cannot ban speech with which it disagrees, as it did in my case.

My attorneys and I presented over seven hundred exhibits to the court that had been used in the district, many of which overtly promoted students engaging in homosexual behavior with each other and with adults.

These materials included sex magazines (with advertisements for pornographic movies and sexual paraphernalia, and personal solicitations), invitations and advertisements for homosexual adult parties and bars, and lists of books containing graphic descriptions of homosexual behavior. (One such book, used frequently in the district, promoted teachers engaging in homosexual behavior with their students. And another, written at about a fourth-grade reading level, advised boys to stimulate their anus and seek an experienced partner for "getting fucked" less painfully.)

There were directions for students to visit adlbooks.com and other such stores, and magazine articles. (One article advocated having sex with persons who are HIV positive, and another exemplified the virtues of, "fuckin' a nigga in his ass.") These are but a small sample from file boxes full of filthy and degrading materials submitted to the court.

The district's defense in this case was that all of these materials were district-approved instructional materials.

Were it not for the harmful nature of the materials and overt bias of the judge, the district's defense in this case would be laughable. If you can imagine a school district claiming that materials which referred to homosexuals as "sadomasochists," "pederasts," "perverts," "fairies," "faggots," "fruits," "cock suckers," and "fudge packers," were intended to dispel name calling. Or that stories which idealize high school boys servicing bath house patrons and contacting adult homosexuals through newspaper solicitations were intended to teach safe sexual behaviors. No reasonable person would believe that the district's materials bore any legitimate pedagogical value.

169

And none but the most calloused would not fear for the children entrusted to the district's care.

The district court judge assigned to our case aided the district with their defense. In fact, at one of our hearings, the judge complained that he was tired of doing the district's work for them. After months of coaching the district and just hours before our trial was set to proceed, the judge issued his decision to deny my right to a trial. Incredibly, he stated that all of the filthy materials that the district had provided were appropriate for teaching tolerance to children.

We appealed the decision to the Ninth Circuit Court of Appeals, which disapproved of our judge's legal rationale, but upheld his ruling in its decision issued on September 7, 2000 (Case #99-56797).

We then turned to the California Supreme Court. However, even though the high court was apprised of the content of the district's materials, which were described in detail and quoted in our submissions, it denied our request to review the lower court's decision.

We then filed a second lawsuit in federal district court using the same filthy materials and were again denied a trial. This time the presiding judge decided, among other things, that public schools cannot be sued for civil rights violations, and that our complaint, which represented over a million people in a class action, was too long and could not possibly be altered to his satisfaction. The Ninth Circuit Court of Appeals upheld his decision and wrote in bold capital letters above its caption that their decision could not ever be published or cited as a precedent.

I wasn't through trying, however. I met with then California Assembly Member Dennis Mountjoy, who used the exhibits as the basis for legislation in January 2002. Once the Democratic majority on the Assembly's Education Committee learned about the nature of our evidence, they quickly curtailed discussion and killed the bill, which simply stated that the promotion of homosexuality in public schools should be prohibited.

My hope is that parents and the public one day become aware of what is being thrust upon innocent and defenseless young children in our government schools. My belief is that parents and taxpayers have the right to know what is taking place, even though the media, public schools, courts, and the legislature strive to suppress such information. I also hope that parents and others armed with this knowledge will stand up and protect our vulnerable children from the homosexual predators who now have unfettered access to them in our public schools.

Rob Downs, Teacher, Los Angeles Unified School District

EDITORS' NOTE: The following excerpts are taken from material produced by the LAUSD's legal staff in response to a federal court order to turn over all items which were on display in its schools for Gay and Lesbian Awareness Month.

In fact, quoting from the LAUSD's Office of General Counsel's memo to all middle and high school principals, the district's counsel wrote: "... a Los Angeles federal court judge ordered the school district to produce by this Friday, July 2nd, all documentation or materials which were posted on school district bulletin boards or displayed in school district display or show case for Gay and Lesbian Awareness Month."[12]

Be advised that the following material is extremely graphic. And while it is a representative sample of what the investigation discovered in the course of the lawsuit, the editors of this book deleted far more graphic material.

The following books are recommended reading for LAUSD students:

> **Young, Gay, and Proud!** In sex there are no rules. One of the great things about being a gay person is that we're not held back by a lot of the limits and fears of heterosexual society. The body is a temple... But it's also a playground. Have a good time, and explore however few or many of the unlimited possibilities for pleasure that you choose... Get to know your body. Use a mirror for all those hard-to-see places... Jerking off is a fun, safe, and healthy way for guys to enjoy our bodies and fantasies... Besides, we can't always find someone else to be with when we're horny!...Gay men can make love in many different ways. Here are just some possibilities: ... Mutual masturbation—that is, holding your own or your friend's penis and pumping up and down, wither together or taking turns, licking each other's bodies, including nipples and penises, sucking each other's testicles and penises, taking care to use a condom or, at the very least, to stop sucking before your partner ejaculates. Then jerk him off until he comes. Do not swallow your partner's semen... Anal intercourse

isn't the only way to enjoy the feelings of your anus. You can use fingers, either your own or someone else's. Try it with yourself at first to get a feel for it. Some people like to use dildos… If you are interested in anal sex, you should always insist on using a condom and water-based lubricant, whether you are the insertive partner…or the person getting fucked. Your first few times having anal sex might be a little hard. You may have to practice a bit before it starts feeling really good… Anal sex is just a matter of becoming familiar with relaxing the muscles around your anus…"[13]

One Teenager in Ten (This story was from a sixteen-year-old girl describing her first encounter with her dance teacher who "brought me out.")

…she slipped the leotards over my shoulders… leaving the costume hanging at the waist with my breasts bare… she licked her index finger and began rubbing my left nipple, making it hard. She did the same with the right one…Then she took a nipple in each hand and rolled them between her fingers…I began sucking her tongue… She moved her hands down to my butt, massaging, and pushing my pelvis into hers… she concentrated on my clitoris with a circular motion, slipping her middle finger between my lips and occasionally into me… She positioned me on the bed, with my head on a pillow and my legs spread as wide as she could get them… she encouraged me to relax… Before long she was getting her face closer to me and kissing me; using her mouth and tongue on my clitoris, giving me a feeling I had never felt before…We continued that night, all weekend and for almost three years until I had to move with my family.[14]

The following books are listed in LAUSD's resource guide, Educating for Diversity:

Know About Gays and Lesbians: Pederasty[15] may even have begun in the Stone Age, stemming from the ancient belief that semen was a powerful life-force. In our society, sex—heterosexual or homosexual—between a teacher and student is generally condemned. But this practice was a normal part of development among Greeks…Transgenerational homosexual activity (that is between males of unequal ages) is known to exist in Africa, South America, New Guinea, and other places. Among the Sambia of New Guinea, boys traditionally entered into prescribed homosexual relationships, which lasted for many years, until they married or became fathers…Plato thought that pederasty between students and teachers could be justified if it helped the learning process... Among those who engaged in homosexual activities were some well-known artists, for example, Leonardo da Vinci and Michelangelo, each of whom took younger lovers. It was customary for many adult males to consider boys interchangeable with women.[16]

Looking at Gay and Lesbian Life characterizes man-boy homosexual behavior as normative in many modern day cultures:

Major aspects of this model of intergenerational male sexuality are evident among the Samuria of Feudal Japan and the Mossi and Azande civilizations of the African Sudan... In addition, up to approximately 1950, the Siwans of the Libyan Desert followed this model...

All men and boys engage in anal intercourse...Prominent Siwan men lend their sons to each other, and they talk about their masculine love affairs. (Ford and Beach, pp.131-2)

When the youth reaches marrying age, he takes a wife and acquires a young male lover of his own. The society of Melanesia... maintains strict rules dictating avoidance between males and females. At early puberty, young males go through secret initiation rites where they are separated from all females for an extended period of time, sometimes for a number of years. Older bachelors train young novices to the ways of the male group, and homosexual relations are essential to this process.

For the Karaki of New Guinea: Bachelors...universally practice sodomy and in the course of his puberty rites each boy is initiated into anal intercourse by the older males. After his first year of playing the passive role he spends the rest of his bachelorhood sodomizing the newly initiated. This practice is believed by the natives to be necessary for the growing boy. (Ford and Beach, p. 312)

... Some societies place less emphasis on anal intercourse and instead focus on oral-genital contact...In Marinnd of Irian Jaya, youths live in forest lodges during the day with other bachelors. At night the young men sleep with older married men.[17]

Numerous magazines on display in the middle and high schools included announcements and invitations in the "personals" section for gay and lesbian encounters. All of the advertisements contained dates, times, locations, and contact information. The ads included information about "live phone sex," sex toys, homosexual sexually oriented businesses, etc. Mr. Downs also detailed how other magazines on display at a middle school carried advertisements for activities such as Outfest (a gay and lesbian pornographic film festival in West Hollywood) and contained information about how gay and lesbian youth could receive free tickets. The magazine also described in graphic detail dozens of pornographic films, many with the descriptors "NUDITY," "SEXUAL SITUATIONS" "GRAPHIC SEX," "EXPLICIT SEX" and "HOMOEROTIC." He said the magazines also contained photographs showing a variety of partially and totally nude homosexuals with some engaged in sexual acts.

But even more astonishing were flyers that openly announced lesbian and gay events. These weren't for teenagers; they were quite clearly geared for adult homosexuals yet were displayed at middle schools and high schools! One such flyer was for lesbian women and said that topics covered would include: What is it we find attractive about women? How important is sex in a relationship? How close are you to living your dreams? Another flyer touted an "HIV and Men's Monthly Dance Party."

Remember, all of these were found on middle and high school campuses.

A student slapped with a bad grade for her father's activism, a bulletin board banned for presenting both sides of an issue, and an appeals court that lauds enticing children to homosexuality with pornographic material demonstrate that tolerance in today's public schools is not a "two-way street."

CHAPTER NINE

CREATING AMERICAN JIHADIS

I T'S HARD TO BELIEVE *that, in the aftermath of the 9/11 catastro- phe, the textbook publishing industry, school boards, and state education agencies seem to be doing everything in their power to promote a false ver- sion of Islam to America's youth. But that's exactly what is happening.*

Part of this is due to the liberal worldview which believes 9/11 oc- curred because of the West's misunderstanding of Islam and that our failure to understand the religion has prompted hatred by Muslims to- ward our country. This misguided view fails to take into account that the Muslim faith has been at war with the West for a thousand years, long before America was founded. Nevertheless, 9/11 gave impetus to the education bureaucracy to change our textbook standards so that we may "better understand Islam."

The problem is that the education establishment is taking sides, and it's not on the side of the West. A concerted effort has been made to re- write our textbooks to reflect the Islamic view of the world and to por- tray the religion in a way that can only be described as propaganda. It is multiculturalism run amok. The effect on today's youth will be to ill- prepare them for the challenges ahead.

An avalanche of pro-Islamic textbooks, programs, speakers, and pro- jects has buried our schools within the last few years. Please understand that this is not about comparative religious studies, which discuss various religions in factual, unbiased terms. As the stories that follow will show, the current trend presents only a favorable view of Islam without discuss- ing the radical jihadists who practice terrorism in the name of Allah. In some schools, children participate in exercises that go far beyond just try- ing to understand about the religion. (There is a clear distinction between teaching "about" a religion and teaching religion.) Instead, in some class-

rooms, when it comes to Islam, this distinction has been ignored and what is being taught is more about indoctrinating students in the Islamic faith while ignoring parents and teachers who complain.

Students have been asked to build model mosques and to pretend they are Muslims for weeks on end by dressing like them, memorizing parts of the Koran, and most disturbingly, reciting Muslim prayers to Allah over and over. As one of the more popular student guides states, "You and your classmates will become Muslims."[1] There is no doubt that if teachers carried out similar exercises using the Christian faith instead, the American Civil Liberties Union (ACLU) would have lawsuits filed that same day!

The textbooks on average devote far more space to Islam than to other faiths. The books rarely mention the Jihadist element in Islam, or mention how the violent Wahabbi sect funds and dominates the faith. The books also fail to mention the dozens of passages in the Koran calling for the elimination of infidels (anyone who is not a Muslim). The Crusades are treated as a purely offensive set of battles when, in fact, they were a reaction to the violent Islamic takeover of previously Christian lands.

Indeed, the failure of the Islamic hordes to conquer Western Europe had a lot to do with their preoccupation with battling the Crusaders. What's shocking is that many of the key battles at Tours, France; Vienna, Austria; and Lepanto are omitted from the texts, even though they were critical in stopping the Muslim conquests from spreading westward, thus preserving Western civilization. Instead of teaching about the heroes of these battles such as Charles "The Hammer" Martel, the texts venerate obscure Muslims who had little bearing on Western achievement.

Had such key battles not been won by the West, it's very likely that America would not have been founded by Puritans and Pilgrims but rather by Muslims. It's doubtful that had that happened, America would ever have had a Constitution, a Bill of Rights, or any semblance of the democracy we now possess.

The texts exaggerate Muslim accomplishments, which compared to the achievements of the West are relatively minor. And nearly all the texts in use today portray Islam as a religion tolerant of other faiths, a falsehood easily confirmed by religious freedom and human rights groups. Indeed, of the forty-one Islamic countries in existence today, freedom of religion is found in only four, and even in those countries it *is very tenuous. In most Islamic countries today, Christians and Jews face persecution and death because of their faith.*

Yes, some Muslims refuse to subscribe to violent, pro-Jihad, anti-democratic views, but textbooks portray this group as the controlling group within the Muslim faith when, in fact, radical Muslims control nearly all the major mosques, schools, and foundations in the Islamic world. "Moderate" Muslims are powerless, yet textbooks portray them as the controlling faction.

The treatment of Israel in our schools' textbooks is also deceitful—no surprise given the anti-Semitism rampant among the Middle East "experts" and consultants often used by publishers. Jews are often portrayed as "occupiers" of Israel even though they have had a presence there for thousands of years. Israel is usually portrayed in negative terms while Palestinian propaganda about their fairly new movement is treated as the whole truth.

Apparently, when it comes to the Middle East and Islam, U.S. schools have decided it is more important not to "offend" certain classes of people than to tell students the truth. How did all this happen? Well, to begin with, a powerful, pro-Islamic lobby now exists in the United States. One of the most prominent lobbies is the Council on American-Islamic Relations (CAIR). In a report on terrorism, the Washington Times reported that "CAIR is among several hundred Muslim groups listed as unindicted co-conspirators in a recent federal terrorism trial in Dallas, which linked CAIR to the Hamas terrorist group."[2]

One CAIR critic, Andrew Whitehead, the director of Anti-CAIR (ACAIR), was sued by CAIR for statements claiming that CAIR has direct links to HAMAS. CAIR cited five statements listed on Anti-CAIR's Web site. The lawsuit was dismissed "with prejudice"—meaning the judge considered the merits of the case—and the statements still appear on the Anti-CAIR Web site.

While CAIR has used its power to influence government policy, another Islamic group, the Council on Islamic Education (CIE), focuses exclusively on influencing textbooks. CIE also espouses an anti-West, anti-Israel viewpoint. Indeed, it has been reported that CIE's board members have made false statements such as "American children need to know that genocide was part of the birth of this nation" and have boasted that its efforts to influence textbooks is the equivalent of waging a *"bloodless" revolution.*[3] *Textbook publishers such as Houghton Mifflin, Teachers Curriculum Institute, Scott Foresman, Glencoe, and Prentice Hall openly list CIE as an organization with which they consult when writing sections on Islam.*[4]

As the American Textbook Council has written in a report, "Islam and the Textbooks," CIE "demands 'ground rules upon which interaction with publishers can take place.' [CIE] warns that it may 'decline requests for reviewing published materials, unless a substantial and substantive revision is planned by the publisher.' For more than a decade, history textbook editors have done the Council's bidding, and as a result history textbooks accommodate Islam on terms that Islamists demand."[5]

Moreover, textbook publishers often contract radical professors from American universities to write their books. Many of these professors are clearly anti-West and are notorious pro-terrorist apologists—such as Susan Douglass, who once praised Pakistan's Taliban-controlled madrassas *as "proud symbols of learning" even though they do not allow girls to attend.*[6]

But the ultimate responsibility for the reckless adoption of propaganda-tainted textbooks lies with our elected authorities. All states have an educational body tasked with selecting texts to place on an approved list from which all school districts then choose. These agencies have allowed themselves to be bullied by Islamic pressure groups. Depending on the state, most of the people who run these agencies are appointed by the governor, legislature, or the state Department of Education. If they are not able to resist such pressure campaigns, then the elected officials who appointed these people need to hear about it.

Last but not least, school boards bear responsibility for the books they select. In most states, school boards have a wide selection of social studies texts so they often have the option of avoiding the worst texts. Moreover, most states also allow schools to select textbooks not on the approved list, with the catch that if they choose a non-approved book, they must pay for it out of their general budget. Far too often, however, school boards hire "Multicultural Trainers"—who sometimes are anti-American and anti-Israel—to advise them on selecting textbooks. This practice needs to stop, and school board members obsessed with promoting multiculturalism over the truth should be removed.

School officials will not inform parents about the content of these texts, so parents are on their own to review them. Fortunately, there are online resources that can help parents ascertain the nature of the books to which their children are exposed, and these resources are listed in the Appendices.

Praying to Mecca in a Public School

It was a normal day, like any other day as a teacher. I arrived at the school on March 8, 2007, to fulfill my substitute assignment. The elementary school was a non-private, non-charter, public school, and the class that I subbed was a segregated seventh- and eighth-grade combination class of Muslim females in the Arabic Immersion Program (this was not disclosed to me prior to my arrival, nor was it included in my sub details). Upon previewing the lesson plans, I came across something that was not familiar to me in my career. It was so unfamiliar; I was not quite sure how to react to it. As I read the lesson plans that the teacher had left for me, I noticed it said the word "Pray." It stated "From 1:00-2:00 the students will pray for about an hour, the teacher's aide will come in and lead this."

I also noticed the American flag was rolled up (as if never acknowledged) and put in the corner with thick and apparent, long-accruing dust on it. The teacher had come in before school and I had asked him about the word "pray." I asked him if it was a typo and was it supposed to say "play." He told me, "No, the students pray." I believe that he noticed the look of confusion, intimidation, and worry on my face—as if to say, "How will I be able to lead this prayer to Mecca?" He told me, "Don't worry, the teacher's aide comes in to pray with them every day." He had disclosed to me that he is a Muslim awaiting his name to be changed and the aide is also a Muslim female. There are two other Muslim employees who assist this program.

For the most part, it was a typical day teaching the core subjects: social studies/geography, language arts, physical education, and mathematics. During my prep period, the students studied Arabic for about an hour. This was ironic because when a teacher has a prep period, no students in the class receive any instruction. Upon my return, the Arabic teacher was completing the Arabic-instruction time, and I resumed teaching the standard curriculum.

Around 1:00 p.m., the aide came in per the teacher's directions. The students astonished me by their reaction to the prayer time to Mecca. Without direction and without a cue from anyone, the children closed the windows, drew the blinds, and proceeded to roll out their Muslim mats for prayer to Mecca. There was religiosity, tradition, and custom in the students' reaction when their instructor entered the room at the designated time for prayer. I left at this point, because I felt intimidated and uncomfortable.

Upon returning approximately forty to forty-five minutes later, the students had to let me in because the door was locked. They were opening the blinds and windows. I resumed with my teaching plans for the remainder of the day.

Following protocol, I notified the principal about the constitutionality of prayer during instructional time and the flag being rolled up and "thrown" in the corner. She indicated to me that, "They pray during their recess time, and I will look into the flag: I did not notice." I explained to her that the students already had their lunch and their recess. She continually persisted that, "It was done during their break, and it was legal; we have to teach religious standards." I told her it is legal for students to pray on their own volition, not during curriculum time and when led or encouraged by a district employee. I stated, "Children don't close the blinds and windows for a typical break or recess."

The principal told me, "It is supposed to say fifteen minutes; I will see that the plans are changed." I asked her, "I noticed that the population at the school is not 100 percent Muslim, have you notified the parents of the goings-on here?" She told me, "I do not have to because there are two separate programs, one for Muslims and one for the other students." I asked her, "Who authorized this prayer?" She told me, "It was a negotiation with the school, because it's an Arabic Immersion Program." The principal told me the students came from a failing charter school in Los Angeles and were "re-routed to San Diego." She indicated that they began "setting-up" at the school.

I notified the board of education about my concerns, and they advised me to contact the superintendent. It took several weeks, but when I did hear back, he seemed unaware and said, "I will look into it." I attended a board meeting to voice my concerns and to encourage the board to investigate the following issues: Was the program approved by the board? If so, when was it approved? How was it funded? Who was assigned to monitor the program? How could the board establish adequate and consistent monitoring? And, finally, how was the public being informed? I was told I would be contacted after the investigation. I was never contacted, and as far as I know, none of the issues were investigated.

The representative from the district explained in an e-mail that the students were from a charter school in Los Angeles. Yet state law requires charter schools to be chartered by the district in which they are located. Since this school was chartered in Los Angeles but located in San Diego, it did not appear to be an authorized school operation. It was explained that all this occurred quite close to the opening of the current school year, so the district wasn't able to charter the school locally. Thus, officials placed the students into this particular school, which serves as an overflow school, and "they began setting up there." It was also disclosed that the district received $405,000 for the Arabic Immersion Program.

I looked into the district's explanation of the charter school, and I spoke with the head of Los Angeles Unified's charter school division, who informed me that no students had been relocated to San Diego and that there was no such charter school that had failed. This just made me question who was monitoring what? I kept asking myself, why is everything so skewed if this Arabic program is law-abiding and there is nothing to hide?

Disguised as Arabic instruction, religious and political indoctrination is invading public schools, and from what I am now finding out from other sources, it appears to be influencing curriculum all over the country. Muslims learn Arabic in order to read the Koran according to Allah's call. Islam is not just a religion; it has a political angle. I wonder what is going on behind closed doors at this school or behind other doors in our children's schools.

I don't deem it the public's responsibility to pay for such luxuries as four Muslim teachers to teach Islamic doctrine or protocol or to learn Arabic to read the Koran. Are Christians being taught Greek or Aramaic to read the New Testament? Are Jewish children being taught Hebrew to read the Torah? This is not an issue of fairness, justice, bias, or even freedom of religion, but rather upholding our country's values and beliefs. For far too long, it seems to me, the freedoms we enjoy in this nation have been taken advantage of by certain groups in order to change our way of life.

But freedom also means that we respect our laws, and if it's illegal to have teacher-led prayer for Christians and for Christians to pray during regular class time, then it's illegal for all other faiths as well. Why do we lean over backwards to accommodate one particular faith in a way that we would never do for Christianity—the majority religion of America—or for any other faith?

My concerns were brought to the attention of the public, thanks to talk radio, but one should not have to create a media scene to force our public schools to follow the law. As a result of all the publicity this controversy created, the superintendent has since ordered staff to discontinue any prayer during instructional time and has discontinued segregated classes at the school.

Mary-Frances Stephens

History Alive! Medieval World

In November 2007, I caught a segment on Fox News one evening that piqued my interest. Sean Hannity was reporting on parents complaining about Islamic content in a middle school history textbook. He commented that in a Lodi, California, public school you can't mention Christmas, but you could teach Islam. At the center of the controversy was *History Alive! Medieval World* (HAMW), the book my own son was using in his seventh-grade history class at the public middle school he attends.

Until I saw a picture of the book on TV, I have to admit I hadn't paid much attention to it. I was aware that California seventh-grade educational standards called for analyzing "the geographic, political, economic, religious, and social structures of the civilizations of Islam in the Middle Ages."[7] But I also knew that other religions, including Christianity, Judaism, Hinduism, and Buddhism, are studied in the sixth grade. Although it did occur to me that there seems to be a disproportionate emphasis on Islam, I was skeptical that a textbook approved by the state of California for use in public school class-rooms would actually teach religion (as opposed to teaching about religion in a historical context).

Because I wanted to see for myself what the brouhaha was all about, I asked my son if I could see his copy of HAMW. After poring over the chapters about Islam for the next few hours, I was shocked. I not only agreed that HAMW includes religious content that has no place in a public school, but thought the book was even more inappropriate than portrayed on Fox News. Not only did the book speak of angels and prophecies and praying with prophets in caves, but it contained inaccurate information, as well as insidious anti-Semitic content.

Some chapters had little to do with presenting historical fact and seemed to propagandize present day political issues. For example, the chapter titled "Muhammad's Teaching Meets with Resistance" suddenly shifts from the year 619 to end with a remark that "to this day Jerusalem is a holy city for Muslims." (Not only is this comment out of context, but it follows a passage that sounds like something from the Koran: "The horse then guided Muhammad through the seven levels of heaven, and Muhammad met Allah."). [8]

Later that night, after doing research on the Internet about other complaints about HAMW, I sent an e-mail to the principal, my son's history teacher, the school district superintendent, and school board trustees, with a link to an article about HAMW having been withdrawn in Scottsdale, Arizona in 2005. I told them, "I was pretty surprised that I agree that (HAMW) does indeed include what I believe to be inappropriate religious content that has no place in a public school." I said that I was considering asking the school district to use a different textbook, and I asked to schedule time to discuss this further.

The next day, I sent out another message clarifying that, "I understand that studying about Islam is part of the state standards for history. That is not my concern. I believe that *History Alive!* not only contains explicitly religious content, but material that is biased and inaccurate."

The principal never responded, even to date. However the superintendent called to schedule an appointment, so I sent her a letter in preparation for our meeting in early December, which stated in part:

> While the seventh grade California standards call for teaching *about* Islam, *History Alive!* teaches Islam in a religious manner. For example, describing *jihad* as, "the human struggle to overcome difficulties and do things that would be pleasing to God," and discussing *hadiths* which instruct Muslims how to fulfill a *jihad*, appears to be describing how to be a good Muslim rather than describing the relevance of *jihad* to the expansion of Muslim rule through military conquests, which is part of the actual standard.
>
> ...There are sections of the text that portray Jews negatively when compared to Muslims. For example, in reference to Jews and the Crusades, Jewish people are described as "killing their children" and refusing to "give up" their religion, while Muslims are portrayed as being willing to "give their lives" and "protect" their families and their religion.
>
> *History Alive!* often references history from a religious perspective, e.g., from revelations to Muhammad from the angel Gabriel. It would be entirely unacceptable if information about other religions was similarly presented, e.g., the words of Jesus from the Sermon on the Mount, or what God said to Moses in the Burning Bush.

Although the superintendent initially seemed responsive, my meeting with her was frustrating. A school board trustee who also attended tried to assure me that she was attempting to understand my complaint. However, the superintendent made several offensive comments to me. When I tried to discuss my concerns about some of the content in HAMW—and the confusion it might cause for a twelve-year-old studying for his *bar mitzvah*—she told me, "There are Jews that don't feel the way you do."

I later got an e-mail from my son's history teacher, who offered to let my son use another text for some of the chapters on Islam. However, the teacher emphatically stated that he "cannot unilaterally decide to skip certain standards because some parents don't feel they're appropriate." He said, "I am not willing to design an alternative curriculum...for the entire year." I realized that he not only misunderstood my concerns when he told me he thought I was saying that "students should not learn about Islam at all," but that he believed I was preventing my own son from being properly "educated."

He also wrote:

> If there are a few sections or chapters of the book that you don't want him to learn about, I can provide alternative assignments at those times... It is simply impossible to teach effectively about world history without addressing the major religions of the cultures the course covers. Since the beliefs and practices of a religion strongly affect a region's history, it is essential to know what the key beliefs are. In fact, I believe that you cannot call yourself an educated person if you do not know at least something about each of the world's major religions.

The teacher also contacted a representative of TCI, the publisher of HAMW, and then told me that he assigned *Across the Centuries* for my son to use for chapters on Islam. (Note: It has come to my attention that *Across the Centuries* has also been criticized for its Islamic content. I personally feel that ATC is not nearly as problematic as HAMW. After reviewing the chapters on Islam, I told the teacher that it was acceptable for my son to use it.)

Following are excerpts from my response addressing both the teacher's and TCI's e-mails:

> ...N. has not addressed my primary complaint, i.e., that rather than teaching about Islam and the spread of Islam in the context of history per California standards, *History Alive!* contains overtly religious content inappropriate for a public school setting.

> ...Students in public school history classes should not be studying about the [Koran] and the Pillars of Faith in depth, any more than they should study the Torah and the Ten Commandments. Nor should they be asked theological questions, e.g., to comparing Allah to the God of the Jews and the Christians. It is just as inappropriate to ask public school students about God, angels and judgment from a Muslim perspective as from a Jewish, Christian or any other religious perspective.

> ...*History Alive!* definitely presents some of the material in a biased manner that portrays Jews negatively compared to Muslims... I also find *History Alive!* to be imbalanced in that there is no mention, for example, of the role *jihad* plays in the Crusades, military conquests and the spread of Islam, while the concept of

dhimmi is glossed over as a "special tax" with no mention of the oppression or religious persecution it represents. Also, *History Alive!* interjects inappropriate political commentary, e.g., an out of context sentence that states that Jerusalem is important to this day for Muslims in a section that is supposed to be about historical resistance to the spread of Islam."

As I am writing this in January 2008, it is unclear what action, if any, the school district is ultimately going to take. Just the other night I attended a program at my son's school (not his class), entitled, "Islam: A Presentation for Parents." What I saw was deeply disturbing. The students had difficulty distinguishing historical fact from religious myths and stories, as they told about Muhammad accompanied by the angel Gabriel, flying on the back of a winged horse to Jerusalem, praying with Abraham, Moses, and Jesus, and being carried up to heaven by Gabriel to meet God. Although these same students supposedly learned about Judaism and Christianity last year in sixth grade, they were not asked to build models of churches and synagogues, to research biblical prophecies, or to spend an evening telling their parents about the Ten Commandments or the Gospel according to John.

Not that that would have been appropriate either. However, I am sure that if there had been a similar event about another religion in a public school, there would have been a huge outcry. Therefore, I have to ask: Why a presentation specifically dedicated to Islam? I can't help but wonder why teachers in America's public schools are so intent on teaching American students about Islam that they are overlooking our American Constitution, which not only guarantees freedom of religion, but is supposed to protect from the risk of religious indoctrination.

Anne

A Publicly Funded Islamic School

An Arabic language and cultural school opened in Brooklyn, New York, on September 4, 2007. It is a public school supported with taxpayer dollars. There are two main concerns I have with this school: 1) that it is supported with taxpayer dollars, and 2) questions about the purpose of the school.

Supposedly, the school is designed to help students better understand the culture and language of the Middle East. Its executive summary says, "The curriculum will provide exposure to a wide variety of cultures and perspectives but will have a primary focus on learning about the richness and diversity of Arab culture and history." It also reveals in the summary that a minimum of forty hours per year of social activism is required. It says that the activism will be devoted to community projects and "Town Meeting Coordination" involving "community members."

Supporters of the school claim that U.S. students need to gain an understanding of the Middle East and children from Middle Eastern families need to reconnect with their culture and find a sense of community.

But an August 15, 2007 report by the New York Police Department, called *Report on Radicalization*, states that the marginalizing of Muslims creates the atmosphere for breeding terrorist cells. It says that isolating students based on a specific culture impedes their opportunities to co-mingle with peers of many backgrounds and describes certain venues as providing the fuel for radicalization. It calls them "radicalization incubators." The report further mentions student associations as one particular area of concern. Also worrisome is the finding that "Middle class families and students appear to provide the most fertile ground for the seeds of radicalization."[9] As a school teacher, it was apparent to me that helping young immigrants to assimilate and become Americans was not the school's goal.

After reading the NYPD's report, I had to ask myself if the school's "purpose" encourages its students to form allegiance to the United States or to the Middle East. And while it certainly is the purpose of public education to educate students and give them exposure to a wide array of different cultures, the emphasis should be to cultivate a deep pride in their own country and culture. Why do we use public funds to promote and encourage an allegiance to a culture that is so diametrically different than that of the U.S.?

The active participation of Islamist organizations partnering with the school includes the Arab-American Family Support Center and the American-Arab Anti-Discrimination Committee. Another partner is the American Middle Eastern Leadership Network about which the school's executive summary says, "[it] will organize cultural exchange programs to stabilized areas in the Middle East as well as other countries with significant Arab populations."

What would happen if a group of Christians asked for the same funding in order to focus their attention on Christ and the contributions and culture of Christianity? What if they, or a Jewish school, expected taxpayers to fund trips to the Middle East to study their religious heritage and culture? You can bet the ACLU and others would immediately file lawsuits to stop such a violation of "separation of church and state."

Also evident in the school's stated ideology is the desire to isolate their community within a public school setting. Given the Islamist ideology of the participants, this is a perfect opportunity for *da'wa*, an invitation to Islam. In fact, the Web site of an *imam* who sits on the school's board openly states: "Allah is our goal. The Prophet Muhammad ibn 'Abdullah is our leader. The Koran is our constitution. *Jihad* is our way. And death in the way of Allah is our promised end."[10] It is certainly understandable that as taxpayers and Americans we should be concerned that this religious philosophy could permeate the school.

Concern over the overall tone of the school is especially relevant when one considers statements made by the school's founding Principal Dhabah "Debbie" Almontaser. She is on record as saying about the United States' involvement in fighting terrorism, "...I would like to see Norway taking the risk demanding that USA stops the killings, spreading suffering, emergency, and fear in countries as Afghanistan, Iraq, Venezuela and Sudan... I would like to see Norway show its guts in the Security Council and protest against unfair and racist policies. Stop the sanctions against Iraq..."[11]

Almontaser's name may sound familiar because it appeared in newspaper accounts over the controversy she created when she appeared to support the use of the word *intifada* on T-shirts sold at the time with the words "Intifada NYC" on the front. Almontaser gave an interview to the *New York Post* in which she said *intifada* merely meant "shaking off oppression."[12] However, the word is widely interpreted in the United States and around the world to mean rebellion.

For a woman who has lived in the United States from the age of three, and whose reputation is supposedly based on promoting "sensitivity-training," Almontaser's support for the shirts and the use of the term "Intifada NYC"—especially in New York— showed at the very least a remarkable lack of sensitivity.

As a result of the public outcry over the T-shirt controversy, Almontaser lost her job at the school. However, Danielle Salzberg, an administrator who had created the school's vision side by side with Almontaser, was appointed interim principal. So it is easy to assume that she shares Almontaser's views and goals for the school. (Almontaser subsequently sued in an effort to regain her position at the school but a Manhattan federal judge, Sidney Stein, ruled against her.)

The school's religious advisory board—appointed by Almontaser—is what originally prompted me to attend one of the first P.T.A. meetings held in the building intended for the school. I asked questions about the curricula, textbooks, lesson plans, Web site resources, teacher handouts, and about the special *halal* food to be served in the cafeteria. Another gentleman in the audience, comprised primarily of parents, stated that he was terribly disappointed that Mayor Bloomberg, apparently aware of the controversy surrounding the school, continued to support it, as evidenced by a *New York Times* report.[13] All of these concerns were ignored by the chief executive of the New York City Department of Education's Office of New Schools. I spoke with him after the meeting and again raised some concerns about the school's main partner and on-site supervising agency, the Arab American Family Support Center. I pointed out that their Web site linked to the Council on Islamic Education (CIE), which clearly holds a very biased viewpoint about Islam. He laughed in my face.

Parents in local school districts across the country are raising the alarm that their public school curricula and textbooks are being compromised by Islamic educational organizations that adhere to *shariah*, Islamic law. This is not just a New York City issue.

Islamist political extremists believe in the superiority of Islamic law over our own U.S. Constitution.

Because of the disturbing nature of the school and curriculum invading America's classrooms, parents and teachers, with support from the Catholic League and the Friends of Gibran Council, formed an organization called Stop the Madrassa Coalition. The public response has been overwhelming. With national media coverage, several hundred people responded immediately and Stop the Madrassa became a national organization that is still growing. We now receive calls from parents across the country also fighting the Islamic indoctrination in their local schools. If you would like more information about Stop the Madrassa, visit www.stopthemadrassa.org.

Sara Springer

Worshipping Allah for Extra Credit

When we moved to a small country farming town to raise our family, I never expected that my children would be educated in a liberal school system. There were hints during the elementary years. For instance, in second grade, my son came home one day to inform me that Christopher Columbus was a criminal. Other incidents like this occurred throughout the primary years. But nothing prepared me for the indoctrination that would be inserted into my son's seventh-grade social studies class under the guise of "cultural" education.

In August 2006, my eldest son brought home his syllabus for that year's social studies course. The units to be covered included world geography, Islamic culture, Europe, and Asia. We were also asked to sign the syllabus, as it was part of the grade. One of the topics raised a red flag for me, so I immediately contacted the school to ask what was going to be taught in Islamic culture. I met with my son's teacher and the teacher in charge of setting the curriculum for the school. I was assured the unit was required by the state and that they would be teaching only material out of the text.

World geography was covered in one week, then came Islam. Three weeks into the Islamic culture unit, my son came home to tell me that an American Muslim was coming to speak to the class. The speaker arrived that day in full Islamic garb. She brought extra traditional dress for the class to try on. The kids were then offered extra credit if they would put on the *burqa*—the *hijab*. She brought in her Koran, and the students were told not to touch it for "it" was holy.

Two textbooks were used in my son's class, *Journey across Time* and an alternative, *Across the Centuries*. The books explain that *jihad* is an inner spiritual struggle and that Muhammad was a prophet of God. One class activity required students to dress as Muslims and act out the "five pillars" of Islam in five-minute sketches. The students were graded on this activity. I objected, so my son was sent to the library to write an essay on the Prophet Muhammad's life.

Throughout the unit I was very uncomfortable, so my husband and I decided to address the school board. The Friday before the school board meeting, the district sent a letter to everyone in the community detailing their side of the story. It stated that Oregon standards require that they teach the course. The benchmark requirement says: "Discuss the rise of Islam and how it affected Western Europe." Since there are well over one hundred benchmarks that need to be taught to students during their middle-school years, how does the district justify spending a total of six weeks on this one unit, when so many others need to be taught?

The letter also told parents that they had received "[a] consent form describing course content and class rules." The syllabus said nothing of the sort. The letter also said that only one family complained. That, too, was incorrect. My husband and I and two other parents went before the school board. We were outnumbered by the teachers and administrators there to defend the school's policy. We were called bigots, and it was inferred that we were country bumpkins who had never been off the farm. I tried to explain that I had no problem with teaching "about" Islam as long as it was taught in context and they taught "about" other religions in the same context. Neither Christianity nor Judaism was taught that year.

We were told that tolerance is so important in today's world and that we need to educate our children about different cultures, but if this was truly their goal wouldn't they want to teach about all religions equally without putting such an emphasis on one?

Our complaints fell on deaf ears and the following year my second son was also forced to do and learn almost the same material. I sat in on a few classes during the 2007 year. The teacher taught that the reason Muhammad had so many followers is because he brought a new message of "one God and the afterlife." My son raised his hand to ask if it wasn't true that the Jews believed in one God eighteen hundred years before Muhammad taught that concept. Since the students aren't taught Judaism or Christianity in chronological order, isn't it easy to assume that these twelve-year-old minds will believe that Muhammad was the first to teach these truths?

One of the class assignments was to watch a PBS documentary on Islam. The children were taught that Christians, Jews, and Muslims believe in the same God and that their religions were similar. During the documentary, I recall that one student felt sorry for Muhammad because he was being persecuted. Yet the movie never showed the persecution of Jews and Christians at the hands of Muhammad. During the skit portion of the class, one of the children stood on a chair and did the call to prayer.

My husband and I have now been labeled "troublemakers" at the school and the teachings continue. And while the school says it is all about equality, my son's class this year spent two days discussing Christianity. And even then the teacher didn't really teach about it but instead handed out two worksheets for the students to work out on their own. The words Jesus Christ were never spoken. It wasn't discussed how Christianity has influenced the world's culture, and nothing was said about the ties with the Jewish faith or how other religions have copied many of the same concepts.

NOTE: *This winter the school district could not use the words "Merry Christmas," but the greeting "Feliz Navidad" was used on both of the school's flashing marquees. When I asked why, I was told that they were asked to "take it easy" on using "Merry Christmas." I guess in today's world it is all right to celebrate Christmas, but only if you speak Spanish.*

Kendalee Garner

Memorizing the Koran for a Grade

One day during the 2006 school year, my daughter, then in seventh grade, was in her room doing her homework. I walked in and happened to glance at what she was doing. I don't do this often, as she is a great student and her homework is often too advanced for me to follow. However, the title of her paper caught my eye and I nearly choked: "The Life of Muhammad and the Great Religion of Islam." I not so calmly asked her what in the world she was writing. She said, "Yeah, I know, Mom; you should read the garbage my history book says about Islam." So I did. To say I was shocked would have been an understatement. This book was overly positive about Muhammad and Islam and explained how Islam is such a peaceful religion, and how Islamists don't believe in violence or blowing up government buildings, etc.

The title of the book is *History Alive! The Medieval World and Beyond*, published by the Teachers' Curriculum Institute (TCI). After a little research, I learned that this publisher has a history of publishing anti-West, anti-Israel, pro-Islamic textbooks. As the Textbook League reported:

> This material consists of overwhelmingly Islamic religious propaganda. It includes blatant preaching as well as deceptive claims and extensive fraudulent narratives dealing with the beginnings of Islam, the life of Muhammad, and the inception of the Koran. These claims and narratives are disguised as accounts of history...[14]

The amount of space devoted to Christianity and Judaism pales in comparison to Islam.

My daughter then pointed out to me I should read Chapter 9.1.1 on *jihad*, which ignores the common interpretation by terrorists of waging war to advance Islam.

> The word *jihad* means "to strive." *Jihad* represents the human struggle to overcome difficulties and do things that would be pleasing to God. Muslims strive to respond positively to personal difficulties as well as worldly challenges. For instance, they might work to become better people, reform society, or correct injustice.[15]

Isn't that sweet? I could not believe what I was seeing. How did this get into our schools? The Teach and Learn projects the teachers were required to assign were even worse. My child was asked to make a Koran with scriptures that she would have to memorize for a grade. This was only one of many Teach and Learn projects recommended in the TCI material. Another suggested project was to visit a local mosque. My daughter's teacher informed me that she only chose the least controversial Teach and Learn projects. Obviously, this didn't make me feel much better.

I told my daughter to stop working on her project. If they wanted a report on Muhammad we would give them one, but not the version from the text. If they wanted scriptures from the Koran, we would give them some, particularly the ones about beating women into submission to start with.

I e-mailed her teacher and called the principal; I wanted a meeting. The vice-principal was more than happy to meet with me. He was a history major, but he seemed totally unaware of the contents of the text. He had never even read the book; neither had my daughter's teacher. This was the first year for this text, so it was new to everyone.

The school showed me our state's history standards for the seventh grade, which appear to be part of the problem. There is nothing in the standards that require publishers to say anything about Islam that isn't flattering. The standards apparently have not kept pace with the dual nature of some religions; i.e., that politics often intertwine within religious beliefs. Therefore, the standards do not require that while teaching about Islam, schools should also mention terrorists point to Islam as the reason for killing and that where Islam is widely practiced, there is often abject poverty, a lack of basic freedoms, and the exploitation of women.

My options were limited because the tests administered by the state are linked to the standards and thus to the books. The whole process is rigged to indoctrinate students. I told the principal I was shocked at the lies being shoved down my daughter's throat. I said that if a textbook praised Christianity, or had students create a Bible, visit a Christian church, or do a report on

Jesus, there would be a tremendous outcry by liberal groups and lawsuits filed to put a stop to it.

Apparently a board approves these books for the school district, but they either don't read the book and its supplementary materials before approving them, or are sympathetic to the views of these pro-Islamic books. The TCI book has been approved for use for the next six years in our school district, and I'm told there is nothing that can be done about it.

I told the principal my daughter would not participate in anything on these chapters. I wanted him to come up with another plan so it would not affect her grade. He said he would talk to the teacher and get back to me. At our next meeting a few days later he agreed to just wipe out the zero grades she had received so that it would not affect her grade either way. He was understanding, and I was happy with it being handled that way.

I also contacted an acquaintance on the school board and told her what was going on, and she gave me the name and number of the school district representative in charge of curriculum. In the meantime, I contacted a legal group which defends the rights of parents called the Pacific Justice Institute, and they informed me that someone had already tried to sue a school district based on this issue and it went all the way to the Supreme Court, which refused to hear the case. In the meantime, my daughter's class had moved away from that chapter, so I let the matter drop. I did, however, inform everyone I knew about this textbook.

If there was anything good to come of this, it was a lesson for my daughter. I wish all children could learn this. As I told her, just because something is mentioned in a book and a teacher is teaching it to you, that doesn't make it so. Do research on your own, and come to your own conclusions.

To me, the scariest part of this issue is that a trusted teacher and an official school textbook teaches a version of Islam espoused by those who want to destroy our way of life. How many kids are going to believe this propaganda without their parents even knowing about it?

Colleen (Last Name Withheld by Request)

Islamic Indoctrination in Arizona

On the morning of September 22, 2004, my seventh-grade daughter informed me that in school she learned that AD and BC were no longer the way to refer to dates. She said that now everyone was supposed to say CE and BCE. This was news to me.

In order to find out what was going on, I went to the school to speak with the teacher. I was able to get a copy of the textbook, titled *History Alive! The Medieval World and Beyond*, published by Teachers' Curriculum Institute, also known as TCI.

While leaving the school, I glanced through the textbook and noticed a two-page spread featuring timelines. I saw that Islam had its own timeline and that it spanned both pages. This focus on Islam seemed odd to me, and no other religion was showcased in this way. I discovered that the class was actually supposed to read *Across the Centuries* published by Houghton Mifflin.[16] The school never notified parents of the switch, and refused to allow students to take the textbook home.

As I began reading the textbook, I quickly came to realize that there was far more wrong with it than the promulgation of CE/BCE. I found that *History Alive!* was heavily biased towards Islam. The book showcased Islam everywhere and never mentioned anything negative about Islam.

Beginning to suspect the veracity of everything in the book, I decided to learn as much as possible about how a book like this came to be and how it ended up in the hands of unsuspecting and impressionable middle school children.

I discovered that bias in favor of Islam and the rewriting of history to glorify Islam was a pervasive problem within school textbooks. From what I was learning, it appeared that the Islamization of American textbooks had gained notoriety for quite some time.[17]

In response to my questions, I was directed to the official in charge of the district's science and social studies curriculum for grades K-12. When we met, she insisted *History Alive!* was a great product from Stanford and highly recommended. She also informed me that I was the only one who had complained.

I argued I already had found enough red flags to warrant erring on the side of doing no harm and removing this textbook from the classrooms until further investigation could be done. I sent to her the research that I was gathering.

I spoke with the district official several times and remained serious and persistent in my efforts to convince her to remove the textbook. She had not even read it.

In response to my queries about the CE/BCE issue, the official informed me that all learned people used this dating and that all educators and publishers did the same. She said that the *Chicago Manual of Style* mandated the use of CE/BCE.

Suspecting that this was not true, I decided to find proof.

During my search for an expert to refute the propaganda and misinformation regarding the crusades section in the *History Alive!* textbook, I found Dr. Thomas F. Madden, a professor of history at Saint Louis University and director of its Center for Medieval and Renaissance Studies. A specialist on the crusades, he critiqued the book's presentation of the subject and directed me to the *Chicago Manual of Style* which, in fact, does not mandate the use of CE/BCE.

I sent this information on to the district official.

On October 24, 2004, I received the district's official position that the textbook would stay in the classrooms and that it fit the Arizona state social studies standards. I was also told that, since I had concerns regarding TCI's products, I could volunteer to serve on the district's upcoming textbook adoption committee. TCI would present their products to this committee for official adoption by the district. I volunteered and looked forward to serving on this committee.

After receiving the district's official position that *History Alive!* would stay in the classrooms, I redoubled my efforts. To accomplish my goal of getting this textbook out of the classrooms, I felt that I needed an independent, educated, and reliable critique. I had hopes of finding a professional to review the book.

While researching, I found two well-respected textbook reviewers. I sent inquiries to William Bennetta of the Textbook League and to Gilbert Sewall of the American Textbook Council. I learned that it would take time to do a proper and thorough report of this textbook and its associated materials.

To further complicate things, one reviewer also was having continuing difficulties obtaining the materials that he needed from the publisher, TCI.

On January 28, 2005, Mr. Sewall posted a preliminary report in "Islam and the Textbooks" on his Web site,[18] and Mr. Bennetta later released his comprehensive report, titled, "How a Public School in Scottsdale, Arizona Subjected Students to Islamic Indoctrination."[19]

While waiting for the textbook reviews to be completed, I continued researching and took note of what was transpiring in the classroom.

The following timeline details the events that occurred in the classroom, as the students studied Islam, using *History Alive!*:

> January 3, 2005—Monday—The students officially began studying Islam in the classroom.
>
> January 19, 2005—Wednesday—The students were told that Muhammad was voted the most important person in the history of the world.
>
> In the *History Alive! The Medieval World and Beyond Interactive Student Notebook*, the students did an exercise that required them to vote for whom they thought was the most influential person in the history of the world. Their *Interactive Student Notebook* provided the students with a list of names from which to choose.
>
> Most of the students voted for Jesus, thinking that this was the correct answer. The teacher then told them that no, Muhammad was the most influential person in the history of the world. To drive this point home, the teacher obtained and used Michael H. Hart's highly controversial Top 100 list which places Muhammad as number one, Sir Isaac Newton as number two, and Jesus as number three.
>
> January 25, 2005—Tuesday—I sent my official letter to the superintendent of the district and to the school board, requesting that they remove TCI's materials from the classrooms. I also included the research that I had gathered.
>
> February 1, 2005—Tuesday—The school hosted two professional Muslim speakers from the Islamic Speakers Bureau of

Arizona, who presented Islam to the entire seventh grade. This took one whole day.

During my research, I was impressed with three articles by Daniel Pipes, and I sent an e-mail to him, telling him of my problems with this textbook and with the school district.

Dr. Pipes wisely suggested that I make my statement public, which I did.

On February 27, 2005, I posted my comment on Pipes' Web site.[20] This was a pivotal move. Pipes marked it as an outstanding comment and from his Web site, my reader comment spread to other notable Web sites, touching many readers. By sending e-mails and letters to the school board, these concerned readers were instrumental in motivating the district to remove TCI's materials from the classrooms, which occurred less than two weeks later.[21]

March 9, 2005—Wednesday—Publisher presentations to the textbook adoption committee began. When I arrived to watch presentations to the lower grades, I was told that all TCI materials were being pulled from consideration by the textbook adoption committee. It wasn't mentioned that TCI's materials were also being pulled from district classrooms.

March 10-11, 2005—Thursday/Friday—*History Alive!* and any associated materials were removed from all classrooms in the district!

Janie White

EPILOGUE: *November 2005—TCI's products, including* History Alive!, *were adopted by the California State Board of Education for use in all California classrooms.*[22]

Promoting Islam Is Fine; Reading the Bible Is Illegal

The following story originates from a Knoxville, Tennessee family, but because the case was being litigated at time of publication, their attorneys, Nate Vellum and Jon Scruggs, wrote their story. Both work for the Alliance Defense Fund. Contrast the promotion of Islam in public schools with how the Bible is treated.

All ten-year-old Luke Whitson wanted to do was bring his Bible to school and talk about it with his friends during recess.

But one parent complained, and Luke's principal at Karns Elementary School in Knoxville, Tennessee, cracked down on Luke and his friends as if they were reading obscene material at recess. She told Luke that he not only had to close his Bible immediately, but that he had to leave it at home and never bring it to school again.

Her rationale? Banning the Bible was in the "best interest" of keeping children "safe" and allowing the Bible reading would be a violation of the so-called "separation of church and state."

Luke was crushed. He asked himself, "What's wrong with reading the Bible and talking about it with my friends? Is there something bad about my Christian faith that I don't know about?"

When he shared what happened with his mother, she knew that the principal had violated Luke's constitutional rights. Luke's parents contacted an Alliance Defense Fund (ADF)-allied attorney, who sent a letter to the principal, simply asking her to allow Luke to exercise his First Amendment freedom to read and discuss the Bible with his classmates during noninstructional time.

What should have been an open-and-shut case wasn't. The principal and the school district ignored the letter and dug in their heels, claiming recess was "instructional time" and therefore the Bible could not be discussed during that time. Ironically, other students were allowed to talk about Harry Potter books and American Girl catalogs during such "instructional" time. The principal also said that if she allowed Bibles to be brought to school, she would have to allow "the Muslims to do their thing."

The Whitsons felt they had no other choice but to ask ADF Senior Counsel Nate Kellum to file a lawsuit (*Whitson v. Knox County Board of Education*) on behalf of their son, Luke, to defend his First Amendment freedom.

But after suit was filed, the principal responded by upping the ante. She filed a slander lawsuit against Luke—asking for three million dollars.

Now, three years later, Luke is a teenager, and the case continues, residing in the United States District Court for the Eastern District of Tennessee.

From a legal perspective, there seems to be little rationale for the principal and school district to continue this case. The school's position regarding recess time being "instructional time," therefore justifying the Bible ban, is untenable. Courts have routinely treated recess as noninstructional time and by allowing the reading and discussion of other material during that time, it is clear that it is religious activity that is being isolated and targeted for a specific ban.

In addition, the principal's actions were not only in direct violation of the First Amendment, but also run contrary to the principles expressed by the United States Supreme Court in the landmark student speech case, *Tinker v. Des Moines Independent School District* (1969). In its decision, the court held that "[i]n the absence of a specific showing of constitutionally valid reasons to regulate their speech, students are entitled to freedom of expression of their views" and students do not "shed their constitutional rights to freedom of speech or expression at the schoolhouse gate." The Court also asserted that the First Amendment protections afforded students extended to the "cafeteria," the "playing field," or simply "being on campus during authorized hours," so those protections are extended to the playground as well.

When the principal censored Luke's Bible reading, they offered no legitimate reason for doing so, only a vague statement regarding "safety" at school. In fact, the principles laid out in *Tinker* affirm that Luke's reading and discussion of the Bible during free time is protected by the First Amendment.

The result is that the principal and school officials engaged in viewpoint discrimination, singling out one viewpoint for censorship, while allowing all others. This is unconstitutional. The U.S. Supreme Court held in *Good News v. Milford Central Schools* and *Lamb's Chapel v. Center Moriches Union Free School District* that religious groups cannot be denied access to school facilities during noninstructional time if all other groups have the same access. That same principle applies to religious speech, as in Luke's case.

When one sifts through all the facts in the Whitson case, it becomes undeniably clear that the school district's actions show a blatant hostility towards religion. When a school official tells a student to not only put his Bible away but also to never bring it to school again, making reading of the Bible subject to reprimand, and then sending a letter to parents that any form of Bible discussion was strictly prohibited, a reasonable person will come to the conclusion that the school's actions demonstrate a disapproval of religion.

Nate Vellum and Jon Scruggs, Alliance Defense Fund

Textbooks that side with Islam against the West and ignore violent jihad are one thing, praying to Mecca during class time is quite another, frustrating parents and teachers who wonder why we "are leaning over backwards to accommodate one particular faith in a way that we would never do for Christianity—the majority religion of America—or for any other faith."

Violations of Student and Parental Rights

CHAPTER TEN

PARENTAL RIGHTS— GOING, GOING, GONE

WHILE PROPONENTS *of school reform sell the movement to parents and community leaders as a necessity to prepare students for the workforce, in reality, much of it is an effort to inculcate social values, attitudes, and behaviors that have nothing to do with academic pursuits. As a result, lawsuits by outraged parents are increasing.*[1]

In some cases, state laws grant rights to the child—or even schools—that blatantly undermine the rights of parents, and too often, parents find themselves faced with laws and policies they didn't know existed. For instance, how many parents read through all those notices sent home at the beginning of the school year? Lyn Booth, a California mother, was outraged when she read: "You have the right as a parent: To be informed that school authorities may excuse your child from school for the purpose of obtaining confidential medical services without your consent." In other words, the notice tells parents that they have the right to be told they have no rights!

Even state education codes sometimes denigrate and undermine the role of parents. In one debate on the floor of the California Assembly, Assemblyman Baldwin challenged a parental compact bill that undermined the rights of parents. He offered an amendment that simply stated, "The compact shall preserve the role of parents as being primary in the development of their children." The chairwoman of the Assembly Education Committee, Kerry Mazzoni, a Democrat, rose to her feet and asked angrily, "With this amendment could parents assert their right to direct and control the public education of their children?" Assemblyman Baldwin replied, "That's already in state law. Parents do direct and control..." Mazzoni interrupted, stating, "No, they do not in the public schools."

A number of high-profile cases in recent years have highlighted this attack on parental rights:

> In California, a father shared how upset and hurt he was when he learned that the school drove his teenage daughter to a birth control clinic for contraceptives. "As a responsible parent, I like to be involved in important decisions made by my children!" he said.[2]

> In Oregon, a young pregnant student was removed from the school campus without parental knowledge or consent and "against her will was taken to a clinic where an abortion was performed."[3]

> In Pennsylvania, parents were outraged when a middle school authorized a doctor to conduct genital examinations on fifty-nine sixth-grade girls without parental knowledge or consent. The school defended itself by saying it had sent home several consent forms. If parents did not respond, the school "assumed" parental consent and proceeded with the examinations anyway. Some of the girls claimed they were given the genital exams against their will, and when they asked if they could call their parents, they were refused permission. The doctor denied forcing the girls to have the exams. However, in July 1999, the courts agreed with the girls and ruled in their favor.[4]

> A Missouri mother was prohibited from observing a school-sponsored assembly conducted by the Gay, Lesbian and Straight Education Network (GLSEN). She was removed from the room by an armed security guard.[5]

Parental rights are also being undermined in the name of providing health care to underprivileged children. States are increasingly pushing for expanded medical and mental health care services at school-based health clinics. While providing basic health care for at-risk children is a noble idea, parents must be forewarned that laws to expand the authority of school-based clinics are growing. Unfortunately, such expansions mean that more services can be provided without parental knowledge or consent.

In written testimony for the U.S. House of Representatives, Dr. Karen Effrem, a Minnesota pediatrician and researcher, discussed the "provisions of, loopholes in, or goals of" certain federally mandated programs including Healthy People 2000, Goals 2000, and School to Work Opportunities Act.[6]

Her concerns centered on the effects these laws or programs have on children and the rights of parents. Dr. Effrem pointed out:

> The schools are "one stop shopping centers" ... School-based or school-linked clinics (SBCs) are the vehicles and tax dollars, especially through Medicaid, are the funding mechanism. The emphasis in our public schools is no longer on the academic liberal arts education required of responsible citizens in a free republic, but instead on medicalized and psychologized mixture of attitudes, beliefs, feeling, behaviors, and job skills... there are many disturbing consequences ... the massive gathering of personal medical and family data from students resulting in profiles and diagnoses of children for disorders that often have more to do with compliance with the mandates ... than with the medical reality for the child [another consequence is] the loss of parental control in the education and medical care of their own children to the "It takes a village of government bureaucracies to raise a child" mentality ...[7]

Who are these people invading the privacy of families and children? Who gave them the right? And why aren't parents creating waves of protest? How dare schools conduct psychological group counseling sessions during school hours? How dare the school system decide without parents' knowledge that children need to sit around in circles and discuss real or imagined personal or family problems, or answer questions that are clearly designed to elicit personal information from children?[8] Were parents given the chance to "opt-out" their children? Were parents told that participation in these activities might involve their children being labeled at-risk and referred for "appropriate" counseling? Who gave the school authority to make those decisions? The answer, of course, is that legislators have given schools this power. They assume that with the breakdown of the family, all students are at-risk and in need of government intervention. They suffer from the same dangerous and misguided belief held by many educators—that they are the ones that need to step in and make all these sick children well.

But the premise is wrong. Yes, there are dysfunctional families. There have always been dysfunctional families. And there have always been at-risk children. However, is more government intrusion the answer? Unfortunately, current practice—and laws—include all children in programs supposedly designed to serve only at-risk students.[9]

Schools, teachers, and legislators must realize that current reform practices, which shift the primary focus of schools from objective, concrete, measurable academics, to subjective evaluations of children's attitudes, will no longer be tolerated! Schools should not be experimental labs—schoolchildren should not be lab rats.

Psychological Counseling without Parental Knowledge

I'm a single mom raising three children. I have a son in high school, one in middle school, and my daughter is in second grade. I've been very lucky that none of them have given me any real problems. However, the fact that I am a single mom automatically labels me as a less than fit parent, and labels my children "at-risk."

My middle son is quite musically talented. Yet after an episode in band class (which I didn't find out about until almost four weeks later), he was sent to psychological counseling—without my knowledge or consent.

Apparently, he and another boy started hitting each other with drumsticks. No blows were exchanged. The teacher saw it all and didn't intervene. However, my son was sent to the school psychologist while the other boy, who had two parents, was not sent.

I first found out about my son's psychology sessions when I got home from work one Friday night. I walked in the door and found a note from my son saying he was sorry that he was such a burden for me. He said he hadn't realized we didn't have any money, or how difficult it was for me to raise three children. He said he needed to be alone to "think." We didn't find him until almost ten o' clock that night—just wandering the streets.

He told me that the "counselor" had asked him how much money I make; how much his father sent, etc. It took some time before I could make him understand that raising him and his brother and sister was not a "burden," that I loved them and that we were a family—a happy family.

I was furious! When I went to the school on Monday, I learned that he had been placed in the "at-risk "category because I was a single mother. At no time did they call me to discuss their concerns, or ask permission before sending my son for counseling. They didn't notify me about the classroom skirmish; they just decided he was a troubled teenager. I also learned that he was not going to be allowed to participate in band for a few weeks. However, they waited to begin his punishment until after a big concert that was planned. The reason? He was the lead drummer and considered so good that his teacher wanted him in the concert!

My high schooler also had an incident at school. During lunch he and probably thirty-five to forty other students were sitting under a tree. Since we live in a hot climate, it isn't unusual for students to gather under a shade tree for lunch. On this day several different groups ate under a shade tree. The members of each group didn't necessarily know the members of the other groups. They were all just sharing the tree's shade during their lunch period.

Some teachers conducted a drug search, and one of the boys in another group had a "pipe." As a result, all of the students were searched. Nothing else was found. The school called the police and wanted to press charges against all the students. The police refused. However, the school decided that every student under the tree needed drug counseling and wrote reports on every child. My son's report said that he was associating with someone charged with possession. (He didn't know the boy with the "pipe.")

All of the parents complained, but the school insisted on drug counseling for everyone. I was aware enough to know that this report would remain on my son's record, and I wanted it removed. I also knew there was no basis for the charge, and I went (though I was told I couldn't) with my son to his first scheduled session. I told the counselor what had really happened. After she checked out my story, she agreed that there was no basis for counseling. I also insisted that the school give me my son's record. I believe several of the other parents—after hearing about my actions—insisted on their rights too. If I had not known my rights, my son would have had a permanent drug record. How many other students have similar records that parents don't know about?

On another occasion, my daughter came home very upset because she didn't understand her homework assignment. She knew she had done it wrong. I explained that the teacher would help her the next day at school—that teachers were there to help students learn when they didn't understand something. You can't imagine how I felt when I picked her up after school the next day and she was in tears. She said that when she handed her homework to the teacher that morning, she told the teacher she knew it wasn't right. The teacher gave her a big smile and said she was sure it would be fine. When the paper came back, there was a big "happy face" on it. My daughter pointed out that she couldn't have a "happy face," because she still didn't understand the assignment. The teacher again said, "It's just fine, don't worry about it."

My daughter knew her homework was wrong, and she didn't want to hear how "fine" her wrong answers were; she wanted to learn what she had done wrong. If this phony "fine" stuff is supposed to build "self-esteem," it doesn't. Teaching students, helping them learn, and exciting them with the thrill of knowledge builds healthy self-esteem. When will we learn?

If parents think charter schools are the answer, they need to think again. Charter schools are only as good as the charter. If they teach this integrated, feel-good junk, then it's no better than a regular public school.

Name Withheld by Request

Child Protective Services

Throughout my childhood and early adulthood, I was taught to appreciate our country and the freedoms it provides. I admired our legal system and felt secure in my right to live life as I believed God would want. Imagine my surprise when a social worker informed me that the government I was taught to trust had the right to remove my children from school without my authorization!

One afternoon, as I said good-bye to a friend and her little girl, a woman came to my door and announced that she was from Child Protective Services and needed to talk to me about my daughter. Completely confused, I invited her in.

She began by telling me she had been to my daughter's school and had had a conversation with my child. To my astonishment, her next comment was, "Normally, under these circumstances we would take the child into custody and you would have the right to prove your innocence." Innocence? What innocence? What was she talking about? I hadn't the slightest clue what she was referring to; I even thought she must have the wrong family! But as she continued, I discovered that much had occurred about which I knew nothing! I was simply the last to know!

As I listened, I learned that on the first day of school the brand new counselor had gone to each of the classrooms and announced to the children that she was their "special friend." She told them that if they ever had any problems and wanted to talk about them, the teacher would allow them to leave class to talk with her. What better invitation could a creative child have when she wasn't getting her way with her parents? As we later discovered, our third-grade daughter had gone to this woman on one occasion with the complaint that she had been spanked and left with a bruise. When the counselor asked to see the supposed bruise, my daughter said it was "already gone."

On another occasion, our daughter claimed her father had kicked her, leaving a bruise on her ankle which also was gone by the time she mentioned it to the counselor. Nevertheless, our state law apparently doesn't allow the counselor to inform the parents of any accusations made against them. The law also requires that after a second accusation of a supposed abuse, Child Protective Services are to be notified.

To our knowledge, our daughter had never had any bruises. She later admitted she made up the story about the spanking bruise. She did say that her ankle was bruised, and after some discussion, we finally determined how it happened. After sending her to bed one evening she got up repeatedly and was repeatedly sent back. Finally, she entered the kitchen where her father and I were sitting, and my husband grabbed her by the arm and spun her around to face him for a scolding. Her ankle apparently struck my husband's work boot, causing a bruise.

As a result of these activities, our daughter is very reluctant to use her creativity, a talent that previously enabled her to make it to the Young Authors Conference. She is now fearful that anything she writes may be misinterpreted and the authorities might take her away from her family.

We were fortunate; the CPS counselor said that in our daughter's case, it was evident that there were no signs of abuse. However, she did advise us that the complaint would become a permanent record and that if any further reports were ever received, CPS could remove our children from our home. We now live with this threat hanging over our heads.

Christina Dickinson

Parent Arrested

School officials talk a lot about "parental involvement." Well, you can't prove it by me. I tried to get involved in my children's school and was arrested! Not once but twice. My offense? I wanted to observe a teacher in-service training arranged to instruct teachers on how to implement new programs. If my story doesn't alarm parents, I don't know what will.

My friend, Cyndi, and I were arrested for attending a teacher in-service for the new "wellness" program that was to be implemented.[10] These are publicly funded meetings at which a publicly funded curriculum is discussed.

This was not my first arrest instigated by this district. A similar arrest took place four months earlier. Yet on two other occasions I attended similar training sessions and was left alone—apparently the district couldn't make up its mind.

On the morning of the arrest, two friends and I met at the school parking lot to attend a "facilitator training" for the new "wellness" program. When we arrived at the entrance of the multipurpose room, the wellness coordinator was just closing one of the doors. We tried all four doors to the room. Since they were all locked, I knocked on the door the coordinator had just closed. She opened it slightly and said through the crack that this was a private meeting and that we were not allowed. I responded by saying that it wasn't private and that as parents, taxpayers, and community members, we had the right to attend. I assured her we would sit quietly on the side of the room and not interrupt.

I tried to open the door wider in order to enter, but the coordinator shoved me and tried to pull the door shut on my fingers.

Finally, she stepped outside and pulled the door closed behind her. We expressed our concern about the doors being locked during business hours in violation of the fire code.

We also asked her about the secretiveness of the meeting. She said the decision wasn't hers. I questioned this statement and suggested that she ask the school administrators for clarification. I knew that if she really didn't mind our attending, there would be no resistance from the administration. She said that topics would be discussed that she wanted kept private. Then she went back into the room and left us standing outside.

We called the fire department to notify them about the locked doors and then stood outside trying to decide what to do. The principal walked toward us and asked if we were attending the training. We said yes, so she unlocked the door and invited us in.

We took chairs at the side of the room, and I began taking notes. After five minutes, another trainer asked us to join them. She asked us to introduce ourselves, so I gave her my name and said that I was there as an observer. Cyndi agreed. The trainer asked the attendees if anyone had a problem with us staying. Everyone seemed to agree that it was okay. At this point, the coordinator approached us and told us that we couldn't stay. She started pushing and poking at me. I finally maneuvered my chair so that I could sit down. Cyndi sat next to me.

Then we were told that the afternoon session was confidential, and were asked not to attend. We agreed with their wishes. The trainer then began teaching various "ice breaking" games. She stated that the "training packets may seem sparse, but the bulk of what you will be learning is not in your worksheets—the stuff you will take back to your support groups." We assumed "the stuff" referred to was the information she would be giving during the seminar.

Some time later, the coordinator came into the room with her walkie-talkie and announced that it was break time and instructed everyone to go out the back exit to the teacher's lounge. Cyndi and I started toward the exit but were blocked by the coordinator. She threatened me by shoving me backwards down the stairs. I asked her to stop, because she was hurting me.

As Cyndi and I returned to the multipurpose room, we were met by two police officers. They said they were there to place us under "citizen's arrest." When I asked for the name of the "citizen," one of the officers gave the name of the assistant superintendent. I tried to show them documents which proved that the district had no policy excluding parents or community members from these in-service training sessions. I also had proof that the district attorney had chosen not to prosecute me for an earlier, similar arrest.

As I stood to leave, the officers handcuffed us both. They hadn't indicated that they were planning to arrest us. We offered to leave then, but they took both of us to police headquarters, and I was jailed. Cyndi is a diabetic and was displaying signs of low blood sugar, so she was released and taken home.

What was so secret about the wellness curriculum? Why did the school coordinator feel she had to conspire with other school employees to have us falsely arrested in order to remove us from a teacher training session? What are they teaching our children that they don't want us to know?

The following excerpts from *Wellness Is Our Way of Life* are instructions to the teacher:

> Objective: To help students become aware of the ineffectiveness of punishment as a motivator for long-range, positive change.
>
> Materials: "Where did we ever get the crazy idea that in order to make people *do* better, first we have to make them *feel* worse?"
>
> Adults often are disrespectful and discouraging to children in many ways without realizing it. Any form of punishment or permissiveness is disrespectful and discouraging to children...
>
> Ask students to think of a time when someone tried to motivate them to do better by making them feel worse. Tell them to remember exactly what happened as though they were reliving the event and to remember how they felt. As a result of that experience, what did they decide about themselves, about others, or about what to do?...
>
> These adults are fooled into thinking they are right if the misbehavior stops for a while because of punishment.[11]

Connie Youngkin

Psychological Counseling without Parental Knowledge

When our eight-year-old daughter made honor roll at her elementary school, we were proud of her. She has set high goals for herself and wants to be like her older sister, who was a multiyear honor roll student before she passed away in an automobile accident four years ago.

We want people to understand that our daughter is neither troubled nor an underachiever. Yet her teacher selected her, along with eleven other students, to go across campus to meet with the school district's counselor. Our daughter thought she had done something wrong because when she asked why she was being sent to the counselor, the teacher would not give her an answer. Instead, the teacher just told our daughter to go along with the other students to the counselor's office.

When our child arrived at the counselor's office, the counselor sat with the rest of the group and asked a number of personal questions about our home life:

> Are your parents divorced?
>
> Do your parents still see each other?
>
> Do you see your other parent on regular visits?
>
> Did you have a death in your family?
>
> How did it happen?
>
> How do you feel about it?
>
> Where do you feel safe?

After thirty minutes, the group returned to the classroom. Our daughter asked again why she had been sent to the counselor's office, and again did not receive an answer. The teacher did tell her not to speak to anyone outside of the classroom about the counseling group. As soon as our daughter arrived home, she told us what had happened.

Over the course of a few days, we contacted the counselor, vice principal, and principal in an effort to get straight answers about why our child was cross-examined without parental notification or consent. We heard everything from, "It was a glitch," to "Your daughter asked to be in the group." When we asked to review our child's counseling records, we were first told the records did not exist, then were told that the records were in group form and could not be accessed, and then again, we were told they did not exist. Meanwhile our daughter was suffering. The teacher was so angry with us that she was punishing our child in retaliation. We had to remove our daughter from the class and place her in another.

By this time, I was beginning to wonder if this situation had happened to any other parents. I distributed fliers in our neighborhood. Within the first two days, we received more than ninety calls from parents whose children had experienced the same situation—some dating back four years. One parent said she had been threatened by the counseling staff because she made an issue of the lack of parental consent. We dug deeper and learned that, in one year, 50 percent of the student body was involved in this counseling group.

We arranged to meet with the director of counseling. During the first half of the meeting, the counselor told us how good the counseling program was, yet he avoided answering any of our questions. Frustrated, I finally pointed out that our rights had been violated. The director said: "We work for the state, Mr. Rogers; we set the policies, and we don't need your permission." It was then that I suggested an initiative, to be named after our daughter, which would require the counseling center to get written consent from parents before the counselor asked any personal questions of children. We were promised it would be voted on by the Site Governance Committee.

We attended the voting and were not surprised that committee members did everything they could to make us look like the "bad guys" because we opposed the counseling program. Our daughter's teacher was the committee chairman. She was accompanied by the counselor and the director of counseling, and although we tried to persuade the committee to address the topic of written consent, they were not interested. It soon became apparent that the committee had no intention of voting on our proposed initiative. (The school continues to operate with total disregard for parents and parents' rights.)

During the hearing, my wife managed to ask the counselor a few questions. The answers angered parents in the audience who had heard one thing prior to the hearing and something entirely different at the hearing. (These are the people we are told to trust with our children's well being and education.) In our opinion, we were all told lies; however, we do not intend to give up. We are taking the problem to the Board of Education. If that fails, there are other avenues to follow. We received local news coverage about this controversy and will go to the mainstream media if necessary. We don't want other children to suffer, and want as many parents as possible to be forewarned about their local schools.

For too long, parents have buried their heads in the sand and let other people decide what is best for our children. I will not let the state teach my children morals because the state has no morals. As parents, we are the role models for our children, and I intend to fight for that principle. People have a right to seek counseling, but when our child is taken out of class and cross-examined by a stranger without our consent, we must draw the line. Sooner or later, we will prevail in the interest of our children and our rights.

Interestingly, the president of the school Parent Teacher Association told us that the organization does not get involved in "these" matters. They involve themselves with issues such as smaller classroom sizes and more teachers' aids; they don't look into problems with school counselors, teachers, and parents.

Martin and Lynda Rogers

EDITORS' NOTE: Mrs. Rogers said that when she requested a copy of the notes taken during her daughter's counseling session, the counselor told her she "threw away the records."

Battling to assert their parental rights, two moms shut out of a teacher training session found they had reason to be suspicious, as educators discussed a "wellness program" that aimed to "help students become aware of the ineffectiveness of punishment as a motivator for long-range, positive change." The threat to their authority comes as no surprise to other parents who live in fear of a knock on their door by a Child Protective Services armed officer with a fresh tip from school officials.

CHAPTER ELEVEN

NO SECRET IS SAFE

D O NOT WRITE *your name on this survey. All of your answers will be kept private. No one at school or home will see them,"* says the cover of a ninth-grade survey about sexual behaviors.[1] *You'd think the survey was anonymous wouldn't you? Guess again. Page twenty-one asks for a series of identifying facts, such as the first initial of Mom and Dad's first names, their birth dates, the last digit of their phone numbers, and zip codes. (Any computer database with half a brain knows exactly who these kids are.)*

While the survey asks students to comment about what they "think" their friends are doing sexually and whether they are using birth control, etc., it also wants to know about their own sexual behaviors. But after answering twenty-seven questions, students are finally told that the next several questions are about their personal sexual behavior and are given four choices. They are:

> I am willing to answer these questions.
>
> I have never been sexually active and I prefer to skip these questions.
>
> I have been sexually active but I prefer to skip these questions.
>
> My parents sent in the letter saying I should not fill out this survey. I think I received it by accident, so I prefer to skip these questions.

Students who choose not to answer the questions are instructed to jump over to question forty-three on page nineteen. Did you get that? Even with a letter from parents denying permission for the survey, students are still required to answer forty-eight of sixty-two questions. Even if students don't answer questions thirty through forty-two, you can bet they read them.

Below is a sampling of just one of the optional survey questions asked. For each statement, the students choose one answer: "never, 1 time, 2-5 times, up to more than 20 times."

Question #32: Now think back over the past year... During the PAST YEAR, how many different times did these activities occur? (Emphasis in the original.)

A girl played with your penis.

A boy played with your penis or you played with a boy's penis.

You played with a girl's vagina/clitoris.

A girl put her mouth on your penis until you ejaculated (came).

A boy put is [sic] mouth on your penis until you ejaculated (came) or you put your mouth on a boy's penis until he ejaculated (came).

You put your mouth on a girl's vagina/clitoris.

You put your penis in a girl's vagina.

You put your penis in a boy's anus (butt) or a boy put his penis in your anus.

You put your penis in a girl's anus (butt).

This obscene series of questions then asks the whole series once again but this time asks if a condom was used. After subjecting ninth graders to all these offensive questions, the last question asks: "How many questions in this survey did you answer honestly?"

A West Virginia survey given to junior high students without parental permission, asked these true-false statements:

Frequent masturbation causes emotional problems and harm to your body.

Young women who have more than one sex partner are easy.

Too much sex stretches the vagina. Intercourse is the best kind of sex.

The average flaccid (soft) penis is 3-4 inches long.[2]

Other surveys probe into the lives of students and their families. For instance, My Beliefs—My Parents' Beliefs, *asks pupils to reveal their attitudes about their families as they comment on various topics such as "Par-*

ents should be the only ones allowed to give certain information to their children" and "Religion should be an important part of everyone's life."

Another survey, given to sixth graders in Pennsylvania, also delves into each student's family life. It asks:

> I fight with my parent(s) often.
>
> My parents treat other children in my family better than they treat me.
>
> I have too many responsibilities at home.
>
> My parents fight a lot.
>
> My parents are headed for divorce.

It isn't unusual for children to sometimes think that a parent treats one child better than another. Yet if asked, it also isn't unusual to discover that a brother or sister also has these same feelings. But what might happen if after reading one of these subjective surveys someone at the school decided that a child was being abused or the family was "at-risk"? Would the child be sent to the school counselor? Or maybe a social worker might show up on the family's doorstep.

The Material World Questionnaire seeks personal information about various aspects of each family member.

> List the members of your family (include name, age, occupation, and grade/level of education).
>
> How much money does each family member earn/month?
>
> Family possessions: What is each family member's most valued possession?
>
> What types of sacred objects are around the house?
>
> Alcohol, tobacco, and firearms: Are they available and what family members use them?

A California survey with no title (apparently teachers sometimes come up with their own surveys) asked the following questions about families:

> If your mother promised to be home at 2:00 in the afternoon to take you to the movies but didn't show up until suppertime and didn't even phone, what would be a good punishment for her? Would punishing her be likely to make her on time in the future?

When you are mad at your parents and want to get back at them, what little things do you do to anger or embarrass them?

If you woke up tomorrow and by magic were already grown-up and had kids of your own, how would you treat them differently from the way your parents treat you?

If you could change any one thing about your parents, what would it be?

Talk about violation of personal privacy! But school surveys and questionnaires are prevalent in schools today.

Tim Zerger, a registered art therapist, said, after viewing several of the surveys and curricula mentioned, that he believes they are "designed to elucidate their [the students'] thought processes, value judgments, and how they make moral choices ... the academic realm is now tampering in the area of the therapeutic realm."[3]

Drug, Alcohol, and Tobacco Self Reporting Surveys

Our son and his friends were laughing uproariously. When I asked what was so funny, these twelve-year-old boys said they had been "drug tested" at school.

Appalled by visions of school-administered urine tests, I asked what type of drug testing had been conducted. The boys said the teacher had told them to stop taking an academic test (!) and fill out a survey about their personal cigarette, alcohol, and drug use. They thought it was hilarious to facetiously answer "yes" to all of the questions.

I telephoned school district officials to ask why the district hadn't informed parents that a survey would be administered and why the district neglected to send parent permission slips home. I was told that the district did not need our permission as this was the state attorney general's annual survey. (More on this later.)

Five concerned parents from our district, including me, obtained copies of previously administered surveys. We strenuously objected to questions that asked for exceptionally personal, self-incriminating information about the student's participation in behaviors considered illegal in our state.

In August and September, the county Board of Education proposed seeking waivers from the state Department of Education so that they could continue administering the survey without parental permission.

Contrary to our district's position that survey answers were confidential, the information gleaned included definite means of identifying individual students. These included: initials, school, grade level, the language spoken at home, parent's income, parent education, ethnic background, grade level, GPA, and sex. At one meeting, a survey proponent generated considerable anger from parents when she stated that the proponents wanted to "go back and survey the same students again." So much for anonymity!

Another chilling moment occurred when a uniformed police officer stated that he didn't know anything about "this self-incrimination stuff" but that they, the police officers, needed the kids to fill out the surveys so they could "find out where the drugs are."

We do not send our children to school to become police informants or to forego their constitutional protections against self-incrimination. Therefore, we demanded to know what was being done with the completed surveys. We learned that nine thousand actual student surveys (raw data) were not kept in storage at the district offices, but at the Department of Health Services, Drug and Alcohol Division offices.

We repeatedly requested district officials, the county Board of Supervisors, and numerous state officials to authorize the destruction of the reprehensible, deceptive, and inaccurate surveys. We also suggested that letters of apology be sent to the nine thousand families. Officials informed us they would "review" our request for destruction of the surveys under applicable laws.

As our children matured, they became aware of our state's "zero tolerance" policies as they relate to adult opportunities in this state. They worried that answers given facetiously at the age of twelve could return to haunt them at sixteen when they apply for driver's licenses, education opportunities, or jobs. How could parents reassure their children that they had no reason for concern when officials arrogantly disregarded parental demands that the surveys be destroyed?

The Board of Supervisors informed us that the surveys were scheduled for destruction. To date, no public or personal apologies have been issued to the nine thousand families who deserve this courtesy.

NOTE ON THE ATTORNEY GENERAL'S ANNUAL SURVEY STATEMENT: County and school district officials deliberately misled parents by stating that they followed guidelines established by the state attorney general (AG). AG office staff forwarded a mountain of information including: model parent permission forms which clearly stated that not only is parental permission encouraged but required when conducting surveys.

Tura Avner

Values Appraisal Survey

During my son's freshman year, he took a Values Appraisal Scale survey in his Careers and Technology Class—required for graduation from high school and part of the School-to-Work program.

He read the first few questions and realized that they were extremely personal. He knew I would not want him to answer them and also knew that the school had no right to ask the types of questions listed on the survey.

Since this was a "careers" class, I couldn't understand what the following questions had to do with a career. There was a total of one hundred questions. Here are a few examples:

I have a regular physical checkup by my doctor every year.

I will regularly take my children to church services.

I have a close relationship with either my mother or my father.

I have a regular dental checkup every year.

I believe in a God that answers prayers.

I believe that tithing (giving 1/10 of one's earnings to the church) is one's duty to God.

Someday I would like to live in a large, expensive house.

I pray to God about my problems.

I like to spend holidays with my family.

I care what my parents think about the things I do.

I believe there is a life after death.

I love my parents.

I respect my mother and father.

I believe that God created man in his own image.

I am kind to animals.

When my son saw these questions, he asked permission to call me. The teacher said "No," and told him to sit down. He did go back to his seat, but a few seconds later he walked out of class, went to the admissions office, and was then sent to the vice principal's office, where he called me. I wasn't home at the time, but when I returned and checked my answering machine, I heard him crying. He said he was in the vice principal's office and had walked out of class because of a test he knew I wouldn't want him to take.

This was only his third day at a brand new school and, as a freshman, my son was very hesitant to assert his rights. The school made him feel he had no business questioning the teacher. I immediately went to the vice principal's office where I was told that the survey was not meant to offend anyone. While it may not have been their intent to offend, the questions were extremely offensive and a clear violation of state law which holds:

> No test, questionnaire, survey, or examination containing any questions about the pupil's personal beliefs or practices in sex, family life, morality, and religion, or any questions about the pupil's parents' or guardians' beliefs and practices in sex, family life, morality, and religion, shall be administered to any pupil in kindergarten or grades 1 to 12, inclusive, unless the parent or guardian of the pupil is notified in writing that this test, questionnaire, survey, or examination is to be administered and the parent or guardian of the pupil gives written permission for the pupil to take this test, questionnaire, survey, or examination.

Not only did my son's school not ask my permission, they also made him feel that he was wrong in asserting his rights. He was very upset, as I was, not only about the survey but also the teacher's refusal to allow him to check with his mother when he asked to do so.

I contacted an attorney who wrote the school a letter on our behalf. The district's assistant general counsel replied saying that the school had adopted educational programs to "better prepare our students to meet the employment challenges of the 21st century..." She went on to say that the school had developed a Career Exploration course which teaches students "self-awareness and decision-making skills." However, she added that the present teachers had not developed that program, and the material came from previous courses. (I have since learned that this survey has surfaced in four other states.)

The attorney for the district noted that the survey wasn't graded nor was the document kept by the teacher; it was "only marked for completion." She pointed out that the two students who complained were given alternate assignments. She refused to address the "content of the survey," and she ended by saying that, in the future, written notices would be sent home and that these "... [would] also fully comply with the requirements of [the state education code]."

I still have questions about how this situation was handled and how it will affect future students: 1) Will they disclose the full content of the survey when they send home notices? 2) Why are these types of questions needed for students to explore career options? 3) Why, if the surveys were only for student use, were they required to sign their names? 4) Why was a scan-tron survey form used?

Karen Wood

Do you pray? Do your parents fight? Are they headed toward divorce? Do you take drugs? A twelve-year-old who jokingly answered yes to the last question shockingly found intrusive school surveys—often given without knowledge or permission of parents—are no laughing matter.

CHAPTER TWELVE

WHAT CAN PARENTS DO?

A RE YOU FRUSTRATED? *Are you fed up with creative spelling, death education, math scores in which feelings count, guided imagery designed to "challenge" your child's values, and graphic presentations by condom ladies? Have you decided your daughter has attended her last "anti-bias" program? Are you prepared to no longer tolerate* jihad-*appeasing textbooks and surveys that probe the state of your marriage?*

Are you suffering along with a son who can't do basic algebra, because his textbook is filled with lectures on endangered species, air pollution, how to make chili, and "facts about the Dogon people of West Africa"? Or, worse, are you grieving for a child robbed of his innocence, or even his life, because he was exposed to images and ideas even adults should never bear?

You are not alone. You can join parents and grandparents across America already engaged in the battle to restore quality education in our public schools. If you find yourself rebuffed by a teacher or adminis-trator who insists the grievance was an anomaly, you are not alone. If you're labeled a troublemaker and told, "You're the only parent with this problem," you are not alone.

Now is the time for parents to reassert their rightful position as the true guardians of their children. Now is the time to take back control of public schools from the unelected elites who, with the blessing of school boards, impose their tradition-bending worldviews on children. Now is the time to challenge educators who believe public schools exist primar-ily to shape our children emotionally and psychologically.

Many teachers, in fact, will gladly return to the role of educator if par-ents will participate in their children's lives and take ownership of their education. The problem is not that the majority of parents do not care—it's that they don't know what is going on in their children's classrooms.

Parents commonly have not read their children's textbooks or con-sidered basic questions such as: Does the school violate my values?

Has my child been told his parents' belief system is wrong? Does my state allow children to receive health services without my knowledge or permission?

Your battle may be limited to your child or to his or her school. Success may be opting him out of offensive curricula or blocking the introduction of materials into her class.

But, ultimately, state and federal laws mandate many of today's educational practices. You can make temporary changes at the local level, but to win the war, parents must learn to fight at the state and national levels. This battle will be won by parents and concerned citizens who contact their local representatives—from school officials and state legislators to members of Congress—and present the facts, give evidence, and insist that schools return to the business of teaching objectively measured academics—not attitudes, values, beliefs, and behaviors.

Take an active role in your child's education. Following is a list of practical Dos and Don'ts that parents will find helpful when dealing with problems in their public schools.

At the Local Level:

DON'T Sign All School Forms

Do not sign any forms that give the school permission to conduct medical or psychological examinations or treatment. These may well end up in your child's permanent file that will follow your child throughout his or her academic life and could become available to your child's future employer.

DO Notify Schools

Do notify your child's school—in writing—that your child is not to be given any surveys, questionnaires, or curricula that ask personal questions about his or her personal beliefs, family life, religious beliefs, attitudes, feelings, sex, drugs, etc.

In an effort to diffuse parents, an attorney with the Office of General Counsel for the National Education Association (NEA) wrote a legal opinion for teachers in the February 1996 issue of NEA Today. In his article, the attorney spoke about the federal Protection of Pupil Rights Amendment (PPRA), sometimes referred to as the Hatch Amendment.[1] He wrote it because so many parents cited PPRA in an attempt to opt their children out of personally offensive courses. One teacher triumphantly handed the article to a parent and said: "Read this. You don't have the rights you think you do."

The legal opinion stated that while PPRA does give parents some rights, those rights are extremely narrow and apply only to surveys, analyses, or evaluations and then only if they are actually funded by the U.S. Department of Education.

Unfortunately, the NEA attorney was right. Unless the material is directly tied to federal dollars, federal protections don't apply. However, most states do have laws that give parents these rights. Check your state laws. For the most part, parents aren't exercising the rights they do have. As an example: California state law §51513 prohibits administering invasive surveys and questionnaires without parental permission.[2] The problem is that most teachers are either unaware of the law or ignore it and give the surveys without notifying parents. It is imperative that parents know the laws in their state and exercise the rights they have!

Your state legislator's office should be able to access all applicable laws. If your state has repealed your rights, work with a friendly legislator to get them back! (A few years ago, in California, legislation was passed to "sunset"—repeal—Education Code §51513. A small group of outraged parents contacted a state legislator who quickly drafted legislation to restore those rights.)

Don't Sign Compacts/Contracts

Do not sign any compacts/contracts. Schools that accept Title I funding from the federal Improving America's Schools Act (IASA) also accept the federal mandate to: "...develop with parents for all children...a school-parent compact..." The law does not say that parents must sign it. However, many schools send home notices either telling parents they must sign and return the contract/compact or implying that a signature is required.

The stated purpose of these compacts, of course, is academic improvement. But as with so many nice-sounding "reform" platitudes, you need to ask yourself, "Where is this headed?" Beware of the proverbial "wolf in sheep's clothing." Compacts are agreements between parents, teachers, students, and sometimes, principals. Basically, they are agreements between the signing parties to form a partnership. In this case, compacts are suppos-

229

edly for the educational benefit of the students. The idea sounds good. However, as a parent, do you really want to sign a contract that gives the school the power to join you as a partner in raising your child? A voluntary contract/compact between parents and their own children is fine. However, when schools get involved, far too often the school assumes the role of dictator by placing the parent in an untenable position.

One father reported that while he was running for a position on the local school board, he ran across a "permission form" for a program called Remedial Academic Progress. While it wasn't a contract, he was shocked at the way the "form" was worded.

He called it a "shocking display of institutional arrogance" and said that the form, after stating why the school felt that the student in question was in need of remediation, required the parent to check one of two statements at the bottom, and then sign it. The two choices were:

_____Yes, my child will participate in the RAP program.

_____No, even though the RAP program is critically necessary to my child's future academic success, he or she will not participate. Reason: _____

How would you like to be on record signing that form?

What happens if you don't live up to your contract?

A Florida mother who signed a compact filed a federal lawsuit because her kindergarten son was kicked out of school when she missed too many mandated meetings with the school. Why did Mom miss the meetings? She has kidney disease and must report for regular dialysis in order to live. Her son's public school evidently didn't think this was a good enough reason. The time has come to seriously question the government's interpretation of "parental involvement."

If you haven't heard about "parent/school compacts," you will shortly. They are either already in your local school, or coming soon.

Do Check Out the Curricula, Textbooks, Speakers, etc.

Ask to see all of the teacher's guides and supplementals. You can't always rely on the materials your child brings home. Viewing teachers' material is a must. Also ask for a list of any outside speakers, their credentials and the topics to be discussed.

NOTE: To obtain copies of these materials, call your district or county education offices to find out if they carry copies of the texts, handouts, teacher's manuals, etc. If not, get them directly from your teacher or school. Unfortunately, parents are sometimes given the run-around when they ask for these materials. If this happens to you, you can file a "State Public Records Request." A sample letter and explanation on how to file this request is provided by the United States Justice Foundation in the Appendices.

Do Read What YOUR CHILD Is Reading

Is the textbook really teaching math? History? Spelling? Does it promote politically-correct attitudes, i.e., "correct" attitude toward the environment, gun control, etc. (Beware—much of the environmental information found in schools is not backed by sound science. If in doubt—ask the experts!)[3]

Get a group of parents together. Divide up the "Recommended Reading" list; go to the library, check out the books that are recommended for your children, and read them yourselves. Are they really age appropriate? Is it something you want your child to read? If not, say so. Ask, or demand, if necessary, alternate assignments for your child.

NOTE: If your child is not reading by Christmas of his or her first grade year, teach him/her yourself with any of the excellent phonics based programs. Some experts say that if your child is not reading by the end of first grade, chances are he will never read at grade level! Make sure your child reads by the end of first, not third grade!

Do Complain

Whenever you protest curricula, methodology, outside speakers, etc., make sure you follow your district's policies and procedures.

1) Decide what you want to accomplish. Do you want to remove inappropriate material? Opt your child out of courses with offensive content? Draft new policies? Or something else?

2) First, take your concerns to the teacher.

3) If that doesn't give you satisfaction, make an appointment to see the principal.

4) If that fails, either: a) address the school board at a general school board meeting during the general comment portion, or b)

call your district office and ask to be placed on the school board's agenda at the earliest possible meeting. Find out their rules and follow them. (If you are not on the agenda, the board will not be able to address your concerns during the meeting; however they can make it an agenda item at a subsequent meeting.)

5) Work with other concerned parents. Form a parents' group—there *is* strength in numbers.

6) If your school board adheres to the three-to-five-minute rule and you need more time, have other parents speak. Divide your comments so that all areas are covered.

7) Present evidence. This may take the form of curricula, surveys or teaching methods, guest speakers, etc. Know your state law. If your district has violated the law—make it known.

8) Make sure every board member gets a copy of your examples.

9) Always send copies to your state representatives. They need to know what is going on in the classrooms of their districts.

10) Parents can also file complaints with the Commission on Teacher Credentialing. (Contact your state Department of Education to find the contact information for your Commission.)

11) Join policy-making committees. If they won't let you join— attend the meetings.

12) Make your voice heard.

NOTE: An excellent example of how to present curriculum or survey violations is listed in the Appendices. The example was successfully used against the textbook Holt's Health.

Do Talk with Your Child

Tell him/her not to answer any questions of a personal nature without checking with you. To take the pressure off the student, tell your child to say something like, "I'll be glad to answer this, but would you please call my mom or dad and get their permission first?"
SPECIAL NOTE FOR FATHERS: *Get involved in your child's education. Recent studies say that children whose fathers help them with homework, attend back-to-school nights, etc., do much better overall than students whose dads are not involved.*

Do Know the Law—State Laws

Find out what your state law says about parents' rights, the practice of psychology by unlicensed persons, and other relevant laws. (Your state legislator can provide you with all these laws.) Another helpful law is one that was passed by California in 1996. This law, introduced by Assemblyman George House, prohibited anyone other than a licensed, credentialed psychologist from engaging in psychological practices with students.[4] Prior to its passage, California law stated that no one could engage in psychological practices without a license except for public school employees. Check your state law to see if you have similar "loophole" verbiage.

Does your state law specify that explicit systematic phonics be used to teach children to read,[5] or computational math,[6] or accurate history, etc.?

Legislation? Me? How?

Are you convinced that you need to change your state's laws? Yes, you can make a difference. You can be instrumental in bringing about needed change.

1) Collect examples of parental rights abuses, invasive questionnaires, inappropriate and/or illegal curricula, etc.

2) Find a legislator who will listen to you. (Ask friends, etc. for references. He/she may not necessarily be your own local state representative.)

3) If you know someone in the legislator's district—ask that person to help you make an appointment and accompany you on the visit.

4) Don't expect to meet with the representative at the first meeting. While it may be possible, be prepared to have your initial meeting with a legislative aide.

5) Present your case. Show your examples. Be concise, calm, and knowledgeable.

6) Once convinced, the legislator may introduce a bill or find another legislator to introduce one for you. (If possible, have a copy of the type of legislation you'd like to see enacted.)

7) You can help by generating testimony and support for the bill.

Federal Laws

It is imperative to understand the laws that have had such a great impact on today's reform movement. The following bills can be accessed online.

Elementary and Secondary Education Act (ESEA), Public Law: http://www.ed.gov/legislation/ESEA/index.html

(The 1994 Act that helped implement Goals 2000 and STW): www.ed.gov/policy/elsec/leg/esea02/index.html

(The 2002 version that authorized the No Child Left Behind Act)

Improving America's Schools Act (IASA), Public Law 103-227: www.ed.gov/pubs/Final/index.html

More Info on No Child Left Behind: www.ed.gov/policy/elsec/leg/esea02/index.html

Litigation

Nothing you've tried has worked. Now what do you do? Litigation should always be your last course of action. However, sometimes it is necessary. Anytime you believe your rights have been violated and the teacher, principal, and/or district will not take appropriate action, you may need to seek the advice of legal counsel.

Gary Kreep, executive director of the United States Justice Foundation, has the following advice for parents reading this book and who may be considering legal action:

If you believe that you have done everything you can to resolve the problem, short of litigation, contact an attorney or a legal organization well versed in Education Law. Unfortunately, most, but not all, of the private attorneys involved in Education Law work for school districts or law firms under contract to school districts. Fortunately, however, there are individuals and legal organizations that litigate school-related issues on a regular basis [see list below].

You need an attorney well versed in Education Law to advise you as to whether you have grounds for litigation and what your chances of success are. Unfortunately, there are circumstances where, despite the fact that a family has been wronged or a law violated, there is little or nothing that litigation can do. The only recourse may be legislation, usually by way of adoption of a policy by the school district's board of trustees.

Given the control that the teacher unions and the educrats have over most school boards, this is usually unlikely.

In the Appendices that follow, you will find guidelines and strategies to employ with officials at all levels of government. Change, you will discover, can be put in motion with a tactically crafted phone call, e-mail, or a letter to the right person. But patience and persistence must follow. And for that you will need the co-laboring and encouragement of other awakened parents responding to their call as stewards over every aspect of their children's lives.

To contact the authors or to share your own public school horror stories, go to www.fromcrayonstocondoms.com.

APPENDICES

Is Legal Help Available?

The following organizations are listed for resource and informational purposes only; they have provided no creative, legal, or substantive review of the book; and make no representations of any kind in connection with the publication unless so stated in other sections.

For the most part, these organizations provide their services at no charge, although contributions to help with the cost of litigation are appreciated. Please remember that all these organizations have budget constraints, and that they may not be able to take every case brought to their attention.

LEGAL FOUNDATIONS

Advocates for Faith and Freedom
24910 Las Brisas Road, Suite 110
Murrieta, CA 92562
Local: (951) 304-7583
Toll Free: (888) 588-6888
E-mail: info@faith-freedom.com
Web site: www.faith-freedom.com

Alliance Defense Fund
15100 N. 90th Street
Scottsdale, AZ 85260
Phone: 1-800-TELL-ADF
E-mail: www.alliancedefensefund.org/adfresources/contact/general.aspx
Web site: www.alliancedefensefund.org

American Center for Law & Justice
P.O. Box 90555
Washington, DC 90555
Phone: 1-800-296-4529
E-mail: www.aclj.org/Contact
Web site: www.aclj.org

Liberty Legal Institute
903 E. 18th Street, Ste 230
Plano, TX 75074
Phone: (972) 423-3131
E-mail: info@libertylegal.org
Web site: www/libertylegal.org

Pacific Justice Institute
P.O. Box 276600
Sacramento, CA 95827
Phone: (916) 857-6900
E-mail: pji.org/request
Web site: www.Pacificjustice.org

Rutherford Institute
PO Box 7482
Charlottesville, VA 22906-7482
Phone: (434) 978-3888
E-mail: tristaff@rutherford.org
Web site: www.rutherford.org

Texas Justice Foundation
8122 Datapoint Drive, Ste. 812
San Antonio, TX 78229-3273
Phone: (210) 614-7157
E-mail: info@txjf.org
Web site: www.txjf.org

United States Justice Foundation
932 D Street Suite 2
Ramona, CA 92065
Tel: (760) 788-6624
E-mail: usjf@usjf.net
Web site: www.usjf.net

Who Can Tell Me if My Child's Curriculum Is Academically Sound?

History/Social Studies
The Textbook League: www.textbookleague.org
American Textbook Council: www.historytextbooks.org
Education Research Analysts: www.textbookreviews.org
National Council for History Education: www.nche.net
Core Knowledge Foundation: www.coreknowledge.org

Math Methodology
Mathematically Correct: www.mathematicallycorrect.com
HOLD: www.rahul.net/dehnbase/hold
Saxon Math: www.Saxonpub.com

Reading Methodology
National Right to Read Foundation: www.nrrf.org
Association for Direct Instruction: www.adihome.org
The Phonics Institute: www.readingstore.com
Center for Applied Research: darkwing.uoregon.edu/~bgrossen/
Abeka: www.abeka.com

Other Resource Links

Sex Education
The Medical Institute (formerly the Medical Institute for Sexual Health)
Web site: www. medinstitute.org
E-mail: medinstitute@medinstitute.org
Dr. Judith Reisman: www.drjudithreisman.com
Diane Fessler: www.fessler.com/SBE/health.htm
Sex Respect: www.sexrespect.com

Curriculum: Islamism
The Textbook League: www.textbookleague.org
American Textbook Council: www.historytextbooks.org
Blessed Cause: www.blessedcause.org
Stop The Madressa Coalition: stopthemadrassa.wordpress.com
American Values for Kids: www.americanvaluesforkids.org

New Age/Paganism in Curriculum
Mission America: www.missionamerica.com

Homosexual Issues
Pro-family sites:
Mission America: www.missionamerica.com
Americans for Truth about Homosexuality: www.americansfortruth.com
Day of Truth: www.dayoftruth.org/comingsoon.htmp
Exodus: www.truthandtolerance.org/truth
Corporate Resource Council:
www.corporateresourcecouncil.org/white_papers/Health_Risks.pdf
PFOX: www.pfox.org/educationnews.htm

Pro-homosexual sites:
Gay, Lesbian, Straight Education Network: www.glsen.org
Safe Schools Coalition: www.safeschoolscoalition.org/safe.html

Obscene Literature Assignments and Texts
Parents against Bad Books in Schools: www.pabbis.com
Family Friendly Libraries: www.fflibraries.org

General School Reform
Center for Education Reform: www.edreform.com
American Policy Council: www.americanpolicy.com/educ/main.htm
Eagle Forum: www.eagleforum.org/educate
American Family Association: www.afa.net/education
Ed Watch: www.edwatch.org
The Education Deform Watchdog Page: www.arthurhu.com/index/edreform.htm
Thomas Fordham Foundation: www.edexcellence.net/foundation/ global/index.cfm

Christian and Private Education
Alliance for the Separation of School and State: www.schoolandstate.org
Gateways to Better Education: www.gtbe.org
Christian Educators Association: www.ceai.org
Discover Christian Schools: www.discoverchristianschools.com
Citizens for Excellence in Education: www.nace-cee.org

Home School Resources
Family Centered Learning: www.familycenteredlearning.org
Home Ed Magazine: www.homeedmag.com
Home School: www.homeschool.com
Homeschool World: www.home-school.com

Bilingual Education
One Nation: www.oneNation.org

Research on Teacher Unions
Education Policy Institute: www.educationpolicy.org
Education Intelligence Agency: www.eiaonline.com
Education Watch: www.capitalresearch.org/ew/index2.html
Evergreen Freedom Foundation: www.effwa.org
Landmark Legal Foundation: www.landmarklegal.org

Psychoactive Drugs
Kids, Drugs, & Guns: www.geocities.com/jurist6/drugkids.htm

Anti-Day Care
Day Cares Don't Care: http://www.daycaresdontcare.org

School Checklist: Questions Parents Can Ask

The following questions are designed to help parents assess the quality of their child's school. It is reprinted with the permission of Chris Patterson and the Texas Public Policy Foundation. Our thanks to them for allowing it to be reproduced here. For a copy of the complete *Parents' Handbook for Successful Schools*, write to: Texas Public Policy Foundation, PO Box 40519, San Antonio, TX 78229, www.texaspolicy.com.

Answer YES, PARTIALLY, or NO to each of the following questions.

ELEMENTS OF GOOD INSTRUCTIONAL PRACTICES

Are students given clear, written expectations for classroom learning and behavior?

Are students required to meet these expectations?

Do teachers maintain orderly classrooms and discipline?

Are disruptive students removed from the classroom?

Are teachers (not students) responsible for planning and directing classroom learning?

Do students have as many opportunities (or more) for individual learning as for group work?

Is homework assigned regularly which must be completed outside the school?

Are assignments corrected by the teacher and returned to the student in a timely manner?

As students progress to higher grades and more advanced courses, is a greater amount of homework assigned?

Does instruction balance laboratory work or project-based learning with the study of concepts and theories?

Does instruction focus equally on developing a foundation of facts and skills, as well as concepts (e.g., students must know major dates, battles, and generals of war, as well as the causes of conflict)?

Are core subjects (math, social studies, science, and English) taught as separate courses? Or if courses are combined (interdisciplinary courses), does testing show that students learn as much when the courses are taught separately?

In core subjects, does instruction focus on the specific subject rather than extraneous matters such as environmentalism in math, gender equity in English, and political activism in science?

Does the school limit block scheduling (nontraditional class lengths) to laboratory sessions and to subjects that are not core foundation courses (such as math, science, social studies, and English)?

If classes are taught in mixed age groups (not specific grades), does testing show that students are learning at their expected grade levels for achievement?

Is most of the school day (75 percent) devoted to studying core academics (math, science, English, and social studies)?

Does the school provide parents the opportunity to identify an academic program best suited to their children and to plant the sequence of courses?

Must all students take every core academic course that is listed as a graduation requirement (without being able to obtain a course substitution such as "Life Skills Math" instead of "Geometry")?

Are nonacademic activities (such as volunteer service, football practice, and yearbook editing) scheduled before or after the academic school day?

Are nonacademic activities such as community service voluntary and not required for graduation?

Do teachers distribute or make available a syllabus for high school courses (listing learning objectives, units of study, instructional timelines, assignments, tests, textbooks, and supplementary materials)?

Is advanced instruction available to students in core academic courses (*e.g.,* honors or pre-advanced academic [AP] courses)?

Is tutoring or remedial help provided to students who are not achieving on grade level?

Are high school students provided the opportunity (but not required) to select career and vocational instruction as elective courses?

Are students encouraged to take Advanced Placement and Dual Credit College courses?

Can students meet school requirements on the school campus or at home (without being required to participate in such activities as community events or business functions)?

Are students encouraged to participate in academic contests (*e.g.,* University Interscholastic League [UIL] competitions and science fairs)?

Are students recognized and rewarded for winning or placing in academic competitions?

Are awards given for outstanding or highest academic achievement in core academic subjects?

Does the school recognize class rankings for salutatorian and valedictorian?

Does the school's mission statement identify academic learning as its primary function and high academic achievement as its primary goal?

ELEMENTS OF GOOD MATH INSTRUCTION

Does the school have clear, explicit expectations for math knowledge and skills that students are expected to learn for each grade and each course?

Are students required to master and to automatically use specific facts and processes (*e.g.,* number facts; multi-digit multiplication and division; manipulations with fractions, decimals, and percent computation with positive and negative numbers; use of exponents and logarithms; solving linear equations by transformation; use of letters to represent unknown quantities or variables; converting written descriptions to algebraic expressions or equations; and factoring)?

Are students required to learn mental computation before using calculators (reserving calculators for middle and/or high school)?

Are correct solutions to problems required and credited?

Are students encouraged to use math symbols to represent numbers and solve problems (instead of models or concrete objects)?

Is immediate remedial instruction provided during each grade and/or course when a student has difficulty?

Are students expected to master the pre-algebra skills required to study algebra I in eighth grade?

Are students expected to use mathematical reasoning and complete mathematical proofs?

Does the school hold students responsible for attaining expected levels of math proficiency before promotion to the next grade or course?

Does the math program have an established record of success both in the school and in other schools (based upon objective data from large groups over time)?

Does the course material (*i.e.*, textbook and handouts) provide sufficient explanation and direction so that the student or parents can use it for instruction at home?

Do teachers have specific training (or certification) in the math courses or grades they teach?

ELEMENTS OF GOOD ENGLISH LANGUAGE ARTS INSTRUCTION

Are phonemic awareness and explicit systematic phonics used to teach initial reading skills in kindergarten through third grade?

Are phonics-based materials provided to students?

Are students provided direct instruction in spelling, grammar, punctuation, and sentence structure?

Are students encouraged to use correct spelling, grammar, punctuation, and sentence structure in first grade?

Are students provided textbooks or workbooks on spelling, grammar, punctuation, and sentence structure?

Are students expected to read at grade level by third grade?

Are informal reading assessments given regularly and frequently to monitor progress, and is intervention provided when necessary?

Are students required to use English while studying English Language Arts?

Does the school have a plan for systematic vocabulary and concept development for kindergarten through twelfth grade?

Are students required to read a variety of fiction, non-fiction, poetry, and plays (modern and classical)?

Are students required to read periodicals, instructions, charts, and technical manuals?

Are students expected to read historically and culturally significant works from the literary and civic heritage of English speaking peoples?

Are students required to write critical analyses of literature (demonstrating knowledge of themes, plot, character development, genre, symbolism, etc.)?

Are students required to write research papers?

Are students required to write in a variety of formats (*e.g.*, notes, outline, and formal/informal correspondence)?

Are students required to study four English courses in high school (including separate courses in American and World Literature)?

ELEMENTS OF GOOD SOCIAL STUDIES INSTRUCTION

Are students taught to respect their national heritage as Americans, as well as the heritage of other nationalities?

Are students required to recall significant dates, events, places, and individuals?

Are students required to study the ideas of America's founding fathers?

Is the primary focus of study devoted to history and geography (not sociology, psychology, or environment)?

Are original documents and sources used as the basis of instruction (such as the Bill of Rights)?

Do instruction and curriculum materials furnish a balance of perspectives without revealing bias or judgment?

Are students required to learn the history of their state in middle school?

Are students required to learn the history of their nation in high school?

Are students required to take four years of social studies in high school (including separate courses in U.S. Government and Economics)?

Are students taught to value the governance, economic, and cultural foundations of America (including constitutional democracy, free enterprise, representative government, free markets, Judeo-Christian principals, heritage of western civilization, and individual as well as states' rights)?

ELEMENTS OF GOOD TEXTBOOKS AND EFFECTIVE TEXTBOOK USE

Are textbooks furnished to each student?

Are students encouraged to take textbooks home?

Do teachers use textbooks (and/or independent materials) to organize and sequence what students are expected to learn?

Are textbooks factual and objective (offering a balanced perspective)?

Is the content of the textbook directly related to the subject of the course (*i.e.*, career awareness is not included in a science book and environmental problems are not included in a math book)?

Do textbooks include original materials where appropriate (such as Lincoln's Gettysburg Address instead of an account of the speech)?

Are review questions provided at the end of chapters or sections?

Are textbook assignments and chapter tests designed to promote individual accountability (rather than the efforts of a group)?

Do textbook assignments and tests require students to demonstrate theoretical knowledge and skills learning as well as applied learning (*e.g.*, projects or exhibitions)?

ELEMENTS OF GOOD TESTING AND GRADING

Are most grades based upon an individual student's (not group) performance?

Are grades furnished at regularly scheduled points in the school term and given as a letter or number?

Are tests corrected by teachers and returned to the students?

Do grades reflect that students have fully met all of the requirements for the course or grade?

Do grades reflect the actual level of student achievement without grade inflation?

Are students allowed to fail courses? Are teachers encouraged to fail students who have not met course or grade level standards?

Is learning tested by both standardized exams and "authentic assessment" (projects, demonstrations, or exhibitions of learning)?

Do tests require students to demonstrate their knowledge rather than just the ability to produce projects and exhibitions?

Do tests require students to demonstrate their knowledge without aids such as open books, formula charts, and programmed calculators?

Are grades based upon objectively scored, standardized tests, as well as written essays?

Do tests assess academic knowledge and skills identified by curriculum standards (rather than personal, social, or psychological traits)?

Are tests designed to measure the extent of learning above grade level achievement (not just minimum competency)?

Are students promoted because they have achieved passing grades?

Are nationally-normed standardized tests (which will provide achievement comparisons between schools, counties, and states) administered annually?

Does the high school exit test assess twelfth-grade-level material (rather than tenth-or-eighth-grade level)?

Do some students score at a level of 4 or 5 on Advanced Placement tests which are offered in high school?

Do SAT and A score mirror (or align with) high school grade point averages? Do "A" students do well on pre-ACT tests?

Do students with As and Bs in high school do well on college proficiency or entrance exams (achieving scores that exempt them from having to take remedial courses)?

Holt's Health Textbook vs. State Education Codes

The following comparison was used by a parent in her district to defeat the adoption of Holt's Health. She compared textbook sections to California's State Education Code. (Similar comparisons can be made with other states' laws.)

PAGE TEXT	CODE VIOLATION
"In between the labia minora is the clitoris. Like the penis, the clitoris is the source of greatest sexual excitement and has the capacity to become erect. It is covered by a hood of skin that is connected to the labia minora [Health—Student book].	State of California Education Code Violation 51553(a): "All material and instruction in classes that teach sex education and discuss sexual intercourse shall be age appropriate." This discussion is sexually stimulating. There is too much detail given to the subject which has little documentation.
"Anal intercourse is when a man puts his penis into the anus of another person. It is possible for either person to transmit the virus to the other. HIV can get through the mucus membranes of the anus, the rectum, or the opening in the penis [Health—Student book].	State of California Education Code Violation 51553(a): "All material and instruction in classes that teach sex education and discuss sexual intercourse shall be age appropriate." The text should mention that sodomy is illegal, and that it is dangerous with or without a condom. The passage needs to specify that anal sex is one of the most dangerous activities, according to the Center for Disease Control.

FILING A FEDERAL "FREEDOM OF INFORMATION" REQUEST

The Federal Freedom of Information Act allows citizens to obtain records and documents that may not normally be available to citizens. All states have their own versions of this law. The United States Justice Foundation (USJF) has developed the language below to assist citizens in obtaining records from federal or state governments under the Freedom of Information Act.

A request should be made in writing and delivered personally (if hand delivered, have a copy of your request date stamped and initialed by the person who receives it) or sent by mail (return receipt requested, if possible) to the federal or state agency that you wish to obtain a document from.

Keep in mind, however, that each agency will likely have its own procedures for obtaining documents. As such, the sample letter may have to be adapted in order to comply with any particular agency's rules. Most federal and state agencies will have a Freedom of Information Office which you can contact to obtain information as to where and to whom to direct a specific request.

Generally, if the documents you seek were produced or funded by a Federal agency then you use the Federal FOIA law. If the agency you are seeking documents from is a state agency, then you need to comply with that procedure. Your state legislator will provide you with this info if asked. Unless the program is a federally funded program, most school programs and activities would come under a state Freedom of Information law.

Sample Federal Agency Request:

Date
Name and address of the governmental agency
RE: Request for Documents [Freedom of Information Act—5 U.S.C. 552]

Dear Sir or Madam:

Pursuant to 5 U.S.C. 552(a)(3), I respectfully request copies of the following item(s) from [name of agency].

1) [example: The Minutes to the October 1, 2007, school board meeting at the XYZ Unified School District];

2) [example: The receipts for travel expenses between January 1, 2006, and December 31, 2006, of Assistant Superintendent Jane Doe];

3) [example: Any and all correspondence between the United States Department of Education and the XYZ Unified School District concerning _____ between January 1, 2007, through and including February 28, 2007]

4) [example: Any and all policies, and/or regulations, concerning the determination of the level of English proficiency of bilingual teachers whose native language is other than English]

As per 5 U.S.C. 552(a)(6), kindly make a determination of the accessibility of these documents within twenty (20) business days and notify me as to the status of the request. If the above request is not in accordance with published rules stating the time, place, fees (if any), and procedures to be followed, please mail me a copy of said rules. Upon receipt of an invoice, I promise to pay the fees associated with this request. How-

ever, if the fees exceed $_____, please notify me before proceeding further. Thank you for your cooperation in this matter.

It is important to keep a copy of your request as well as any correspondence from the federal agency. Should the agency ask for clarification and/or additional information, it is important that you respond as soon as possible as the agency will likely not proceed until they receive your response. Under limited circumstances, a waiver or reduction of the fees for the search, review, and duplication of documents may be granted if it has been requested [5 U.S.C. § 552(a)(4)(A)]. Each agency is required to have its own regulations regarding fee waivers [5 U.S.C. § 552(a)(4)(A)(i)]. As a result, it may be to your advantage to obtain information from the agency regarding its particular rules for fee waivers before you proceed. A good place to begin is to contact the agency's Freedom of Information Office and ask for a copy of the rules pertaining to fee waivers and a fee waiver application. It is also advisable to ask for a copy of the agency's fee schedule.

If your request for documents under the Freedom of Information Act is denied due to a claimed exemption by the agency, ask for a citation of the law upon which the exemption is based. Further, the denial should list the names of the individuals who made the decision on your request [5 U.S.C. 552(a)(6)(c)]. A denial of a request under the Freedom of Information Act is subject to appeal and the agency must inform you of the appeals process [5 U.S.C. 552(a)(6)(A)(i)]. Further, the Freedom of Information Act is enforceable in Federal District Courts [5 U.S.C. 552(a)(4)(B)]. Should you need to seek enforcement in court, it is advisable to hire an attorney.

Sample Legislation

Use the following laws, or proposed legislation, as guidelines to craft your own legislation. Take it to a friendly legislator in your state who can have it written to the language specifications of your state. (Note: Some of the following language passed in California but has been repealed—just another reason for parents to remain ever vigilant.)

PARENTAL RIGHTS: (California Education Code #51513)

> No test, questionnaire, survey, or examination containing any questions about the pupil's personal beliefs or practices in sex, family life, morality, and religion, or any questions about the pupil's parents' or guardians' beliefs and practices in sex, family life, morality, and religion, shall be administered to any pupil in kindergarten or grades 1 to 12, inclusive, unless the parent or guardian of the pupil is notified in writing that this test, questionnaire, survey, or examination is to be administered, and the parent or guardian of the pupil gives written

permission for the pupil to take this test, questionnaire, survey, or examination.

PROHIBITION OF PSYCHOLOGICAL ACTIVITIES BY UNLICENSED PERSONS: (Original text of bill is listed here; California Education Code §49422. Penalties for violations should be added in any law you try to pass. These should be commensurate with existing penalties in other areas.)

Any person who is an employee of an academic institution, public school, or a governmental agency who does not meet the requirements of subdivision (a), and who is not a licensed psychologist or a graduate student or psychological intern in psychology under the direct supervision of a licensed psychologist, shall be prohibited from engaging in activities of a psychological nature including, but not limited to, utilizing psychological methods, and administering psychological materials, including questionnaires and surveys with psychological content, in the course of his or her employment.

ABSOLUTE RIGHT TO ACCESS:

Parents of currently enrolled or former pupils have an absolute right of access to any and all pupil records related to their children, which are maintained by school districts or private schools. The editing or withholding of any such records, except as provided for in this chapter, is prohibited.

Each school district shall adopt procedures for the granting of requests by parents for copies of all pupil records pursuant to Section 49065, or to inspect and review records during regular school hours, provided that the requested access shall be granted no later than five days following the date of the request. Procedures shall include the notification to the parent of all official pupil records if not centrally located and the availability of qualified certificated personnel to interpret records where requested.

FEDERAL—PROTECTION OF PUPIL RIGHTS ACT (PPRA): (Nevada enacted a state law that made this act the state's parental rights law.)

§ 1232h. (a) Inspection of instructional materials by parents or guardians

All instructional materials, including teacher's manuals, films, tapes, or other supplementary material which will be used in connection with any survey, analysis, or evaluation as part of any applicable program shall be available for inspection by the parents or guardians of the children.

Limits on survey, analysis, or evaluation-

No student shall be required, as part of any applicable programs, to submit to a survey, analysis, or evaluation that reveals information concerning—

(1) political affiliations;

(2) mental and psychological problems potentially embarrassing to the student or his family;

(3) sex behavior and attitudes;

(4) illegal, anti-social, self-incriminating and demeaning behavior;

(5) critical appraisals of other individuals with whom respondents have close family relationships;

(6) legally recognized privileged or analogous relationships, such as those of lawyers, physicians, and ministers, or

(7) income (other than that required by law to determine eligibility for participation in a program or for receiving financial assistance under such program),without the prior consent of the student (if the student is an adult or emancipated minor), or in the case of any unemancipated minor, without the prior written consent of the parent.

The following is the actual bill as it was introduced.

BILL NUMBER: AB 170: CHAPTERED PHONICS

INTRODUCED BY Assembly Members Alpert, Burton, and Conroy Co-author Baldwin

JANUARY 23, 1995

THE PEOPLE OF THE STATE OF CALIFORNIA DO ENACT AS FOLLOWS:

SECTION 1. Section 60200.4 is added to the Education Code, to read:

60200.4. (a) The State Board of Education shall ensure that the basic instructional materials that it adopts for mathematics and reading in grades 1 to 8, inclusive, are based on the fundamental skills required by these subjects, including, but not limited to, systematic, explicit phonics, spelling, and basic computational skills.

(b) It is the intent of the Legislature that the fundamental skills of all subject areas, including systematic, explicit phonics, spelling, and basic computational skills, be included in the adopted curriculum frameworks and that these skills and related tasks increase in depth and complexity from year to year. It is the intent of the Legislature that the instructional materials adopted by the State Board of Education meet the provisions of this section.

SEC. 2. Notwithstanding Section 17610 of the Government Code, if the Commission on State Mandates determines that this act contains costs mandated by the state, reimbursement to local agencies and school districts for those costs shall be made pursuant to Part 7 (commencing with Section 17500) of Division 4 of Title 2 of the Government Code. If the statewide cost of the claim for reimbursement does not exceed one million dollars ($1,000,000), reimbursement shall be made from the State Mandates Claims Fund.

Notwithstanding Section 17580 of the Government Code, unless otherwise specified, the provisions of this act shall become operative on the same date that the act takes effect pursuant to the California Constitution.

SEC. 3. This act is an urgency statute necessary for the immediate preservation of the public peace, health, or safety within the meaning of Article IV of the Constitution and shall go into immediate effect. The facts constituting the necessity are:

The poor performance of pupils who took the California Learning Assessment System (CLAS) and the National Assessment of Education Progress tests indicates that it is imperative that steps be taken immediately to ensure that all pupils in grades 1 to 8, inclusive, are learning to read, write, and compute. To ensure that these steps are taken at the earliest possible time, it is necessary that this act take effect immediately.

NOTES

Foreword

1. Cited in Russ Wise, "Education and New Age Humanism," Probe Ministries, 1995. Accessed April 9, 2008 at http://www.leaderu.com/orgs/probe/docs/newageed.html.

Introduction: It's a National Problem

1. Brian Cutting, *Language Is Fun: Teacher's Book, Level One, Book One* (Desoto, TX: Wright Group, 1991), 19.

2. See Carol Ann Lindsay's story under "Curriculum of Social Engineering."

3. Senator Robert Byrd of West Virginia, speech before Congress, "A Failure to Produce Better Students," Congressional Record, June 9, 1997, S5393.

4. Personal interview with editor Karen Holgate.

5. U.S. Department of Education Office of Education Research and Improvement, Study of School-to-Work Initiatives: Studies of Education Reform, 1996, pg. xii.

6. Eric A. Hanushek, "The Impact of Differential Expenditures on School Performance," *Educational Researcher* 18, no. 4 (May 1989): 45-62.

7. Marcy Stein, et. al., *The Beginning Reading Instruction Study* (Washington, DC: U.S. Government Printing Office, 1993).

8. Part of the new education reform movement that believes students should construct their own knowledge.

9. Rob Reiner, *Equal Time*, CNBC, January 9, 1997.

Chapter One

1. Andrew Mollison, "After 25 years, Education Department is here to stay," *Phi Delta Kappan* 86, no. 9 (May 2005): 666-673.

2. Brian Cutting, *Language Is Fun: Teacher's Book, Level One, Book One* (Desoto, TX: Wright Group, 1991), 19.

3. Debra Saunders, "Truly Loco in Loco Parentis," *San Francisco Chronicle*, October 5, 1994.

4. Jerry Moe and Peter Ways, *Conducting Support Groups for Elementary Children K-6* (Washington, DC: Johnson Institute, 1991).

5. A common practice when parents confront proponents of new school reforms.

6. Susan Jo Russell and Rebecca B. Corwin, *Sorting: Groups and Graphs, A unit of study for grades 2-3 from Used Numbers: Real Data in the Classroom,* Developed at Technical Education Research Centers and Lesley College, p. 4.

7. Ibid., 68.

Chapter Two

1. A compendium of common "authentic" literature books used in public schools can be found at www.pabbis.com. Do not allow children to see this Web site as it features extremely vulgar books used in our schools.

2. Brian Cutting, *Language Is Fun: Teacher's Book, Level One, Book One* (Desoto, TX: Wright Group, 1991).

3. Arturo Islas, *Rain God* (New York: Avon Books, 1984).

Chapter Three

1. Personal interview with editor Karen Holgate.

2. Debbie Pelley in her testimony before the Arkansas Joint Interim Education Committee, November 19, 1998.

3. The California Learning Assessment (CLAS) is no longer given in California. However, many of the concepts promoted in CLAS are incorporated in classrooms across the nation.

4. After parents and legislators protested the outrageous story prompts and the prohibition against parents or legislators from viewing the tests, California's Department of Education was forced to drop the assessment testing.

Chapter Four

1. Liz Twardon and Tarek Hamada, "2 Canton Township boys found hanged," *Detroit News*, March 27, 1990.

2. Quoted in *Blumenfeld Education Letter*, "The Nalepa Case: Educators Can Now Cause the Death of a Child and Get Away With It," vol. 10, no. 1 (January 1995).

3. Ibid.

4. Ibid.

5. "What you need to know to help safeguard your child," http://www.realsexedfacts.com/what-you-need-to-know-to-help-safeguard-your-child.html. Last modified August 7, 2007.

6. AB 3188, Assemblyman George House. Relevant language from the bill can be found in the Appendices. An amended version is now CA Education Code §49422.

7. Channel 13 TV news, in which editor Karen Holgate was also interviewed, 1997.

8. Private interview with editor Karen Holgate after samples of school surveys were submitted for his review.

9. David Shaffer, M.D., et. al., "Practice Parameter for the Assessment and Treatment of Children and Adolescents with Suicidal Behavior," *Journal of the American Academy of Child & Adolescent Psychiatry*, vol. 40 (July 2001) Sup. at http://www.aacap.org/clinical/suicide.htm.

Chapter Five

1. Eagle Forum, "Gifted and Talented Curriculum Program Raises Concerns," *Education Reporter*, no. 141, October 1997.

2. Jerry Moe and Peter Ways, *Conducting Support Groups for Elementary Children K-6, A Guide for Educators and other Professionals* (Washington, DC: Johnson Institute), 131.

3. Ibid, 25.

4. Richard Core, "Schools Ban Hypnotists after Carlsbad Incident," *Los Angeles Times*, May 14, 1992.

5. Harold Rose, MD, *Encyclopedia Americana*, vol. 14 (1995): 480.

Chapter Six

1. Susan Brinkman, "Sordid Science: The Sex Research of Alfred C. Kinsey," *Catholic Standard & Times*, August 14, 2005, http://www.drjudithreisman.com/archives/2005/08/sordid_science.html.

2. Judith Reisman, "Reliance of the U.S. Catholic Church on the Discredited Field of Human Sexuality and on Sexology Advisors Whose Scientific and Moral Foundation Deviate Radically from That of the Church," Institute for Media Education, Unpublished Report, 2002.

3. Centers for Disease Control and Prevention, "One in Four Female Adolescents Is Infected with at Least One Sexually Transmitted Infection,

New CDC Study Finds," March 11, 2008, http://www.cdc.gov/stdconference/ 2008/media/summaries-11march2008.htm#tues1.

4. Life Dynamics conducted a study in which staff impersonating minor girls called Planned Parenthood clinics and informed them they were minors. In numerous cases, Planned Parenthood counselors not only assured the girls that they could get an abortion, but promised them anonymity in violation of state child molestation reporting laws (www.lifedynamics.com). Also, the Attorneys General of Kansas and Indiana have charged Planned Parenthood with servicing minor girls and concealing the identities of pedophiles (http://prolifeamerica.com/AG_investigation_of_abortion_clinics.cfm).

5. Lawrence K. Altman, "Sex Infections Found in Quarter of Teenage Girls," *New York Times*, March 12, 2008.

6. Both Planned Parenthood and NARAL maintain Political Action Committees in many states for the purpose of supporting or opposing local candidates.

7. *Positive Prevention: HIV/STD Prevention Education for America's Youth.*

8. Ibid, 237.

9. Cited in William L. Roper, MD, MPH, Herbert B. Peterson, MD, and James W. Curran, MD, MPH, "Commentary: Condoms and HIV/STD Prevention—Clarifying the Message," *American Journal of Public Health* 83, no. 4 (April 1993): 501-503.

10. Medical Institute for Sexual Health, "The Facts about Sexually Transmitted Infections (STIs)," www.medinstitute.org/content.php?name=stifacts.

11. National Institute of Allergy and Infectious Diseases, National Institutes of Health, U.S. Dept. of Health and Human Services, Scientific Evidence on Condom Effectiveness for Sexually Transmitted Diseases (STD) Prevention, July 20, 2001.

12. NPCFR Press Release, July 2001.

13. Ruth Bell, *Changing Bodies, Changing Lives* (New York: Random House, 1987), 102.

14. Ibid, 117.

15. Ibid, 116.

16. Ibid, 114.

17. This was originally an affidavit submitted in support of the Budnick case in which teachers exposed children to graphic pro-homosexual presentations. See Budnick story on pages 130-132.

18. CA law no longer requires that "honor and respect for monogramous heterosexual marriage" be taught in public schools. The amended law

merely requires that abstinence be taught as the "only certain way to prevent unintended pregnancy [and] sexually transmitted diseases..." Education Code §51933(b)(8).

Chapter Seven

1. Louise Derman-Sparks and the A.B.C. Task Force, *Anti-Bias Curriculum: Tools for Empowering Young Children* (Washington, DC: National Association for the Education of Young Children, 1989).

2. Ibid, 12.

3. Ibid.

4. E.D. Hirsch, Jr., "Restoring Cultural Literacy in the Early Grades," *Educational Leadership* 45, no. 4 (December 1987/January 1988).

5. The terminology used in Goals 2000 and STW is "integration."

6. Chicano activists adopted "Aztlan" as a symbol of their belief that the lands annexed to the U.S. after the Mexican-American War belong to Mexico. Aztlan was a mythical Aztec land.

Chapter Eight

1. Jessea Greenman, Gay and Lesbian Student Education Network, e-mail message, March 2000.

2. Brian Burt, "Gay Leader Says Dream Is to Promote Homosexuality in School—GLSEN Speakers Tout Gay Lessons for Kindergartners," *Lambda Report*, January/February 1998.

3. *Family News in Focus* (FNIF), Focus on the Family; http://www.family.org/cforum/fnif/news/AOO12250.html.

4. Robert Hogg, Steffanie Strathdee, Kevin Craib, Michael O'Shaughnessy, Julio Montaner, and Martin Schechter, "Modelling the Impact of HIV Disease on Mortality in Gay and Bisexual Men," *International Journal of Epidemiology* 26, no. 3.

5. Just the Facts Coalition, *Just the Facts about Sexual Orientation and Youth: A Primer for Principals, Educators, and School Personnel* (Washington, DC: American Psychological Association). Retrieved from www.apa.org/pi/lgbc/publications/justthefacts.html.

6. Focus on the Family, www.family.org; Exodus International, www.exodus.to; exodusyouth.net; Parents and Friends of Ex-Gay and Gays, PFOX.org (PFOX does not offer reparative therapy but does offer support

for families of ex-gays). This is only a partial listing of groups or individual therapists who help people leave the homosexual lifestyle.

7. Paul Cameron, "Gay obituaries closely track officially reported deaths from AIDS," *Psychological Reports* (2005; 96: 693-697).

8. The Eagle Center, an "alternative" school, was created by the Los Angeles Unified School District. (Kit R. Roane, "Two White Sport Coats, Two Pink Carnations: One Couple for a Prom," *New York Times,* May 22, 1994.)

9. Harvey Milk High School, New York City. See *New York Times,* "The Harvey Milk High School," August 3, 2003 http://query.nytimes.com/gst/fullpage.html?res=9C01E1D8133EF930A3575BC0A9659C8B63.

10. Robert Skutch, interview with National Public Radio, *Here and Now,* May 3, 2005.

11. Copies of e-mails and phone records now verify this contact.

12. Mary Kay Jackson, Los Angeles Unified School District General Counsel, Memo to all middle and high school principals, June 27, 2000.

13. Don Romesburg, ed. *Young, Gay and Proud!* (Boston: Alyson Publications, 1995), 80-83.

14. Ann Heron, ed., *One Teenager in Ten: Writings by Gay and Lesbian Youth* (Boston: Alyson Publications, 1983), 60-62.

15. Sexual relations between an adult male and a boy.

16. Margaret Hyde and Elizabeth Forsyth, *Know About Gays and Lesbians* (Broodfield, CT: Millbrook Press, 1994), 23-27 (reading level grades 5-6).

17. Warren Blumfeld and Diane Raymond, *Looking at Gay and Lesbian Life* (Boston, MA: Beacon Press, 1993), 105-106 (reading level grades 8-9).

Chapter Nine

1. *Islam: A Simulation of Islamic History and Culture* (Lakeside, CA: Interaction Publishers, 1991).

2. Bill Gertz, "CAIR has lobbying task for Conyers," *Washington Times,* National Weekly Edition, November 26, 2007.

3. Ali A. Mazrui, "'Multiculturalism and Comparative Holocaust,' One Nation, Many Peoples: A Declaration of Cultural Interdependence," *New York State Social Studies Review* (June 1991), 41.

4. Gilbert Sewall, Islam and the Textbooks, American Textbook Council www.historytextbooks.org/islam. See also: Textbook League, www.textbookleague.org/113centu.htm; Lee Kaplan, "Textbooks for Jihad,"

FrontPageMagazine.com, March 19, 2004, www.frontpagemag.com/Articles/Read.aspx?GUID=(3F8C053C-53D2-49CC-B393-85F4CD79A32B); Daniel Pipes, "Think Like a Muslim," *New York Post*, February 11, 2002, www.danielpipes.org/article/118.

5. Gilbert Sewall, Islam and the Textbooks, American Textbook Council www.historytextbooks.org/islam.

6. Paul Sperry, "Look Who's Teaching Johnny about Islam," *WorldNetDaily*, May 3, 2004, www.worldnetdaily.com/news/article.asp?ARTICLE_id=38304.

7. History-Social Science Content Standards for California Public Schools, Kindergarten Through Grade Twelve, Grade Seven, 7.2.

8. Bert Bower, *History Alive! Medieval World and Beyond* (Rancho Cordova, CA: Teachers' Curriculum Institute, 2004), 87.

9. New York City Police Department, *Report on Radicalization*, August 15, 2007, http://www.talkingpointsmemo.com/docs/nypd-report/?resultpage=1&.

10. http://www.mosqueofislamicbrotherhoodinc.org/aboutus.html.

11. Ellen Stokland, "Speaks Out Against Bush," Amnesty International Norge, January 10, 2002, http://www.amnesty.no/web.nsf/ac1a1a01ea7194a3c1256a07004fad10/ffac5a3601aba908c1256c3d004ef7c5?OpenDocument.

12. Chuck Bennett, "Intif-Adios to School Chief Quits City's Arab HS Over T-shirt Talk," *New York Post*, August 11, 2007.

13. Julie Bosman, Head of City's Arabic School Steps Down Under Pressure, *New York Times*, August 11, 2007.

14. The Textbook League, "How a Public School in Scottsdale, Arizone, Subjected Students to Islamic Indoctrination", www.textbookleague.org/tci-az.htm.

15. Bert Bower, *History Alive! Medieval World and Beyond* (Rancho Cordova, CA: Teachers' Curriculum Institute, 2004), Chapter 9.1.1. A discussion of this particular passage can be found at: www.historytextbooks.org/islam.htm.

16. Daniel Pipes, "Think Like a Muslim [Urges 'Across the Centuries,']" *New York Post*, February 11, 2002, http://www.danielpipes.org/article/118.

17. Bob Unruh, "Why Johnny is reading Islamist propaganda. Critics charge Muslim radicals determining textbook content," *WorldNetDaily*, October 26, 2006, www.worldnetdaily.com/news/article.asp?ARTICLE_ID=52623.

18. Gilbert Sewall, Islam and the Textbooks, American Textbook Council, www.historytextbooks.org/islam.

19. William J. Bennetta, "How a Public School in Scottsdale, Arizona, Subjected Students to Islamic Indoctrination," The Textbook League, www.textbookleague.org/tci-az.htm.

20. Janie White, "Islamic Indoctrination in Scottsdale, Arizona Public School: Reader comment on article: 'Spreading Islam in American Public Schools,'" February 27, 2005, www.danielpipes.org/comments/20546.

21. Daniel Pipes, "Daniel Pipes' Weblog 'History Alive!,' Scottsdale Schools, and a Reader's Comment," April 6, 2005, www.danielpipes.org/blog/439.

22. Gilbert Sewell, "California Textbook Adoption," American Textbook Council, www.historytextbooks.org/california.htm.

Chapter Ten

1. Lawsuits initiated by parents Bob and Barbara Tennison, OR, Paul and Jodi Hoffman, FL, and Pam Angelo, CA, are just a few.

2. Personal interview with editor Karen Holgate.

3. Ron Sunseri, *Outcome-Based Education: Understanding the Truth about Education Reform* (Sisters, OR: Multnomah Books, Questar Publishers, Inc., 1994), 140.

4. Cheryl Wetzstein, "Genital exams at school irk parents," *Washington Times*, April 27, 1996.

5. Matt Pyeatt, "Mom Sues Over Ejection From School Assembly On Homosexuality," CNSNews.com, May 13, 2002.

6. Dr. Karen Effrem received her medical degree from Johns Hopkins and her pediatric training from the University of Minnesota.

7. Karen R. Effrem, M.D., The Role of Federal Education and Labor in School Based Health Clinics, written testimony for the Subcommittee on Oversight and Investigations, Committee on Education and the Workforce, U.S. House of Representatives, June 6, 2000.

8. Jerry Moe and Peter Ways, *Conducting Support Groups for Elementary Children K-6, A Guide for Educators and other Professionals* (Washington, DC: Johnson Institute, 1991), 25. "During some group meetings, children will be taking a look at parts of their lives they may rather not explore... they begin to reveal themselves...".

9. The Improving America's Schools Act passed in 1994. At a Title 1 conference held in San Francisco, October 20, 1996, this writer was amazed at the number of speakers who stressed "all means all" whether the students were "at-risk" or not. The consensus was that the funding under Title 1 could be used for programs that would include "all" students. Quotes included: "All students

have needs…we value all children more…serve the total child…[it is the] federal government's job to protect children."

10. Dr. Linda C. Dawson, Mary Hritz, Sharon Jahn, ed. *Wellness Is Our Way of Life, Student Assistance Team Team Training, Workshop Guide.*

11. Ibid, 105-106.

Chapter Eleven

1. High School Student Survey (Male), produced by Rand, administered to ninth-grade boys in Santa Monica High School, California, April 1992.

2. *Are These Myths?*, published by Junior League of Minneapolis, 1989, adapted from the St. Paul Maternal and Infant Care Program. Used in Roosevelt Jr. High School, Charleston, WV.

3. Private interview with editor Karen Holgate after samples of school surveys were submitted for his review.

Chapter Twelve

1. Michael D. Simpson, "What's a Teacher to Do?" *NEA Today*, February 1996. The PPRA is included in the Appendices beginning on page 251.

2. See CA Ed. Code # 51513 in the Appendices, page 250.

3. Referrals for experts listed on pages 237-241.

4. See Appendices for relevant language of the bill. (California passed an amended version.)

5. After California's disastrous experimentation with whole language, California passed a law requiring explicit, systematic phonics. A copy of this law can be found in the Appendices.

6. After a bitter battle over California's math standards in which the State Superintendent of Public Instruction's standards would not have required students to learn double-digit division, members of Mathematically Correct (MC) drafted some of the nation's strongest math standards. MC's standards were adopted for the state by the State Board of Education over the protests of the state's superintendent. MC's contact information can be found in the Appendices.

Explore these "Good for your kids" books from WND!

The Sky's Not Falling: Why It's OK to Chill about Global Warming
By Holly Fretwell
Kids Ahead Books, $17.95
Paperback: ISBN 9780976726944

For ages 8 and up! You've heard the claims that the earth is warming up
because of cars, factories, and the many other
wonders created by humans. But is it really true?

Sure, our planet is changing, but it has before and
will again. There's more to the global warming
story than you may have heard! Can we adapt to a
changing world in ways that help the earth while
keeping people working and countries going
strong? Of course we can! Yes, it's OK to chill
about global warming. Let *The Sky's Not Falling*
show you why.

What's Right about America: Celebrating Our Nation's Values
By Rep. Kay Granger, with a Foreword by Sarah Ferguson, Dutchess of York
World Ahead Books (now WND Books), $21.95
Hardcover: ISBN 9780977898404

For ages 12 and up! Texas Congresswoman Kay Granger was enroute to the
Middle East to help Iraqi women learn democratic principles when it
occurred to her: *How can we teach others about the principles of freedom when
we're not teaching our own kids about them?*

What's Right about America is Rep. Granger's
exciting, eloquent tribute to those principles, told
through the lives of great Americans. Some of these
individuals are well known; others toiled far from
history's spotlight.

Far from citing dry historical facts, Rep. Granger
digs deeper, showing how these heroes' most courageous acts brought out
the best in themselves and others. Here's the perfect antidote to dull, often
inaccurate, intermediate and high school history texts.

Available online and at all major bookstores.